An Infantry Battalion in Combat

> "The discovery of unforgettable facts had never been encouraged in the armies, who treated their history as a sentimental treasure rather than a field of scientific research"
>
> –CAPTAIN B LIDDELL HART

"The accounts of various actions fought by the battalion have been described with heartening accuracy, blend of truth and authenticity, though it looks acrid, harsh, frank and even bitter at places, but that is what it is. The book delves deep into the causes, roles, results and merits of each case and that makes it hardheaded assessment and as such worth reading."
—**Lt Col Ravel Singh**

"I find the entire account very accurate, true and very revealing – slamming all the way for hard facts. Flops and bad patches are given for correct appreciation of the situations, without which the posterity will be bereft of useful lessons. I wholeheartedly appreciate the efforts in producing readable and very useful book." —**Lt Col MS Punia**

"The book will be of absorbing interest to the commanders at all levels, who prepare, train and fight battles. It is a comprehensive study of operations at section, platoon, company and battalion levels. The most captivating point is the description of the phenomenon of fighting at last 200 yards and beyond, which is missed in most historical accounts." —**Col Hardial Singh SM**

"The subject matter has been dealt with, in an art of the fact manner, by following a researching theory. It goes deep into the psychology and thinking of a fighting infantry soldier and critically analyses the issues. The lessons to be learnt are really a storehouse of wisdom, which will be of immense value for new generations." —**Col Sansar Singh, VrC**

"Publication of such a book, should have been much earlier. It was really overdue. It is a typical case of an infantry battalion being involved in all operations of war in one campaign – a very rare phenomenon. Besides, the book puts the records straight in respect of all actions fought and removes misconceptions based on false premises and speculations." —**Maj Santosh Kumar**

An Infantry Battalion in Combat
A Critical Appraisal of Battle Situations Encountered by an Infantry Battalion

Lt Col (Dr.) Sube Singh Ahlawat

Lancer • New Delhi • Frankfort, IL
www.lancerpublishers.com

LANCER

Published in the United States by

The Lancer International Inc
19558 S. Harlem Ave., Suite 1,
Frankfort, IL. 60423.

First published in India by

Lancer Publishers & Distributors
2/42 (B) Sarvapriya Vihar,
New Delhi – 110016

© Lt Col (Dr.) Sube Singh Ahlawat, 2013

All rights reserved. No part of this publication
may be reproduced, stored in a retrieval system or transmitted,
in any form or by any means, electronic, mechanical, photocopying,
recording or otherwise, without the prior permission of the publishers. For
additional information, contact Lancer. Printed at Sona Printers, New Delhi.

Printed and bound in India.

ISBN-13: 978-1-935501-36-7 • ISBN-10: 1-935501-36-4

Online Military Bookshop
www.lancerpublishers.com

IDR Net Edition
www.indiandefencereview.com

Col Bhagat Singh (then Lt Col) raised 7 SIKH in 1963, led it in 1965 War and got the Battle Honour of OP Hill. 1965 and Theatre Honour of J&K – 1965 for the Battalion

CONTENTS

	Preface	7
	Abbreviations	13
1	Preamble	17
2	First Things First	26
3	Irony After Irony	38
4	Jammu and Kashmir, British and Pakistan	52
5	Punch and its Specific Importance	64
6	1947-48 War and Afterwards	70
7	Testing of Mettle and Might at Rann of Kutchh	80
8	Infiltration by Guerrillas	89
9	Defence at Sauji	100
10	Capture of Mandi	108
11	Battle of Gali	128
12	Engagement at Molsar Ridge	151
13	Raid at Kabar-Ki-Dheri	158
14	Operation – Phanne-Shah	164
15	Battle of OP Hill	186
16	Phenomenon of Gibraltar and it's Crumbling	223

17	Young Commanders and Leaders	235
18	Junior Leadership	257
19	Honours and Awards	267
20	Last Few Yards	281
21	What Makes a Man Fight	297
22	Lessons Learnt	310
23	Dealing with Pakistan	325
24	The Last Word	335
	Bibliography	361
	Index	364

PREFACE

I take pleasure in presenting this account of exploits of 7 SIKH Regiment pertaining to Indo-Pak War – 1965, as a case study for the book titled "An Infantry Battalion in Combat." It is a critical appraisal of battle situations that are likely to be encountered by an infantry battalion during war. It brings out the conduct of operations at infantry section, platoon, company and battalion levels. Infantry being the "Queen of the Battle" has got an important role to play during combat. It seeks the enemy, closes in, engages, kills the enemy, captures and holds the ground.

Demystifying infantry's successes and failures has never been an easy task for any military historian. Infantry's conduct in battle is heavily dependent on intangible human factors like leadership, courage, resilience, bravery and camaraderie. Infantry operations are simple, rugged and soaked in sweat and blood. What makes an infantryman surmount all odds under most unfavourable conditions can only be understood by being a part of an infantry battalion. It is a highly specialised subject, which cannot be learned by playing from outside. Qualities of command and leadership when enmeshed with the elements of duty, honour, courage, discipline and training produce an electrifying effect that motivates an infantryman to fight till the "Last Man: Last Round." It has happened in the past and will continue to happen in the future too, as long as Indian Army has officers and men of strong will and character.

I have delved upon the genesis of Indo-Pak hostilities, the Partition and 1947-48 War in Jammu and Kashmir, which sets the backdrop for Indo-Pak War 1965. 7 SIKH, then a newly raised unit had fought numerous actions with distinction in 1965 in Punch Sector of Jammu and Kashmir. It is a comprehensive account of not only the operations fought by 7 SIKH in that war but also the socio-political situations prevailing at that time in the sub-continent, which had direct effects on operations.

I was an active participant in these actions and as such pen down these memoirs. I have purposely gone into all minute details and described each action with peculiar infantry flair and flavour bringing out earthy lessons. I, with due respect to all, have narrated the strengths and weaknesses of complete wherewithal very carefully without prejudice and malice. I have simply restated and reinstated the facts. I strongly feel that these detailed accounts of various infantry operations will be of learning value to the young officers and junior leaders and useful for others who prepare, train and range troops for battle against the dreaded enemy.

The Author

*Pakistani Intruders
and 7 SIKH,
First in Mandi Valley and then in
Mendhar Valley
In Punch Sector, J&K in 1965 Indo-Pak War
Triumph of Sustained Resistance
Annihilation of the Aggressor*

—**Lt Col (Dr.) Sube Singh Ahlawat (Retd.)**

Dedicated to

Capt Surjit Singh, 2/Lt SS Sandhu, Jem (later Naib Subedar) Makhan Singh, Hav Piara Singh, NK Banta Singh, NK Shangara Singh, L/NK Achhar Singh, L/NK Saudagar Singh, Sep Ram Singh, Sep Pritam Singh and all other brave jawans of 7 SIKH, who laid down their lives for the safety, honour and welfare of India. They all fought heroically, keeping alive the fortitude and courage of a Sikh soldier of Indian Army, whose life and dedication to their profession and the love for the country, forced upon me a reason, to write this account. It should be of immense use to posterity to know as to how a good soldier, officered well, performs his task, in the face of daunting challenges.

My Gratitude to

- Col Bhagat Singh who went through the account of Mandi operations in Punch Sector in J&K, written and submitted in 1973, added the left out but finer details and made me follow it, till it was accepted by Army Headquarters, New Delhi as a Battle Honour/Theatre Honour of Jammu and Kashmir–1965 for 7 SIKH. Thereupon I thought of adding the accounts of all the other actions fought by the battalion, during 1965 War which he again gracefully studied and made me record and write in the form of a book.

- Col DR Nijhawan, who while commanding 7 SIKH in Eastern Sector in 1973 asked me to write the account of Mandi operations as per the requirement of SAO 27/S/72 to be submitted to Army Headquarters, New Delhi, which finally became the basis for writing this book.

- Maj Santosh Kumar, my first company commander, with whom the details of actions were often discussed, insisted that I must record the complete battle account in the form of a book. Factually speaking, he is the main source of inspiration for this small venture of mine. He helped me in adding up lot of minor details, which otherwise I would have missed.

- Col Sansar Singh, VrC the hero of Operation "OP Hill" and a brave heart of 7 SIKH inspired me to include all operations and write a book for preservation of values, which helped our way to fight and beat the Pakistanis first in Mandi Valley and then in OP Hill in Mendhar Valley. He very kindly handed over to me, his own version of actual fighting on way to capturing Jungle Hill, an important part of OP Hill Complex, being a leading company commander, which enriched the contents of this book.

- Lt Col Ravel Singh was a very efficient Mor platoon commander and took part in all operations fought by 7 SIKH in 1965 War. A very brave, enthusiastic and forthright officer, who had since been contributing to various military magazines based on his personal experience and has been my contemporary in this field for quite some time. His frequent discussion of those days provided lot of study material for writing this small but actual history of 7 SIKH of Indo-Pak War 1965. His Mortar Platoon had done a splendid job in the capture of Mandi and in OP Hill.

- Sub Bikkar Singh, was the first JCO to have received me at Kalai Bridge and take me to 7 SIKH, on my commissioning from Indian Military Academy. I had a liking for him due to his soldierly qualities and immense value for military discipline. While I was posted at Dehradun as GSO-3 in an infantry brigade, he came all the way and stayed with me. Knowing my educational qualifications and literary bent of mind, he said:-

"*Sahab tusi larai da itihas likho. Kiyon nahin likhde. Tuhanto bad, kisi nu kuchh pata nahi hona aur 7 SIKH da, 1965 di Larai da, bara sohna itihas loki bhool jange.*"

(Sir, you must write the battle account of 7 SIKH of 1965 War. Why don't you try. After you people are gone, nobody will know anything about it and this beautiful history of 7 SIKH will be forgotten.)

I promised him and though late, I am fulfilling it. He is no more. O God! Convey to him in your own mysterious ways, that I have done my duty. He did well, first in the capture of Mandi and proved himself to be a fearless leader. He was again one of the heroes of Battle of OP Hill 1965, where he broke the crust of enemy defences and went in, evicting them from Jungle Hill, which was the Battalion's objective.

ABBREVIATIONS

Adjt	Adjutant
Arty	Artillery
Appt	Appointment
ADS	Advance Dressing Station
AG	Adjutant General
AWOL	Absent without Leave
AK Bn	Azad Kashmir Battalion (of Pakistan)
Assly	Assembly
Adv	Advance
BC	Battery Commander
Bn	Battalion
Bde	Brigade
Brig	Brigadier
.50 BMG	.50 Browning Machine Gun (acquired by Pakistan in 1964-1965)
Comn	Communication
Coln	Column

Coord	Coordination
CO	Commanding Officer
Col	Colonel
CFL	Cease Fire Line
Capt	Captain
Cas	Casualty
CGI	Corrugated Galvanised Iron
Coy	Company
DF	Defensive Fire
Div	Division
Disposn	Disposition
Ech	Echelon
Ex	Exercise
ERE	Extra Regimental Employment
En	Enemy
FDL	Forward Defended Locality
Fwd	Forward
Fd Bty	Field Battery
FOO	Forward Observation Officer
FUP	Forming Up Place
GHQ	General Headquarters
GSO3	General Staff Officer Grade 3
GSO2	General Staff Officer Grade 2

Abbreviations

HQ	Headquarters
IMA	Indian Military Academy
Info	Information
IO	Intelligence Officer
Inf	Infantry
Jem	Jemadar (now known as Naib Subadar)
JCO	Junior Commissioned Officer
KDL	Key Defended Locality
LMG	Light Machine Gun
Lt Col	Lieutenant Colonel
Lt Gen	Lieutenant General
LOC	Line of Control
2/Lt	2nd Lieutenant
Mtn	Mountain
Mor	Mortar
MMG	Medium Machine Gun
Maj	Major
MBE	Member of British Empire
Ni	Night
No	Number
Org	Organisation
Ops	Operations
Obj	Objective

OP	Observation Post
OTA	Officer's Training Academy
Pl	Platoon
PW	Prisoner of War
Pt	Point
POK	Pakistan Occupied Kashmir
Posn	Position
Recce	Reconnaissance
Rd	Road
Retd	Retired
RL	Rocket Launcher
SSG	Special Service Group (of Pakistan)
SL	Start Line
SHO	Station House Officer

1
PREAMBLE

"While a ship may symbolise the Navy and Aeroplane the Air Force... the only adequate symbol of our Army is the man – the frontline Infantry soldier" —Anonymous

General

Infantry is called the Queen of the Battle. It the basic fighting arm and has got the honour of being the oldest. There are others, who are also being called arms, like the Armoured Corps, Artillery, Engineers and Signals but they are for supporting the Infantry in actual sense. Without infantry, they cannot think of launching independent operations and their existence basically is dependent on the working of infantry. Historically, in the bygone days, for the purpose of growth and development of army these regiments of other arms had been raised, by converting some of the then existing infantry units. That way, we may not be wrong if we say that it is the mother foster of all the arms and thus rightly be called, MOTHER QUEEN OF THE BATTLE. With the progressive development of warfare, the other arms assumed their own significance and developed accordingly. Today though the final job will still be accomplished by infantry, but infantry alone will not be able to withstand the rigours of present day warfare, where the opponents to have highly developed components of supporting arms in their armies. It will be naive to believe that troops armed only with high morale would continue to deliver with obsolete, antiquated and inferior weapons, when pitched against superior technology. In any case the infantry is still loaded with acute responsibilities and will be required to finally capture and hold the ground. It thus has to be valued as the very foundation and nerve of the Army. It is an admitted fact that infantry is the great lever of war and that the Armoured Corps and Artillery are the indispensable accessories. But infantry is required to master two of its most essential conditions, that its men should be great walkers who are inured to fatigue and that the firing with the personal weapon of its men be very well executed. We probably have one of the best infantry in the world and we ought to keep them in high spirits, duly trained and equally motivated. General Slim of Second World War fame had very rightly said, *"when the other arms boasted about their achievements, infantry stood quietly with victory under its feet."*

The infantry men are underdogs, who often are mud-rain-wind boys. They have no comforts and they learn to live without necessities. Their language gets coarse and they live a life stripped off conventions and niceties. Their nobility and dignity conform to the way they live, unselfishly, and risk their lives to help each other. It is the least spectacular arm, but without them you can do nothing. When the smoke clears away, it is the riflemen who settles the final issues on the battlefield.

In the end of the ends, we can say that infantry bears the heaviest burden of battle and requires the greatest sacrifice so also it promises the greater renown, which undoubtedly needs judicious treatment. It is therefore better that the infantry is used most carefully and be fully supported by Artillery and also Armoured Corps at required times. Good infantry without doubt is the sinew of an army but if it is forced to fight for long time against the enemy fully equipped with very superior artillery, it will become demoralised and will be destroyed.

Case Study

This is an account of an Infantry Battalion in Combat against the 'Gibraltars.' All infantry battalions have got the same philosophy of working and macro issues are same every where. Some micro issues could be different depending upon the traits of the various Communities the troops came from. It can be therefore safely assumed that all the issues discussed in this case study of 7 SIKH are applicable to all the Infantry units of the Indian Army.

The Raising Process

This is an account of 7 SIKH, an Infantry Battalion which was raised in 1963 at Meerut by Lt Col Bhagat Singh who baptised it with the motto "To the Top The Hard Way." The nucleus of the trained troops was provided by the old units of the SIKH Regiment. It used to be the prerogative of the provider units to send the rank and file, they could spare and the receiving unit could not be choosy as the donor units were not very many in number. They always tried to pass their none-so-bright, rank and file, to the new raisings. 7 SIKH also got its share. However the Commanding Officer being an old diehard regimental officer was effective and well meaning. Being a Sikh gentleman himself and knowing the troops well, he put everybody in his place and handled the unit affairs firmly. It had taken about three months for all the troops to arrive, assemble and join the training in the new unit. The unit was raised, officially on 1 January 1963. The troops who came from the other units of SIKH Regiment, were sent back number of times and the Commanding Officer, really had to struggle for getting qualified, disciplined and well-trained JCOs and NCOs. As a result, the unit could only carry out elementary, individual, platoon and company training, but it was unable to do the collective training for various operations of war due paucity of time, which is so very important for taping up the drills and making it into a remorseless machine. However, unit after six months of raising and with all possible help from SIKH Regimental Centre, completed its knitting in process, sent the Advance Party and by end August 1965, reached Punch and occupied the posts along the CFL as part of 93 Infantry Brigade. (See Sketch 1)

It will not be wrong to say that to develop, tie up and master all the drills efficiently, inculcate unit's own and a cohesive image, for creating own traditions by breaking new grounds, takes time. There, the unit was deployed on posts, sitting eyeball to eyeball with Pakistanis, where there used to be regular exchange of fire besides the troops often being away on patrolling and raids etc. and thus the practical training for dealing with the enemy started.

Team of Officers

At the time of raising of 7 SIKH some of the officers came from the old units and joined at Meerut, while others joined the unit in the field area directly from Indian Military Academy (IMA), Dehradun and Officer Training Schools (Now Academies) at Madras and Pune. Good percentage of officers was from Emergency Courses with the sprinkling of regular officers, who all,

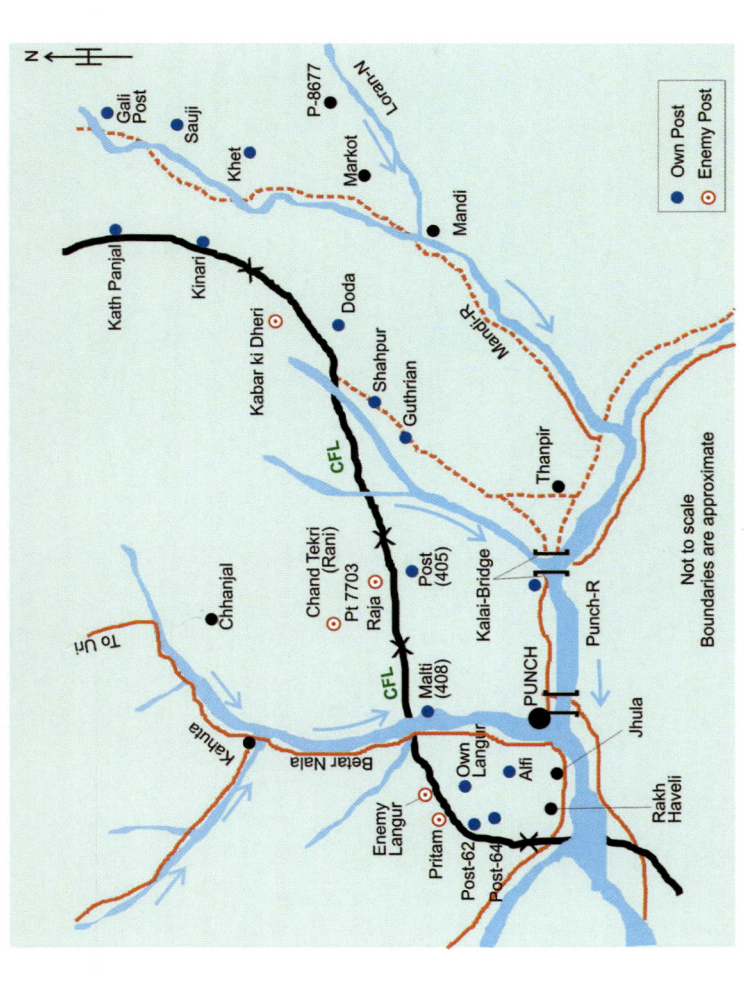

Sketch 1: General Area – Punch Sector Aug-Sep 1965

otherwise had done only six months of training in the academies. The Commanding Officer had established his command in a very effective manner and things were progressing well. To the JCOs and other rank, he had to be rather strict, and ruthless in certain cases, which helped the unit come on to the grid soon. When the 1965 Indo-Pak War started, a good lot of officers was away on courses and other duties and could not be made available to the battalion, when it needed them most. Certain officers like Maj Trilochan Singh, Capt NS Koak and Capt Darya Singh, etc. were away from unit and some of them did not take part in actions fought by the battalion in Mandi valley. Maj Trilochan Singh was on Intelligence Course, Capt Darya Singh on Mountain Warfare Course and Capt NS Koak on Commando Course as the army courses at the Schools of Instructions during 1965 War were not cancelled by Army Headquarters. The unit felt the absence of these officers, who were mostly the professionists rather than careerists. That made a difference in the performance of the battalion during operations initially in Mandi Valley, at Gali Picquet and Sauji and later at Phanne-Shah which are described in detail in respective chapters.

Actions Fought

The unit fought four important actions. The Mandi town, about 20 kms own side of CFL was occupied by the infiltrators on 9 August, 1965 where they attacked the police post, killed the Station House Officer and established their control after looting the weapons. The Task Force comprising of 'A' and 'B' companies, 7 SIKH, suitably equipped with supporting weapons, commanded by Maj KG Belliappa, 2IC, 7 SIKH was detailed to wrest Mandi Township from the infiltrators at the earliest. A and 'B' Companies under 2/Lt SS Sandhu and 2/Lt SS Ahlawat respectively, wrested the Mandi Town and got the civil rule established once again. After that, in thwarting the enemy move in the Mandi valley, the Task Force joined battalion headquarter at Sauji whence defended the area against all odds. One company strength including the element of 7 MADRAS and CRPF fought a gallant defensive battle at Gali Picquet (602), which blocked the enemy's chance of advance on the axis Gali-Sauji-Mandi and Kalai Bridge, on which the enemy had planned to embark upon ferociously. This defensive battle at Gali was one of the very rare actions, fought by officer and men of 7 SIKH with conspicuous bravery and fortitude, holding on for eight days in a God forsaken bowl.

Misplaced Notions at Phanne-Shah

Once the Haji Pir Pass was captured and Uri Punch bulge was in our hands, 7 SIKH was given a task to occupy a feature known as Pir Lahori Shah. It is just close to Pritam (Pakis call it Chakias) Post of Pakistanis, extending northwards tapering down towards Palangi Nala – on the western side of Betar Nala, so that the western flank of road Uri-Punch recently opened after operation at Haji Pir and Raja-Rani, was secured. The operation code named as Phanne-Shah, was not fully successful which was planned on certain misplaced notions. The most notable was the general feeling that next morning i.e. on 22 September 65, the ceasefire will be operative and fighting will stop and we would occupy a feature quietly and then threatening the most important post of Pakistanis – Pritam (Chakias). With these feelings, coupled with the spate in Betar Nala, the move across CFL in this sector for the offensive task was delayed inordinately and the result was, non-occupation of the features by the respective companies at the required time. It was here that the absence of above mentioned officers was felt. Had those officers been there, the outcome could have been different. They themselves, all being the men of convictions, could not have delayed the occupation of the objectives, which were fortunately not held by the enemy. Here, the officers responsible failed the unit. Strength wise also one company that is 'A' Company with Capt Sansar Singh and 2/Lt MS Punia two very capable officers, was at Rajouri for the protection of Divisional Headquarters and for carrying out operations around, against the infiltrators. The unit had about 270 all ranks inclusive, who unfortunately all got concentrated at one place. The enemy's complete Corps Artillery as usual started pounding it and by the afternoon, the battalion was badly mauled, the only consolation for us being that it was not by the infantry of the enemy. It was here we realised that "There are not good or bad units, there are only good or bad officers." The unit which did an excellent work at Mandi and Gali, had to make an heart wrenching retreat under the enemy's ravaging artillery fire. Though it could be said that it accrued due to most accurate and devastating artillery fire but as all the objectives also were not captured even while being unoccupied by the enemy, resulted in heavy concentration only on one feature and hence more casualties. No one could excuse us for this lapse, it included us all. The commanding officer who was a God fearing, and well meaning officer unfortunately could not push respective and responsible company commanders to occupy the given objectives. Initially, on the whole, it was a modest and doable target to capture. The failure on the part of officers of the unit in not capturing and holding on their objectives resulting in shaming retreat filled all ranks with anger, disgust and helplessness, which affected the very soul of the unit. Oh

Good God, what fine troops and such an outcome! To my mind it was because the situation, circumstances and retaliation by enemy was wrongly read by all in the chain and more by superior headquarters (HQs) who had so tasked the unit.

The Last Action

The unit fought the last battle at OP Hill Complex being part of 120 Infantry Brigade. The unit was given task of capturing Jungle Hill, the Ground of Tactical Importance in Phase II of the Brigade attack. The unit had to be launched before time, due to slow progress and the stiff opposition faced by the other battalion in this multidirectional attack. 7 SIKH fought gallantly and evicted the enemy and captured the objective but not without the sacrifices of certain diehard bravodos, specially of 'A' Company commanded by Capt Sansar Singh. This was probably the only brigade level attack launched by Indian Army in mountains in 1965 operations.

Recording of Historical Facts

The unit after the war, moved back to Punch to be again under its parent Formation that is 93 Infantry Brigade. The commanding officer was immediately posted out and the second inning started. The unit got the Battle Honour of OP Hill-1965. The accounts for the other actions fought earlier to OP Hill, however were not recorded. In those operations, seniors were not involved and juniors had no say as usual, being baulked and pushed around. However as late as 1973, the author submitted the account of Battle of Mandi as required by Army HQ, duly recommended by the superior HQ and unit got the much deserved Theatre Honour of Jammu and Kashmir, 1965. However, the details of all the other operations besides OP Hill could not be submitted in time due to one reason or the other and thus the war history of the unit could not be completed. Lately it was noticed, that certain unconnected, unconcerned and unearned actions were shown ascribed and attributed unethically to the unit's account which made the author, advised by the other old colleagues of Punch days, to take the pen, flash out the true account and set the anomalies and distortions at rest.

2
FIRST THINGS FIRST*

"Nothing has really happened until it has been recorded."
—Virginia Woolf

Soldiering and Combat

At the outset, I clarify that this work of mine is neither a tone of high level military planning nor a breezy self justification of my little contribution, in Indo-Pak War 1965, but to bring out efforts of an Infantry Battalion – 7 SIKH thwarting the evil design of our adversary, the Pakistan army, who is constantly fighting costly and seemingly all sorts of interminable wars against Indian Nation, with a aim to grab the State of Jammu and Kashmir. We had to play the hands that were raised on us and had been dealt with effectively. The unit was in a fine fettle and the Good Lord – could not give a believer, a burden it could not handle. It did what a newly raised but trained, infantry battalion, commanded by a matured and professional soldier, does in battlefield, but of course not without misses at places. It undoubtedly will look rather strange for ordinary military man to find an account of actions of an infantry battalion, fought in 1965 War, being published now and when most of the weapons and methods of warfare have undergone significant changes

At the first Battle Honour Day celebrations in peace area at Ferozpur the author on right with (L to R) Capt Mohinder Singh, Capt Darya Singh, Capt SK Singh and Maj Trilochan Singh

towards modernisation as well as obsolescence. Same way the lessons learnt from this study for the posterity, can also be construed differently. But the facts of the case however are a bit different. The accounts which are given here, are mainly of the "Man" who is behind the machine. It is neither about machine nor about the historical manipulation of the self glorifiers, who come on to the stage immediately after the success signal is given. How a battle is managed by seniors and fought by junior officers and leaders in both defensive and offensive operations, is what is brought out here and that is why it is still very relevant and should remain so for all times to come. This account of 7 SIKH, substantially covers almost all operations of war i.e. attack, defence, patrolling, withdrawal, screens and raid etc. in which the unit got involved in Punch Sector in Jammu and Kashmir in 1965 Indo-Pak War and performed with all the pluses and minuses which have been recorded most faithfully with all the time keeping at the back of mind that, "A historian ought to be exact, sincere and impartial; free from passion, unbiased by interest, fear, resentment or affection; and faithful to the truth, which is the mother of history, preserver of great actions, the enemy of oblivion, the witness of the past and the direction of the future."

Causes of Delay in Documenting Battle Accounts

Delay in writing this account has its own story to tell. Unit being newly raised (raised on 1 January 1963) and maximum number of officers being fresh from academies, this operation of 1965 was fought mostly by these very young but enthusiastic and responsible officers. The last action was fought by the unit on night 2/3 November 1965, where it was given the responsibility of capturing the Ground of Tactical Importance of the Brigade, in the Battle of OP Hill in Mendhar Sub-sector, Jammu and Kashmir. Immediately after the battle, the then Commanding Officer Lt Col Bhagat Singh was posted out after about five-six days. New Commanding Officer Lt Col RC Puri took over, who definitely had different priorities as new incumbent will always have. The war had already been over and there were comparatively less activities from across the border for quite some time. It will not be wrong to say that the old chemistry of the unit does change with the new dispensation and 7 SIKH was no exception. Couple of rather most of the senior officers were not very much involved in the earlier actions and as such, they neither knew the details nor were interested in writing about these. Young officers who participated and performed, as usual were busy and had no time for such ventures. In war no soldier is free to say and write what he thinks and after the war no one is concerned what a soldier should think and write and that was exactly what was happening to us all and the unit. After some time they all were posted out on staff, Extra Regimental Employment (ERE) etc. and no one else naturally bothered about it. An inquisitive minded person however could have taken the initiative but unit was derided by the circumstances and the benefit of time was lost. True also as it is, that no successor will go into the success story of his predecessor, because the new one has to give out to the unit that old famous message that, "every predecessor was a... (not as wise as I am)." That way, for a long time the successive commanding officers too came from outside the unit and essence of the unit history and its achievements of 1965 War were lost or I should say ignored, may not be willfully. Now, writing at this stage is really like struggling with the scatterings. However I decided to go ahead. As they say its never to late...

Submission of Mandi Operation Accounts in 1974

In 1973, copy of Special Army Order SAO 27/S/72 was received in the unit, which concerned with the non-submission of the earlier battle accounts and about the action to be taken by units. The unit was in the Eastern Sector and Lt Col DR Nijhawan had taken over as commanding officer. As per the Army Order, the unit was required to submit the detailed accounts of various actions fought during 1965 War to Army HQ, New Delhi. It was required, as, such actions were vividly mentioned in the war dispatches of the Western Command under which the unit fought the 1965 War. Under the guidance of Lt Col DR Nijhawan, the action report of capture of Mandi which was fought on 11-12 August 1965 written by author, was submitted quickly as desired, alongwith the required documents. Consequent to that, the unit was promptly awarded the Theatre Honour of

Jammu and Kashmir 1965, by Army HQ. The action report of the Battle of Gali, Defence of Sauji, Engagement at Molsar Ridge and Operation Phanne-Shah and Raid on Kabar-Ki-Dheri etc. could however not be written in such a short time, and hence not forwarded. The outline account of Battle of OP Hill, the last battle fought, as part of brigade attack, however had already been written and submitted and the unit had got the award of Battle Honour of OP Hill 1965. From there I was posted out on staff like others who had participated and no one else was interested in documenting it and hence neglected for all these years. After some time almost all those who took part were promoted as Lt Colonels & Colonels and took over command of other units. I was posted to 3 SIKH in 1982 and commanded it from 1984-1986 and as such was out of 7 SIKH permanently. I retired in 1990.

Old 7 SIKH (Redesignated as 5 SIKH) vis-a-vis New 7 SIKH (OP Hill)

Old 7 SIKH (Now 5 SIKH) was raised in 1940 and formalities for its redesignation as 5 SIKH were completed in 1959 and formally adopted that name, number and designation in 1960, when it was located at Red Fort in Delhi. Now, the old 7 SIKH is 5 SIKH in all its forms and manifestations. There is a small but interesting incident connected with this change. The SIKH regiment has produced an outstanding military general in Lt Gen Harbakhsh Singh, VrC whose contribution in 1947-48 and 1965 Wars with Pakistan has been tremendous and very decisive. 5 SIKH was raised in 1901 and he had been commissioned in 5 SIKH. This unit was fighting in Singapore, when it fell to Japanese in 1942. Lt Gen Harbakhsh Singh then as a junior officer was seriously wounded and admitted in hospital. Unit became prisoner of

Japanese and as a result was put under suspended animation by British Indian Government. The property and other assets of the old 5 SIKH were kept with SIKH Regimental Centre. Afterwords, neither old 5 SIKH revived nor new 5 SIKH could not be raised due to policies of Government of India, then prevailing. Lt Gen Harbakhsh Singh tried his best, as he was feeling homeless. In the military and particularly in arms like Infantry, Armoured corps and Engineers etc. the unit is considered as a second home. One is commissioned in a unit/regiment and stays throughout and finally would like to takeover the same as commanding officer, if possible. In between he may go for staff, Instructional or ERE duties for about two to three years but finally comes back. Lt Gen Harbakhsh Singh tried and finally was successful but only in getting the approval for redesignation of old 7 SIKH as 5 SIKH. He got a home for his psychological satisfaction and for claiming property of old 5 SIKH which was got done. The old Colours of XLVII SIKHS raised in 1901 (old 5 SIKH) kept at centre along with the Colours of 7 SIKH raised in 1940 (redesignated as 5 SIKH) both were presented, afresh, to the new unit i.e. 5 SIKH at ceremonial parade on 22 March, 1960, at New Delhi. It is now enjoying the rich heritage, legacy and traditions of two battalions i.e. old 5 SIKH and old 7 SIKH. Here goes the history of old 7 SIKH, leaving no chance for anyone to interpret differently for connecting it with new 7 SIKH (OP Hill).

Sanctity of Operational Accounts

During the year 2000, 7 SIKH came to Meerut and had celebrated the Battle Honour Day and also organised reunion. Almost all old officers ex 7 SIKH attended the function. There, it was noticed that the unit had adopted a very unknown Battle Honour by the name of "Peta Hir," 1948 alongwith Theatre

Honour "Jammu and Kashmir 1948." It had also suffixed the word "Choinar" to the name of the unit officially, formally and firmly which otherwise had no relation with the history of the battalion. It, however was objected there and then as these two issues had no connection with 7 SIKH. Peta Hir action, if at all it was an armed action, could be the concern of old 7 SIKH redesignated as 5 SIKH in 1960 whereas present 7 SIKH was raised as a new unit in 1963. It has got no operational relationship of any kind with these actions purported to have been undertaken by then 7 SIKH (now 5 SIKH). We all officers, JCOs and men who fought various actions in Punch Sector in 1965 having been invited for celebrations vehemently condemned these inclusions in the battalion history and requested for their immediate removal from records of the unit. Again, we happened to attend the Battle Honour Day celebration at Mamun in 2006 and found that the same anomalies were still in vogue in 7 SIKH affairs being followed even more enthusiastically. We had to object again in writing asserting more vigorously, but some officers who were responsible for such inclusions did not let, the then commanding officer correct those anomalies and distortions for the reasons best known to them. A few of them seemed to have grossly involved in its manipulation and had felt bad when their exceptionalism was challenged. Unfortunately, no action has been taken by the unit till today, inspite of lot of efforts by couple of old timers. I however have been remonstrating in writing regularly since then. The fact is that unit was known as 7 SIKH (OP Hill) which was based on its well earned Battle Honour of OP Hill 1965. The use of word "Choinar" for the unit in its official records is being made into a case which is totally irrelevant and meaningless which we found formally taken on the leaves of history of the unit. The interested persons did not miss the opportunity even to trash the suggestion by the old timers and rather chastised them by branding as "outdated and obsolete people." Certain senior officers, who have become extra constitutional centres of power, keep driving hard not to let these anomalies be dropped. The crowing irony is that the correct history of the unit is not known or understood by the new lot and the views of the people, who mattered then are ignored and contemptuously rejected. Such an attitude is compounding the impropriety. How can the official history of a unit with its battle account be choreographed. I don't understand. It will be against the soldierly mores.

History of the Unit starts with the First Commanding Officer

Lt Col (Now Col) Bhagat Singh was the first Commanding Officer of 7 SIKH, who raised, fought the 1965 War and got the Battle Honour of OP Hill and Theatre Honour of J&K 1965 for the battalion. He is a father figure for all of us and a revered personality. He got highly disturbed on the issues and requested the then commanding officer Col SS Prasad to do away with the anomalies and not to let the history of the unit be spoiled. Copy of this letter is attached as Appendix-A. But even after all this no action was taken. As I was writing the operational history of 7 SIKH of 1965 War I requested the Army HQs AG's Branch, New Delhi for ascertaining the facts and advising the unit for carrying out necessary corrections and address these monumental issues immediately, drop all fictitious yearnings or earnings if found wrong and not making a travesty of Battle Honour and the history of the battalion. To present the correct history to the posterity to my mind is the soldierly imperative and is so commanding an obligation.

I am reminded of a saying regarding army personnel's dealing with the problems and encountered in general life, "Fauji is right when he is right, and Fauji is also right when he is wrong" and that is the story of this case, where it was tried to be proved.

Publishing of Combat Accounts

As already mentioned, one can imagine as to how the new issues can be added and old altered. I, as a result, thought of putting correct details of actions fought together with the help of other officers so that all the concerned could know about the operational truths. The issue of various additions and alterations had happened because a detailed, actual and true battle account was not available and some enthusiasts started adding new accounts and altering the old one to suit their interests, for self glorification and taking advantage of the situations. I am impressed with the wonderful words of Tacitus who very rightly said, *"this I hold to be the chief office of history to rescue virtuous actions from the oblivion, to which a want of records would consign them, and that men should feel dreaded of being considered infamous in the opinion of posterity, from their depraved expressions and base action."* That is what exactly is being done to the unit's history and I undertook the job of publishing the correct history and accounts of operations of 1965 War. For keeping the pious history of the unit intact something concrete should be available as a reference, so that it is not that easy for self seekers to change it to their taste and whims and fancies. These are the accounts of actions of jawans at Battalion, Company, Platoon and Section levels taking on the dreaded enemy in one to one fight which is seldom available. Individual accounts of some, who get decorations and awards etc. may however be available. There is otherwise nothing that inspires, and strengthens the organisation like reading the unit's history of its actual battle account, whether that account is recorded in the books, or embodied in customs, institutions and monuments. Battle accounts are sacrosanct for an infantry battalion and cannot and should not be glossed over by anyone. To pick up the threads after such a long time from here and there and to make into a presentable and true form is however not that easy. Lot of search and research is required to be done. I have walked the talk with all the officers and numerous junior commissioned officers who took part in various actions and had been to the places of occurrence for facts to collect left-outs, engap missings and restore the misplacings.

Old Pearls of Wisdom

In this writing one finds use of maxims and sayings of important military leaders, social activists and enlightened humanists. The value of each depends on four things, its intrinsic excellence or comparative correctness of the principle it embodies, the subject to which it relates, the extents of its application and the comparative ease with which it may be applied in practice. The old truth answers where sermon fails, as, a well charged pistol will do more harm than a whole barrel of gunpowder, idly exploded in the air. These, therefore cement the actions with the circumstances. Sayings make interesting presentations of our thoughts and feelings in the measured words, brilliantly expressed by the inventors and the scholars. They very clearly put forth all humour, bitterness, tenderness, wit and wisdom in a very special style. They offer delight to find perfect expression to our jumbled structure of unframed words. Such expressions are helpful and are needed by us, when we try to convey appropriateness of the situation. A lot can be said easily by relating a single quotation which at the same time can be appropriately delightful and stimulating. These are the literature of reason or the statements of absolute truth without qualification, like sacred books of each nation and these are the sanctuary of the intuitions. The genius, wit and spirit of a nation are hidden in these sayings and proverbs of its gurus, prophets and educators. In short we can say it is a matter, immensely rich decoded into few words. They have pithy material, which are like nails, which force truth upon one's memory and contain sense, brevity and point which are their essence. Some of them are abridgement of wisdom from experience itself, which is the mother of all sciences. It can therefore be conveniently said that proverbs are in the world of thought, what gold coin is in the world of business, which are of great value in small compass and equally current among all people. Some times these may be taken as false like the coin counterfeit, but in both cases the false proves the value of the true. The wisdom of the wise and the experience of the ages are preserved in them. The author therefore takes pleasure in quoting the sayings in their correct perspective, with the aim of stressing emphasis on a particular situation.

Certain Overlappings

One will find repetition of few facts at couple of places. The reason is simple. Each battle has been described separately with background and there are lot of issues which overlap and cannot be separated. The aim is to clarify the issue in such a way that it does not look as ambiguous. When one point is being pursued, there are others, which are though of little value in that context and look to be subdued, but basically, those points would require to be included. There have been some highs and lows on the part of all, the unit, the officers and the men which is so natural and that has to be taken as such and brought out in a systematic way. But in fact, the sole reason such explaining is that truth is not sacrificed which is so very necessary for upholding the theme of writing the account.

Note

* Issues discussed herein were adopted by someone for diluting the operational history of the unit and as such had to be discarded here only.

3
IRONY AFTER IRONY

"Parting and forgetting? What faithful heart can do these? Our greatest thoughts, our great affections, the truths of our life never leave us – surely they cannot be separated from our consciousness, will follow it whithersoever that shall go and are, of their nature, divine and immortal." —Thackerary

Pangs of Division of Army

The British Indian Army had played a very crucial role in First and Second World Wars. It had earned the name and fame and was recognised as one of the most dedicated and professional armies. British had tacitly accepted that without the Indian element, the outcome of the war could have been different. Indian soldiers had proved their worth and exhibited laudable performance in the most trying operational and administrative conditions. They could dig down and plant themselves resolutely in defence and stick to their posts with dogged determination against most volatile and aggressive enemy, albeit often suffering heavy casualties. Same way, while attacking, moved on to the objective regardless of their own safety, falling down one after the other. This surprised many British officers. It was, however the result of very hard training and strict discipline, and also the fact that

British themselves used to be with the men. Their philosophy of training for warfare was, *"Training cements relationship between officers and men and fighting a war, cements them permanently."*

By the end of Second World War, the number of death casualties of the Indians had risen to about 87,000, a very large number indeed. Their contribution was recognised by British and men were rewarded liberally. It may be pointed out here that irrespective of the differences with the Muslim leadership of India on social and political issues, the camaraderie in the army among Hindus, Sikhs and Muslims was of very high order. The British could create any combination at any time without any hitch, if situation so demanded. They did it and got wonderful results. The key was the hard training and strict discipline. The Sikh Regiment had roughly one third strength of Muslims till 1947. Such cohesiveness effectively worked and proved productive. The catholicity of our armed forces is still being maintained, traditions are upped and loyalty to the government is ingrained in the minds of all. It has helped the army to come out of the pains of its division successfully and it is now serving as one of the important building blocks of national reconstruction.

Shortage of Officers

There came the movement of attainment of Independence for Indian subcontinent. The country was lucky to have inherited such an outfit, but it soon faced the vivisection of the whole war machinery. It was a most difficult period for the army to maintain ethos, standards and camaraderie. The composition changed, ratio changed and the name and number of units changed. Senior Muslim officers, who were quite large in number, almost all, opted for Pakistan Army, forcing a very big gap in the rank structure of officers in the new Indian Army. After having fought together as a part of the same unit for so long and in most inhospitable terrain and most demanding environments, mostly in foreign countries quite away from home, the phenomenon of parting was very painful and the pinch was felt on both sides in the respective armies. But that was destined to be so and in that context Mr Charles Chinevix, in his book, the 'Indian Army and King's Enemies' writes.

> *"The splitting of the regiment, composed of various communities, in most of the cases was poignant beyond words. All over India, Hindus, Sikhs and other communities were giving farewell parties to their departing Muslim comrades, seeing them off at the railway stations, putting garlands around their necks and wiping off their own tears rolling down the faces. And same was happening on the other side, in Pakistan. It was a simple slaughter of the Indian oneness and army suffered its share. In the country, splitting of the units and even the regiments i.e. mother foster organisations, had to face that tragedy, but the biggest solace was the preservation of some of the regiments."*

Parting is sweet sorrow and more so, where the life has been led together in most difficult conditions. Bonds developed during hard days are never erased from our consciousness.

Soldiers are mainly from rural stocks, many of them have the shakiest notion of the cause for which the country commits them in operations. They will perform heroic deeds for the sake of the honour of their units and regiments. The case of self respect and honour of the caste and community too, to which they belong, does merit prime consideration. The combination of good leadership and proud units has always been an important factor for winning the battle and adds substance to above theory. Based on this premise, the new Indian army soon overcame the trauma of division and organised itself, most of it on caste based regiments.

Reorganisation of Army of Independent India

The division of the Indian Army was planned before the declaration of independence, but could only begin a few weeks before, when sectarian killings increased and partition gave rise to various other such problems. The war department had been split on 19 July 1947 and many units had begun the task of moving components to one or the other side of the border, contemplated to be formalised. The number involved was very large. The British Indian Army was some 4,50,000, strong. It was agreed that new Indian Army should be allotted 2,60,000 with balance of about 30% going to Pakistan. Pakistan was not one third of India, but it so happened that almost all Muslim units went to Pakistan, which were very large in numbers and the important and painful factor was the silent proclivity of British towards Pakistan in all arenas of divisional theory. But it was not without a reason. The British had encouraged Muslims to join the army in Second World War, where they came in very large number. 'Mountbatten' by Richard Hough records which amply clarifies the contentions:-

> *"The Muslims had been mainly loyal to Britain during the war and had provided by far the greater number of troops. Congress helped to widen the division by opposing war and Nehru, Gandhi and some 60,000 of their followers were arrested."*

Employability of JCOs and NCOs

As said earlier, alongwith the troops, very large number of senior Muslim officers had opted for Pakistan army and as such there were serious deficiencies in the senior officer's ranks in the new Indian Army. Even the junior officers were not in sufficient strength and some who were there, they were mainly temporary and emergency commissioned officers. However they could shoulder responsibilities with proper support and guidance from senior officers. In such a situation, the promotion to the senior rank became very fast, in certain cases an officer of Major's rank became a Major General in five-six years time. It was a serious problem at unit level which persisted for quite sometime. However, some JCOs and NCOs who were duly experienced and battle hardened proved to be helpful to the commanding officers of units of reorganised Indian Army but certainly could not foot the bill to a desired standard.

Indian Army after partition could not get any respite for organizing, training and administering itself into a cohesive organisation, because of immediate mischief created by Pakistan. It was all due to the devious methods used by British for supporting them, that Pakistan went all out for spoils in Jammu and Kashmir. Both armies came face to face. The comrades of yesterday, whose parting created ripples in the minds and bleeding of hearts, became the worst of enemies – a real tragedy. Initially Indian Army had got committed in dealing with the managing of exodus of civilian people from Pakistan and getting them settled in new areas and help them in all other respects. Then the army was also required in Junagarh and Hyderabad. Though these operations were for brief spells, but did disturb the administering of organisational process of Indianisation of the erstwhile British Army.

Geo-political

Kashmir is a very beautiful place, where nature has showered well. It is paradise on earth with salubrious climate and everything beautiful all around. It was an active tourist destination for large number of foreigners, particularly British. Though the valley was having majority population of Muslims but there was a sizeable population of Hindus, Sikhs, Christians and other communities and a work place for many non-Muslims. It was one of the important states with abundant and varied resources and Maharaja had developed this beautiful land well. It was not for nothing that people used to sing about Kashmir's beauty.

> "Who had not heard of the vale of Cashmere
> With its roses the brightest that earth ever gave.
> Its temples and grottoes and fountains as clear
> As the love lighted eyes that hang over their
> wore" —Thomas Moore

Maharaja was of the opinion that he would do well if stayed independent and could make Kashmir "Switzerland of East." But times had changed and unfortunately he could not understand it. Sheikh Mohammad Abdullah had become very popular and powerful and his National Conference had become a force to reckon with.

Indian Political Leadership and MA Jinnah

The political leadership in India at that time was highly accomplished and was a combination of all sorts. They had shaken the pillars of British Raj using their own ways and means. They cooperated when needed and opposed British, when denied a reasonableness. They fought for freedom in a systematic way, coordinating with all those who were for united India. But Mr. MA Jinnah was out of synchronisation and the Indian leaders could find no way out. He played the Muslim card exploiting their sentiments. Unfortunately our leaders did not deal with him adequately as a lay man thinks. Had they decided that either he agrees to their way or they agreed to his way, some solution could have been found. Jinnah issue was studied and tackled in a most forthright manner only by one person and that was Ch. Sir Chhotu Ram, a powerful minister rather a power centre of Unionist Party in Punjab. This Party was organised by Sir Fazle Hussain in consultation with Sir Chhotu Ram and was led by Sikandar Hayat Khan after former's death. However, it was sustained with utmost care by Malik Khizar Hayat Khan and Ch. Sir Chhotu Ram till death of the later, on 9 January 1945. Sir Chhotu Ram was a very strong voice of Hindu, Sikh and Muslim agriculturists, farmers and rural farm workers. Understanding that Punjab was a Muslim majority state and to face MA Jinnah's Muslim League, he ensured that the premier was a Muslim. In fact, being a very strong pillar of Unionist Party, his name was propped up for premiership of Punjab after the death of Sir Sikander Hayat Khan and he was garlanded symbolising empowering him as such, but Sir Chhotu Ram being a totally selfless worker of the party and a man of masses refused the honour, took out the garland and put it around the neck of Malik Khizar Hayat Khan, surprising both the Mahasabhais and Muslims League. He was a great votary of Hindu, Muslim, Sikh unity and an ardent opponent of Muslim League who wanted the partition of the country.

British and Jinnah

Jinnah was made to run away from Punjab and did not dare enter Punjab till Ch. Chhotu Ram's death on 9 January 1945. Had the Indian leadership dealt with Jinnah, the Chhotu Ram way, the situation probably could have been saved. Reasons may be any, which the research scholars can probe further, but certainly it looks that there was lack of concerted effort on this issue. One can rationalise the thinking on the final outcome and then cannot entirely absolve the Hindus and other interested parties, from the responsibilities of having forced and driven the Musalmans to the cry of Pakistan is another irony. The leadership simply shied away and Jinnah got the country partitioned and went away with Pakistan. In doing so, the British, of course, played their deadly role and derided us. Prime Minister Atlee of England later on when confronted with an awkward question as to "what did you do when all this was happening? Was it not your sacred duty to help the country, you ruled for over two centuries?" He angrily burst out:-

"Jinnah was a little, a very little man, when the Indian political parties could not settle their contentious issues in anyway, what could Britain do under such circumstances except to partition it."

These were very significant observations with highly sensitive revelations. And today having seen the plight of Pakistan and she being a biggest hindrance in the development of India, Atlee's view become weighty. We all including the masses of both the countries and the intelligentsia of Pakistan though privately do strongly feel that Jinnah was wrong and partition was a folly – another ironic imponderable of history.

Problems in Kashmir

Immediately before and during the indecisive period regarding accession of Kashmir, the tribesman coaxed by Muslim league had begun to move towards Jammu and Kashmir. Forays by tribesman were succeeded by invasion by very large number of other troops creating all sorts of problems for the public. It was an indication for a widespread chaos. Sir George Cunningham, newly appointed Governor of NWFP recorded in his diary on 19 October 1947. "A member of my staff told me that there is a real movement in Hazara in North Central Pakistan for a Jihad in Kashmir. They have been busy in collecting fire arms and making definite plans of campaign apparently for seizing the part of main Jhelum Valley above Domel in Western Kashmir. I, on my part have warned all including Afridis and Mohmands of the danger of taking part in anything, it can lead to a war between India and Pakistan. I am not sure enough whether it could be a *casus belli* (cause of dispute) at present, as Kashmir Maharaja has acceded neither to India nor to Pakistan."

Governor made another entry on 24 October 1947 where he mentioned that he disapproved of Maharaja's action for declaring accession to India. It clearly shows, that a man of Governor's stature could not have made such a remark in normal course had the British, not been helping Pakistan both overtly and covertly. Incursions were reported from number of places, which made Nehru to talk to Mountbetten on 24 October 1947. Consequently Mountbetten called the meeting of the defence committee, the next day. Same time Mr. Jinnah Governor General of Pakistan ordered Gen George Douglas Gracy C-in-C of Pakistan to send regular troops to Kashmir in aid of armed tribesmen and invaders, which shows and proves that Pakistan's army was seriously involved in it. But Gracy did not oblige him that day. He was C-in-C of Pakistan, but at the same time he owed his responsibility to Governor General Mountbatten also. He was subordinate to Field Marshal Auchinleck who was Supreme Commander of the forces of both countries. He could not think of ranging troops of both countries against each other, without their open approval.

There were reports of three battalions of Frontier Force Regiment having entered Kashmir in early October 1947. It was confirmed that they were threatening and killing Hindus, Sikhs, Christians and others, forcing them to flee and were commandeering the local Muslim population for invasion. This news convinced Nehru, who in turn requested Mountbatten to send the Indian Army to the valley as early as possible, but instrument of accession had not yet been signed by Maharaja.

Instrument of Accession

On 26 October 1947, when Maharaja declared the accession of his State to India, Mr VP Krishna Menon, Secretary of Ministry of States accompanied by Lt Col Sam Manekshaw (later Field Marshal) were sent to Srinagar to do the needful officially. They found Maharaja in panic. They returned to Delhi with a definite news of advance of Pakistani Tribesman towards Srinagar. They, of course carried with them the offer of accession of Jammu and Kashmir to the Union of India, given to them by Maharaja. Nehru then insisted that Indian troops should be rushed to Kashmir at the earliest. Mountbatten was equally worried about large number of British citizens, who were in Kashmir for one reason or the other. Mountbatten perused the accession document and said that the wishes of the people of the state will be honoured. Mountbatten dashed a letter also to Maharaja, in his private capacity to this effect. It was not responded by Maharaja. He was clear of the offer of joining or not as it was the sole prerogative of the Head i.e. the ruler of the State and public was not involved in it. It is to be remembered that Nehru and Sheikh Abdullah were very popular with the people of Jammu and Kashmir and any decision taken by them, then, was acceptable to Kashmiris. Nehru feeling positive about the outcome accepted in these prevailing circumstances, Mountbatten's views, on endorsement of the clause, though Maharaja had not. Next day troops started landing in Kashmir and the conflict between India and Pakistan began.

Insertions on instrument of Accession

In the meantime, Mountbatten asked for the instrument of accession and on it, he, in his own hand added that :-

"It is my government's wish that as soon as the law and order situation is restored in Kashmir and her soil is cleared of raiders, the question of State's Accession should be settled by reference to the people" —another irony rather very big irony

It is now a well-known fact that sympathies of the British were with Pakistan. They never wanted Pakistan to lose and came to her rescue every now and then. UN intervention and ascertaining the will of the people of the state on final accession inspite of Maharaja having the sole power to decide could not be Nehru's making. It was forced upon him by Mountbatten. Nehru with his maturity and feeling that Kashmiris were with him and they were so then, he accepted it but Pakistan never vacated the area so occupied and intricacies kept on multiplying.

In 1965, the interest of Kashmiris lay in tourists, woodcrafts and papier-mache and all-round development than to go political. It was to take couple of years of alleged rigging and general lack of proper rule, before some element of the Muslims of Kashmir started revolting against Delhi government. Life since then has changed to a great extent. I call this also as an irony.

Some of the other important ironies on the situation prevailing then are given in the succeeding paragraphs which are self explanatory:-

- **Jinnah on Trial of Bhagat Singh, 12-14 September 1929.** Nobody doubted and can say that Jinnah was against granting independence of India. He was a true nationalist at one time. The remarkable feat of his personality was his speech in the central legislative assembly on September 12 and 14, 1929. This was the most forthright statement in defence of Bhagat Singh from among the leading politicians of the time. It is relevant to remember that where principles of law and norms of justice were threatened, Jinnah's voice was that of a fearless Indian. It is the later developments which forced him to adopt different course of action.

- **Letter by Gandhi to Jinnah, 15 September 1944.** I find no parallel in history for a body of converts and their descendents claiming to be a nation apart from the parent stock. If India was one nation before the advent of Islam it must remain one inspite of the change of faith of a very large body of her children. You don't claim to be separate nation by right of conquest but by the reason of acceptance of Islam. Will the two nations become one if the whole of India accepted Islam.

- **Letter by Jinnah to Gandhi 17 September 1944.** We maintain and hold that Muslims and Hindus are two major nations by any definition or test of a nation. We are a nation of a hundred million and what is more, we are a nation with distinctive culture and civilisation, language and literature, art and architecture, names and nomenclature, sense of value and proportion, legal laws and moral codes, customs and calendar, history and traditions, aptitude and ambitions, in short we have got our own distinctive outlook on life and of life. By all canons of international law, we are a nation.

- By this time, he was thoroughly plagued and prostituted by narrow-minded self-seekers, through intense propaganda and foreign trips.

- **Letter of M Iqbal (the great poet) to Thompson of Statesman – 29 December 1930.** "Pakistan plan will be disastrous to British Govt, disastrous to Hindu Community and disastrous to Moslem Community. But I am President of Muslim League and therefore, it is my duty to support it."

- The two letters of Edward Thompson, published in The Statesman and The Nation, stated to be the authority of Sir Muhammad Iqbal that idea of Pakistan had not his (Iqbal's) approval.

- **Louis Fiseher** an independent and fair-minded American observer correctly stated, in his treatise Indo-British Tangle 1942. *"But I carried out of India the definite conviction that if the British wished, they could have a working unity in India within twenty-four hours."*

A stage had come when Britain was forced to grant Independence. Votaries of undivided and divided India could have reached a compromise as we had very strong common heritage, but British never wanted us to stay together. They kept on applying various theories to divide us. I may say in the whole sordid game of partition, the "Referee" was the winner and that was the biggest of the ironies.

4

JAMMU AND KASHMIR, BRITISH AND PAKISTAN

"Study history, study history, in history lies all the secrets of the statecraft." —Sir James Wolfe

Geography of Kashmir

At the time of partition of India in 1947, Jammu and Kashmir was one of the largest states of India. It is in the north and north-western part of India and is bordering with China and Tibet. It acceded to the Union of India in 1947 and became its integral part. Pakistan thinks that it should have gone to her as it was mainly a Muslim dominated area and primarily the Kashmir Valley and Punch area which is with valley connected by Haji Pir Pass and Mughal Road over the Pir Panjal Range. However, no one else than Jinnah himself had suggested in his own statement on 30 July 1947 that "the legal position is that with the lapse of paramountcy on the transfer of power by the British, all Indian States should automatically regain their full sovereign and independent status. They are therefore free to join either of the two dominions or remain independent. The Muslim League (Jinnah's party) recognises the right of each state to choose its destiny" (Dawn 31 July 1947).

The geographical location of the State of Jammu and Kashmir is such that besides that of England, it gains added importance and counts in the geo-political assertions and interests of Russia and China too. For Pakistan, it is a main source of water as all the three important rivers i.e Chenab, Jhelum and Indus meant exclusively for Pakistan as per the provision of Indus Water Treaty 1960, are fed by the tributaries originating from State of Jammu and Kashmir and pass through Kashmir and that is the reason, which has been worrying them most. Besides this, the Kashmir Valley has got its own assets, in its forests, waterfalls, rivers, gardens, hill tops, mountains, rocks and glaciers, with scenic beauty. For centuries, it has been a sacred place for adherents of various faiths, which are firmly rooted here. Its undeniable beauty and climatic conditions have been inviting people, from all over the world and for long. It had its own strategic importance for the world powers as well as for India and Pakistan, in 1947-48 and no less now. (See Sketch 2)

State of Jammu and Kashmir as a whole, is mountainous area with glaciers on top reaches. There are tracts of plain areas also. Kashmir Valley is somewhat more flat and quite developed since long, in comparison to other areas (See Sketch 3). The state has got three distinct areas, which are culturally, linguistically and racially quite different from each other. Approach to Kashmir Valley, from Indian side is mainly through Jammu and the same way, approach to Ladakh is through Kashmir Valley. However before partition in 1947, Kashmir Valley was, maintained primarily from that part of Punjab which is now in Pakistan. Land in the valley is fertile and the main occupation of people is agriculture including, apple growing, animal husbandry, woolen hosiery, papier-mache handicraft and establishing and maintaining the tourists spots, hotels and allied occupations. In other words, Kashmir Valley is almost self-sustaining area. Gilgit and Baltistan during British days were under their direct control but through Maharaja, due to the reason of these being strategically important for safeguarding from the Tsarist Russia. It was manned by Gurkha and Dogra soldiers of Maharaja's army. However, the British had the final say in control over these areas and Maharaja was sort of their protege only.

British Interests in Kashmir

Based on the strategic and geo-political factors Jammu and Kashmir was never out of minds of the British and they kept on playing their game against India till the last day. Even today, as far as Jammu and Kashmir is concerned; they are not out of it. They have deep-rooted ambitions, the reason for such views and mindset on their part are given in the succeeding paras.

Checking of Expansion of Communism

The position of State of Jammu and Kashmir then and even now in the Central Asian context is unique. It was always uppermost in the minds of British that this plateau was the key-stone for catering of their interests in the region. Hunza, Nagar and Gilgit, besides the valley of Kashmir can serve as the launching pad for carrying out any campaign against Russia and China, both then being the strongholds of communism. They were really worried about the expansion of communism. From the very beginning and more acutely with their half-hearted plans of leaving India, they had never taken their eyes off the area and thumbs off its nerves.

Sketch 2: Jammu and Kashmir – Historical

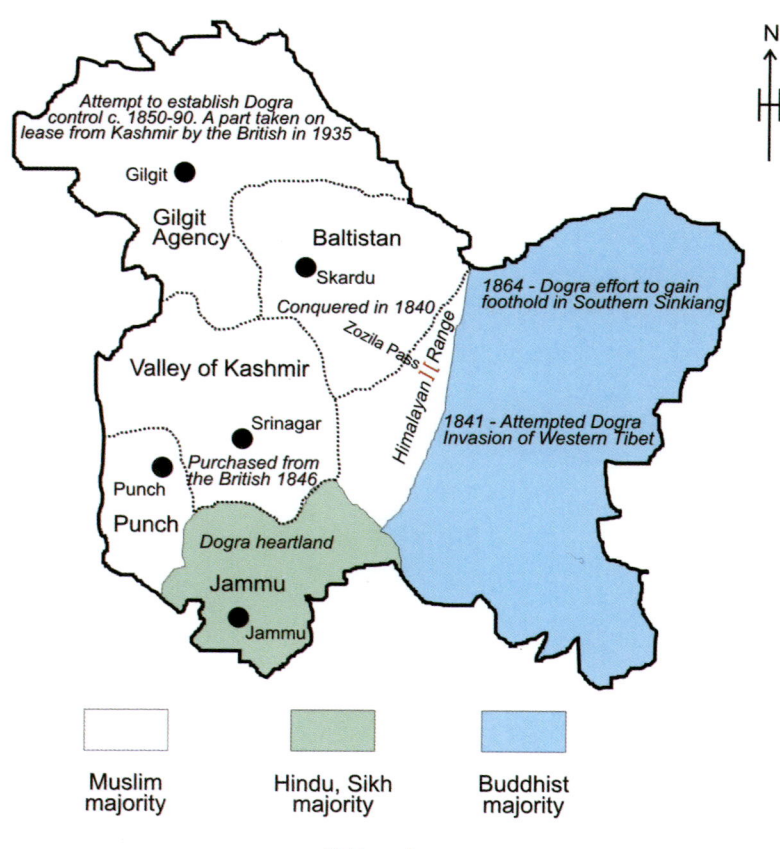

Attempt to establish Dogra control c. 1850-90. A part taken on lease from Kashmir by the British in 1935

Gilgit

Gilgit Agency

Baltistan

Skardu

Conquered in 1840

Zozila Pass

Himalayan Range

1864 - Dogra effort to gain foothold in Southern Sinkiang

Valley of Kashmir

Srinagar

Purchased from the British 1846

Punch

Punch

1841 - Attempted Dogra Invasion of Western Tibet

Dogra heartland

Jammu

Jammu

Muslim majority | Hindu, Sikh majority | Buddhist majority

Not to scale
Boundaries are approximate

Sketch 3: Kashmir Valley

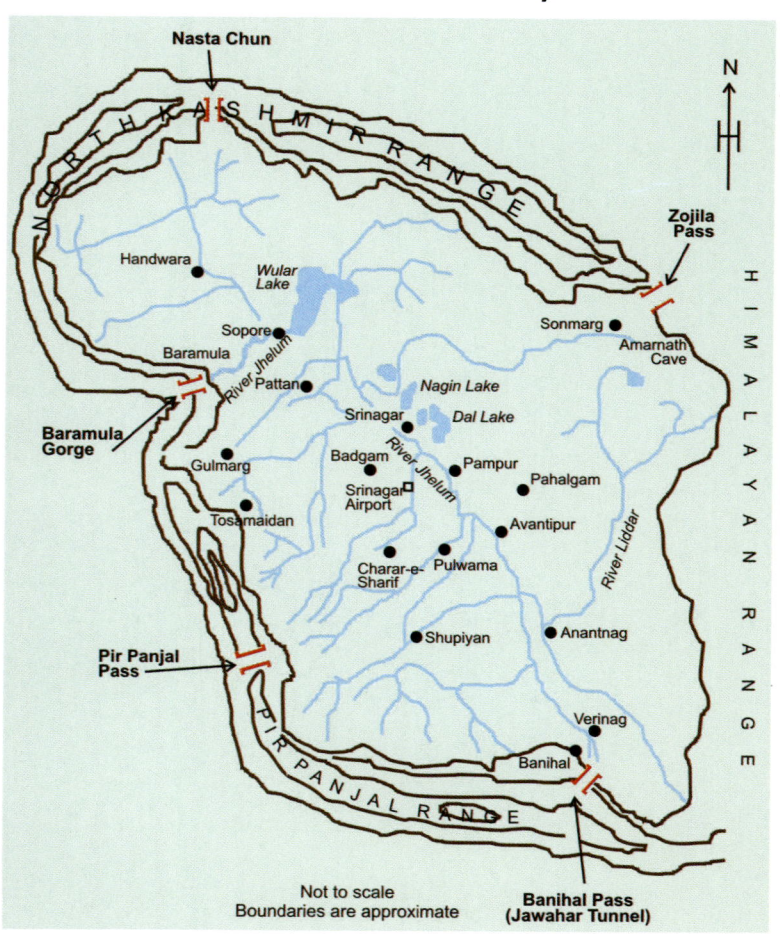

None of the three, India, Pakistan and Maharaja were allowed to have free and frank discussions with each other. Maharaja had been under the obligations and supremacy of the British for long and he had accepted their writ in toto.

In the whole game, the British were prominently seen playing against India. They suspected that based on the history of struggle for independence, Indian National Congress will never play their tune and be a pawn in their hands. They even suspected Nehru to have had leanings towards the communists. They thought that their interest of blocking the communists' expansion could not be served by aligning towards India. These could be best served by being with Pakistan, where Muslim League which was enjoying majority and which had played no part in the struggle for independence, had no problem with British and was always closer to them in comparison to Congress and was thus best suited to deal with.

Middle East Defence Organisation

Another important issue which coloured the views of British and all western powers was that Pakistan being a Muslim country could play an important part for their having control as well as good relations with various countries of the Gulf region and the Middle East Defence Organisation, which they themselves contemplated to organise. They were therefore always pro-Pakistan. India certainly in those circumstances could not have served their cause. All this gave birth to the problem of Kashmir, which was created solely by British. They never wanted that the area of Middle East should go under the influence of Russians or Chinese or both. In view of their natural interests so deeply harboured, they helped Pakistan and propped it up against India particularly over Kashmir. They even saw the free India also being on the same page, with Russia and China. In the game of domination the areas or countries around, the importance of Kashmir Valley, Gilgit, Skardu and Nagar therefore could not be over-emphasised. Even Karakoram Pass and Aksai Chin plateau were never out of the western radar. Any country which had the sway over these areas, could easily influence the Middle East oil rich region, which was so important in the modern age for power, energy and influence in the emerging world. This thinking is still prevalent and almost all the western countries who are under the influence of UK and USA would go with Pakistan. Enormity of this influence has been noticed in the past. It can be said without any prejudice that biased policies of USA, particularly at that time were responsible for making "bluster and bravado" of Pakistan. They could do anything for their 'religion' of self interest.

India for Destroying Pakistan

Western powers were of the opinion that India is against the establishment of Pakistan and she will destroy it, if she had her ways in the region, though Nehru at numerous occasions had made it clear that stable Pakistan was in India's interests. Surprisingly even Field Marshal Sir Auchinlek himself was of the same view and strongly felt that India may invade Pakistan. Most of the Westerners aired their opinion openly about India gobbling up Pakistan, at the first favourable opportunity. Astonishingly the same thinking still prevails with most of the western countries led by USA and UK. They were thus keen that Kashmir should either be with Pakistan or independent but not with India. But Nehru played his game with very cool courage, intellect and active tolerance. He knew their game well and his only aim was that British should be out of India and off the scene, quickly, peacefully and cooly. The Conservatives in England, even wanted that in case India does not behave, Kashmir may be regained again. In view of the above, Pakistan was given all possible help.

Keeping Roots in India

British would have never wanted to vacate this land, had there been no world wars. They had hedged their promises of Second World War but they were forced by the circumstances and shrinking British economy. They were deadly against Indian people and could put hurdles, in the transfer of power. It is a fact that had British not got involved in the affairs of Kashmir, this problem between India and Pakistan, over Kashmir would not have happened. Both countries could have sorted out their problems by now and settled in the new world order. But for serving their own cause, Pakistan was armed by western powers, particularly USA in 1954 and onwards against India. Even now there is no change in their policy. The words of Maj Gen Sir John Malcolm spoken in Parliament Select Committee of England reveal their psychology of staying permanently and of ruling with the sword.

> "The (Indian) Empire had been acquired with the sword and must be maintained by sword. The military plans for the Govt of our Eastern Empire (India) must even be entitled to primary considerations. The local army of India, but above all, the native branch should always be preserved in condition of efficiency and attachment. Our means of preserving and improving our possessions, through operations of our civil

institutions depend on our wise and politic exercise of that military power on which the whole fabric rests"

The policies which were made by British were never for the welfare of Indian people but these were made to rule and loot the country and that sums up their long desire of keeping roots in India. Of course, J&K being strategically important area for domination of world geo-politically, was equally worth committing and uppermost in their minds.

Paying the Debt

Since the days immediately after the Mutiny of 1857 or First War of Independence as we call it, British had realised and made up their mind that somehow the Hindus and Muslims should be kept divided. They were very clear that if these two communities stay together it will not be possible to pursue the policy of suppression and exploitation. The division of Bengal in 1907 on communal lines was the result of this policy. Muslims had been made to send maximum number of recruits in the Second World War and British had felt obliged to their willing participation. They also wanted to pay back their debt to Muslims for not seriously involving themselves in the struggle for Independence. Apropos to that, the British always wanted to favour Pakistan in those formative years and they did, wherever and whenever they could get a chance. Mr HV Hodson, Reforms Commissioner of Viceroy Lord Linlithgow in his eloquent best, had declared, that *"carving out of Pakistan was inevitable, since Hindus and Muslims are two different people and their division is as old as the Arab invasions."* He very conveniently ignored that their culture was indigenous and home-grown in India and there was no difference at all.

Indian Muslims were almost all converted from Hindus over the years, and were maintaining their cultural traditions and ethos with Hindus. During their later years in India, British had endeared Muslims much more than Hindus and Muslims thus served the former better. Most Indians wanted the British to go without any delay but it was not so with all Muslims. Many senior Muslim army officers had served with British and had fine memories of good life spent in association with them. Muslims were never harassed or beaten by the British officered police. They did not have any ill will towards British, rather they had respect and affection for them. Naturally British, never missed such a chance and gave full cooperation to exploit the situation obtaining at that time, in the Indian sub-continent.

Congress and Hindus

Congress wanted a united India and having understood the ground realties had developed strong secular ethos based on the philosophy of Akbar the Great who had said, *"the sovereign of Hindustan is duty bound to become a bridge between Muslims and Hindus of the land. Both are equally our subjects and our responsibility. Mullah, the Them and Us, have no place in our world."* Congress and mainly Hindus, who may be belonging to any political party or organisation were all keen for throwing the British out as early as they could. Congress leaders were very clear in their minds that British will not leave India that easily. Even after Second World War when India had provided recruits on their promise of freeing the country, they started giving confusing signals and the people got very restive.

Indians fought for independence, with determination.

British forces used their might to control and suppress the movements launched by the Indian people headed by Indian National Congress. Their leaders suffered long terms in jails and were treated very harshly. British took Hindus as their opponent. Nehru who was himself a product of British education, culture and upbringing and a foremost nationalist leader of the India fighting for independence of his motherland wanted the British to feel that "we also need a place under the sun." He resented their methods but was cool and wise in his disposition towards them. Mahatma Gandhi and Nehru with their methods of persuasion and conducting various affairs with maturity, coupled with respect, could make a place for themselves in hierarchy of British. The British in general and Conservatives in particular were very upset and were never in favour of granting freedom to India. Congress was blamed by them for getting them uprooted in a systematic campaign. They were all against India. But this band of leaders under Mahatma Gandhi could not be cowed down and never left the line of gentlemanliness required in an adventure involving life and death of the country. British could make certain unpalatable remarks but could not rebut the force of reasonableness which these leaders presented to them. "Trusting our own intuitions that peace will prevail often saves us in different situations" and that was the philosophy of Mahatma Gandhi for his actions towards them.

Jammu and Kashmir – Importance of Pakistan

Pakistan considers the conquering and occupation of Jammu and Kashmir as a key to its survival. Once it is in her hands, it can be a source of permanent trouble for India by being an important launching pad for both guerrilla and conventional warfare against it. Strategically, enhances the depth to its northern part and serves as a great factor for its policies and plans and playing its role in the comity of nations thereby placating the big powers. It feels that particularly, Kashmir part of Jammu and Kashmir is more crucial for its security. Liaquat Ali Khan had once said, "that Kashmir for India is luxury but for Pakistan it is vital for its survival. If it is in India's hand, Pakistan will be at the mercy of India. Having a very long common border, the State of Jammu and Kashmir dominates Pakistan from north and east. It is clear that if it is in India's hands militarily, Pakistan rails, roads and military bases can be threatened and Pakistan can be strategically cajoled effectively for any issue." Jammu and Kashmir has got control over the upper reaches of Indus, Jhelum and Chenab, which are the life lines for the agricultural economy of the Pakistan. The flow of these rivers can be effectively controlled to bring Pakistan to its knees, if needed. In December 1959 President Ayub Khan had said that Kashmir was vital for Pakistan not only politically but militarily also, besides its physical and economic security. Kashmir for them is the head of body of Pakistan for all practical purposes. Pakistan considers Kashmir, as a matter of life and death. Pakistan tries to take the advantage of religion, which plays as an important part for Pakistan's undying wish to annex Kashmir, where the majority is of Muslims though culturally and racially totally different from them all.

Jammu and Kashmir – Importance to India

Kashmir is of utmost importance to India too. The defence of the country will be straightaway jeopardised, if it is in the hands of Pakistan. It can be a source of permanent nuisance and danger to India from defence point of view. The population of Jammu and Ladakh region will face hardship of survival as they belong to different stocks and have different traditions and religions and can be isolated and attacked by any power from any side. For dealing with Pakistan, the occupancy of this area, which is now in India's hands cannot be over-emphasised. Pakistan is a belligerent country and its policy will always be anti-India and it has become part of its character. For keeping the hand and control on the pulse of Pakistan, Kashmir is very important. Any military buildup, by Pakistan can even be "controlled" through the waters of the three rivers and their tributaries. For launching an offensive in Pakistan, the occupation of valley as a base is very-very significant. The security of India can be considerably affected since part of southern boundary of Jammu and Kashmir touching Punjab and Himachal Pradesh are common.

Valley and Convergence of Expeditionary Routes

The state of Jammu and Kashmir lies in the central area of South Asia and is very crucial for the domination of the areas around. Western Countries at the time of partition of India had the fear of the communism and wanted to involve Pakistan in their game plan. Pakistan had joined the western block through various alliances and Kashmir being a problem, created by them earlier, was automatically drawn into this relationship and thus brought into conflict. It was Anglo-American conspiracy, which always put spoils in India's ways to consolidate its position in this most strategic Asian region. British will never miss a chance. They played their dirty trick in the Kutchh arbitration, where we learned the hard way that we in future will never accept third party mediation in our conflicts. (discussed in a separate chapter)

Kashmir is at a convergence of various expeditionary routes and thus gains vital importance. On all its sides, the different types of people with diverse culture are settled, who could be divided and exploited by the powers on various pretexts. Zojila, Nashta Chun, Banihal and Pir Panjal passes alongwith Baramulla gorge are very important landmarks which can dictate number of courses for military adventures for ingress in or from the valley.

5
PUNCH AND ITS SPECIFIC IMPORTANCE

Regions of Kashmir

As has already been brought out in the previous chapters Pakistan was successful in occupying certain areas of Jammu and Kashmir in 1947-48 War, which still continue to remain under its illegal occupation. It is roughly one third of the whole area of State of Jammu and Kashmir of that time, and where lie some of the very important assets like Mangla Dam and Mirpur water bodies with numerous pondages. Firstly, a word about Pakistan Occupied Kashmir (POK) and so-called Azad Kashmir. It is one and the same thing. In India, we call this area of Kashmir, as PoK where as Pakistan calls it Azad Kashmir. The other areas which were or are in the north of the Jammu and Kashmir state intentionally named as Northern Areas by Pakistan where as these are Gilgit and Baltistan and at times, called Dardistan. It is pertinent to note that Jammu and Kashmir had four important regions in 1947 and these were (i) Jammu (ii) Kashmir (iii) Ladakh and (iv) Gilgit and Frontier Illaqas, and Punch formed part of Kashmir region, though on the other side of Pir Panjal Range and part of this region which is under Pakistan is referred

Past History of Punch

Old Jagir of Punch was the part of the then north-western Kashmir Province. Important places in this belt were Punch, Mandi, Kotli, Mirpur, Surankot, Sekhlu, Bagh and some other smaller towns and the countryside around. Punch was a popular place and a Muslim dominated area and British had recruited very large number of Muslims from this area in Second World War. In 1947, Punch as such had very large number of demobilised soldiers and ex-servicemen. It was the first area in Jammu and Kashmir, where revolt was engineered by Pakistan, with the help of ex-servicemen and deserters from Maharaja's army, numbering over 25,000. The net result thus after 1947-48 War, was the loss of Kotli, Mirpur, Bagh and other areas. Punch alongwith Mendhar and surrounding area comprising of Punch river basin short of Kotli was however, secured by the Indian Army. These areas are very fertile and agriculturally very rich. Punch River ultimately falls into Mangla Dam, which is on river Jhelum near Mirpur. It is a most important asset in that area, now under Pakistan's occupation. (See Sketch 4)

Mangla Dam

It is just on the International Border of India and Pakistan, with major portion of the water body being towards Mirpur in Jammu and Kashmir. But as the areas of Kotli and Mirpur are in POK at present, Pakistan has control over the Dam and one Corps of Pakistan Army is located is general area Mangla. One can make out, as to how the Punch basin, south of Doresai plateau is contributing so massively to this project where water, from, upto Pir Panjal Range flows in. Pakistan feels that such a vast catchment area can be controlled by India at any time at number of places and can have terrific effect on the existence and utility of Mangla Dam and, as such, Pakistan will do everything possible to ensure that it does not face a difficult situation during the war. This therefore has always been in their scheme of things for defensive and offensive operations in this area and so far have been successful also in saving the dam, though no serious offensive has been launched by India in that area.

Capturing and Cutting off Punch

Pakistan had planned the 1965 operation to annex specially Kashmir Valley including Punch, though tried to move to other areas also. Their operation was planned on the wrong notions as they could not understand the mood of the people of valley and other areas dominated by people of various origins, the ground realities and the will of Indian people. Just before Kutchh operation in 1965, Pakistan illegally transferred a large chunk of territory of about 25,000 square kilometers, in Shaksgam – Muztagh Valley near Karakoram Pass, unilaterally to China, apparently to get its assistance to build Karakoram Highway and support for any adventure against India. It was in their scheme of things that somehow China should be involved in Jammu and Kashmir affairs, which they succeeded to some extent. Careful study of the happening will reveal that such a big piece of land, ceded to China, without anything in return, was with a specific aim of preparing grounds of an offensive with support, so anticipated from China. It had the tacit support and assuring nod from USA, which was desperately trying to build bridges with China. After the humiliating defeat of India at the hands of

Sketch 4: Punch River Basin

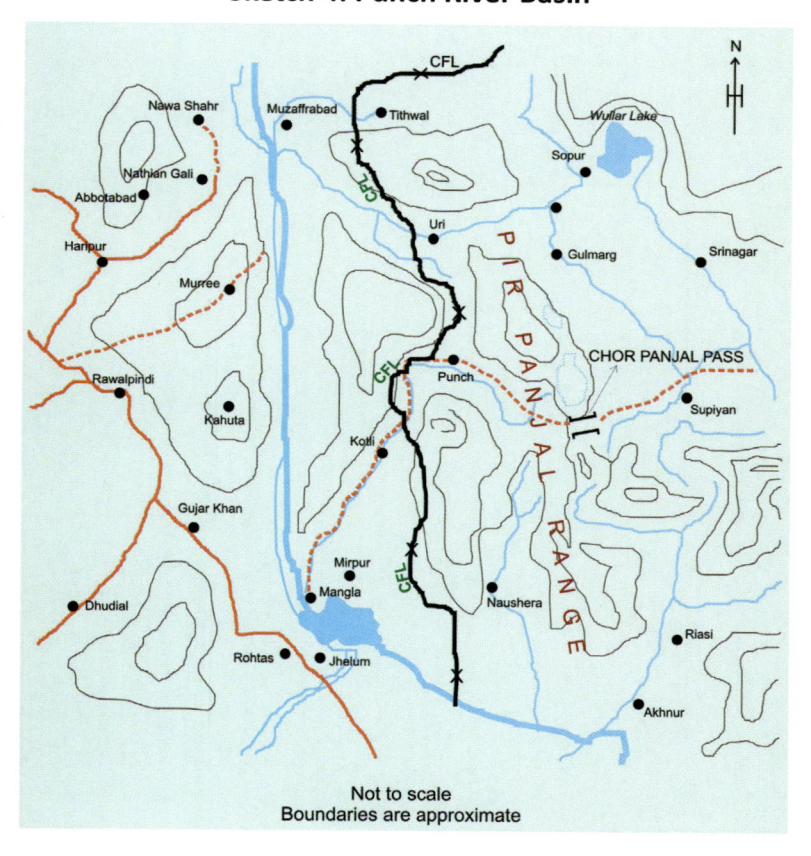

China in 1962 Pakistan took it very convincingly that India was no match then, against her having been armed with the new and flashy weaponry from America and with that background first started trouble in Kutchh and later in Jammu and Kashmir in August 1965. With such backdrop of assistance promised by the high and mighty countries of the world, Pakistan ventured very aggressively for Punch area, besides other places.

Pakistan in 1965 had concentrated heavily in Punch Sector and specially at places against Mendhar and Mandi valleys. Their aim was to cut off Punch projection by linking from both sides at general area of Kalai Bridge – Khanetar Gali. Larger aim was securing the Punch basin area, which is so very important for their Mangla Dam. It was not incidental but the result of meticulous planning that Pakistan had quickly captured Mandi town in north on 9 August 1965, so deep inside and also occupied around 11 August, 1965 the area which later came to be known as OP Hill Complex in south and simultaneously sending a strong column at Khanetar hitting our ammunition depot. Aim was to cut off Punch salient and thwart the Indian threat to the dam on permanent basis. (See Sketch 15)

Lone Unit on Independent Axis

It was here the role of 7 SIKH in thwarting the designs on their northern axis of advance via Mandi comes in. This gallant unit, suffering all sorts of difficulties for about a month, single-handedly, beat the Pakistanis in their game. It wrested back the Mandi town and defended the complete Mandi Valley till last, though not without suffering hardships and casualties. On the

---

Note: For clear understanding of the subject you may properly study Sketch 15 (given with Chapter 15) before proceeding further.

southern axis, the enemy, however was successful in getting a foothold at OP Hill Complex, and could affect every move in Mendhar Valley. With enemy sitting at OP Hill steadfastly their aim of securing the catchment area of Mangla Dam on north and north-eastern side could be a grand success and as a result brigade attack was launched to evict them from OP Hill Complex. It was so incidental that for this Brigade attack too, 7 SIKH was detailed, where it captured the ground of tactical importance, the Jungle Hill in phase II of the operation.

In view of the above, laudable performance of 7 SIKH at both the axes is worthy of note. I may not be very wrong, if permitted to say that in 1965 operations 7 SIKH was the savior of Punch and Punch basin both, first at Mandi and then at Mendhar. If you happen to informally talk to the civilian common gentry with easy demeanours, they will come out with the facts that in 1947-48 War, Punch was saved by Brig Pritam Singh and in 1965 operations it was saved by 7 SIKH. It is still a revered unit in that area.

Conclusion

Punch area is a fertile piece of land. Though it is on the other side of Pir Panjal Pass, it had formed part of Kashmir region which was known as north-western district of Kashmir. It is very important for both India and Pakistan because:-

- It is connected with the valley via Haji Pir Pass but the Haji Pir bulge is with Pakistan, both Uri and Punch are with India and hence vital for India to capture Haji Pir bulge and for Pakistan for isolating and cutting off the Punch salient.

- For launching operations towards Muzzafrabad and adjoining areas of POK, keeping strong presence of armed forces in Punch sector is very important for India
- It is a Muslim dominated area and Pakistan is lured as it can be volatised again as in 1947-48.
- There lies an important asset in the form of Mangla Dam the security of which can be jeopardised if this area is enlarged by India. Punch area if captured by Pakistan can be a great asset for them for advancing towards valley via Uri and Mughal roads.

6
1947-48 WAR AND AFTERWARDS

"To err is human. Even a small mistake committed by a leader transforms a simple headache into a disease"
—JL Nehru in 1962 at Srinagar on Kashmir Problem

Partition and Jammu and Kashmir

Britain had, announced their scheme of partitioning the country on 3 June 1947. Accordingly under the Independence of India Act 1947, they informed all the heads of 562 Princely States and 11 Centrally Controlled Provinces, that they could join either India or Pakistan or even opt for remaining independent. Most of the rulers, had assessed the situation very realistically and agreed to join either India or Pakistan based on factors of their choice. This was the prerogative of the rulers only and no other stipulation for ascertaining the views of public was ever mentioned. Few of them had different notions about the new situation and dispensation and thought that they could remain independent. Maharaja Hari Singh of Jammu and Kashmir was one of them. As a result, he approached both India and Pakistan and sought to enter into a "Stand Still" agreement with both of them. India could do nothing, as they were still at the mercy of British Government, which had the complete control over the levers of power in India till then. While majority of population in the Kashmir Valley was Muslim, the ruler was a Hindu. There was a considerable population of the other castes and communities also. The stand still agreement was signed with Pakistan before 15 August 1947, to be effective from 15 August 1947 onwards.

Pakistan felt and still feels that in accordance with their feelings and principles of partition of the country based on "two nation theory," State of Jammu and Kashmir should have gone to her. India does not recognise and contribute to the idea of two nation theory. The will of the ruler in Jammu and Kashmir therefore was of paramount importance and incidentally none other than Mr. MA Jinnah had suggested that ruler's wishes will be taken as final. It is this point that Pakistan is cornered on and has not been able to negate so far and loses the argument every time. Moreover, the demarcation on communal lines was applicable only to centrally administered state and not the princely states.

In early October 1947, Sheikh Mohammad Abdullah, who had a very good following in the state and specially in the Kashmir Valley, appealed to both the countries not to hustle the issue of Jammu and Kashmir into premature decision, with regards to its future for joining either of the two. India agreed but Pakistan in enthusiasm of grabbing it by hook or by crook, violated the stand still agreement for maintaining of status quo. Pakistan blocked the important route of maintenance of State of Jammu and Kashmir via Muzzafrabad cutting off all the supplies of essential commodities.

Invasion by Armed Looters and Marauders

Maharaja spoke to Mr. Liaquat Ali Khan the Prime Minister of Pakistan, not to resort to this method or else, he would seek assistance from elsewhere. Pakistan however appeared to be firm on its decision and organised armed resources and planned invasion of the State of Jammu and Kashmir. As has already been said Pakistan could not read the mood of the people in valley and elsewhere, who were behind Sheikh Abdullah and Indianess had lot of meaning to them at that time. Pakistan, undeterred, collected hordes of tribesmen from NWFP, ex-servicemen, deserters from State Forces and personnel from Pakistan army and put all under the control of regular officers of Pakistani army, for launching operation in Jammu and Kashmir. On 20 October 1947, Pakistan attacked Jammu and Kashmir from different directions. The task given to them was to capture Srinagar. Unhindered loot were the wages they had been promised – loot and women. There is no exaggeration, some of the nurses in the hospital at Baramula were still surviving to narrate the woes. Complete force was well supplied with arms, ammunition, rations and medicines. It had about 300 civilian lorries at its disposal and enough of fuel was given to them. It is unbelievable and unconceivable that such arrangements could be made without the complicity of the British civil and military officials. NWFP was purposely made to get involved into this, as they had not reconciled to the idea of division of Pashtun area, first between Afghanistan and India and thence making it a part of Pakistan. Pakhtun or Pashtun is an old movement and even today, it is the biggest problem Pakistan is facing, bigger than Kashmir. Muslim League very assiduously thought of diverting their attention and got them entangled in Kashmir taking the lead for arson, loot, plundering and creating mayhem in the valley. Pakistan played its game with them too.

Brig Rajinder Singh and his State Forces

Such a planned operation could not be stopped or faced by

small groups of Maharaja's troops and as such brushing them aside, the marauders reached Muzzafrabad. From there they came to Domel and Uri, destroying, looting and burning whatever they encountered. At Uri they faced Brig Rajinder Singh with a strong company of State Forces. They launched ferocious attack on this company where Brig Rajinder Singh, fighting gallantly, was killed. They reached Baramula on 26 October 1947. There they found the place attractive and went all out with orgy of violence, rape and loot. They did not proceed towards Srinagar but carried on looting and collecting costly stuff and went back to put the loot at some places. They came back for more of it. The author had a meeting with one sister, probably named Parscilla at Baramula in 1977. She narrated the hideous behaviour of the tribal invaders of 1947-48. She told as to how she along with other sisters numbering seven in St. Joseph's Hospital of Baramula were treated. Some of them were treated in a most inhuman manner and appalling indecencies were heaped upon them. It was not only at Baramula, this was their way of behaving and committing atrocities, wherever they could go. She said, something like this about them.

> "It is now like a dream, I do remember most of the incidents but not all details. They were young and old, some of them bearded but other were just young boys. They destroyed all the medicines, that was the worst part. I feel sorry for the men who were killed. I pray everyday for them."

The Accession

Maharaja was really shaken up the first time, when Domel and Muzzafrabad were destroyed There was a great loss at Brig Rajinder Singh's garrison. Everyone was a terror stricken – both civilians and state's military persons. Seeing all this, Maharaja approached the Government of India headed by Governor General Mountbatten, for help. It was argued by them, that it would be wrong and lawfully not tenable to send the troops without Maharaja's accession of his state to the Union of India. Maharaja signed the Instrument of Accession with full support of Sheikh Abdullah and with that J&K became an integral part of India — legally, morally and constitutionally.

Landing of Indian Troops in Kashmir

It was on 26 October 1947, after the signing of the Instrument of Accession that Indian Army started collecting the troops for sending them to the state of Jammu and Kashmir as quickly as possible, as Srinagar was already threatened. The easily available unit was 1/5 GR located at Red Fort in Delhi, but except commanding officer, no Indian officer was posted in, after the reshuffling of units of two countries. But British officers were there who could not be sent. Next unit was 1 SIKH which was deployed in internal security duties near Gurgaon. Consequently Lt Col Dewan Ranjit Rai commanding officer 1 SIKH, was ordered to assemble 1 SIKH, at Gurgaon and reach Delhi at the earliest. This famous unit of the SIKH Regiment and of the Second World War fame, was sent to Srinagar in bits and pieces by civilians and military aircrafts. Lt Col Dewan Ranjit Rai was with the first batch to land at Srinagar airfield on 27 October 1947 and soon started deploying the unit for defence of Srinagar. Finding the Rd Srinagar-Baramula clear of the enemy, the unit did not waste anytime and soon it reached outskirts of Baramula. On getting info of enemy's advance it took defensive position. The unit was soon outnumbered by invaders and it started withdrawing for a better position around Pattan. In that melee the commanding officer

Lt Col Dewan Ranjit Rai was killed and large number of jawans were wounded. However, unit immediately organised defences at Pattan and put a permanent block on enemy's advance towards Srinagar and then gave the historic fight on 29 October 1947. Same day 161 Infantry Brigade started arriving by air with 1 KUMAON, 1 PUNJAB and 4 KUMAON under Brig LP Sen. 4 KUMAON, immediately on landing got involved at Badgam and fought a pitched hand to hand battle where Maj Som Nath Sharma was killed who later became the first recipient of Param Vir Chakra (PVC) of free India.

British Officers in Pakistan Army

The operations were conducted by tribesmen directed by Pakistani Army officers, who were dressed in civil clothes. Punjabi army officers of Pakistan and ex-servicemen joined in fighting. Indian army had organised, though late but once on the move, carried on its operations in winter 1947-48 and gradually established control over the valley of Kashmir. In the northern territory of Gilgit, a British officer, Maj William Brown of Gilgit Scouts declared his intentions and raised Pakistan's flag. Brig Ghansara Singh, who went to take charge from Maj Brown, was arrested and later released in exchange of certain prisoners. It is to be remembered that large number of about 500 British officers and men were made to stay for service in Pakistan Army as regulars and these were the people who played the crucial role in making India to lose large areas in Hunza, Baltistan and Gilgit, because these areas were under British control. These areas had been taken on lease by the British from the Maharaja of Kashmir and were treated as part of British India, administered by a political agent responsible to Delhi. Could Pakistan do it without the tacit approval of British senior officers? No, not at all. Maj Brown was later awarded OBE by the British Government. His role was also finally acknowledged by Pakistan President Parvez Mushrraf who awarded him the title of Sitara-e-Pakistan posthumously. Skardu could not really be helped due to paucity of troops and was occupied by the retreating Pakistani troops. In early 1948, the Indian Army pressed westwards from the valley. All over Jammu and Kashmir, the operations were launched and some area was recovered. (See Sketch 5)

Kashmir was uppermost in the mind of Mr. Jinnah who had himself ordered the then C-in-C of Pakistan, Gen Messervy to send all possible troops to Kashmir. Fighting between Pakistani and Indian forces took place in difficult cold conditions and in inhospitable terrain. Indian Army inspite of initial reverses at few odd places were getting upper hand. Then 163 Infantry Brigade under Brig (later Lt Gen) Harbakhsh Singh, VrC carried on clearing Kupwara, Chowkibal and reached Tithwal covering a distance of 64 Kilometers in five days. In further operations, the incursions were removed, not all but the position was comfortable. Bedori, Kiran, Pandu, Haji Pir and Pritam posts were at one time with us. In the meantime United Nation Commission arrived in India in early 1948 and asked both sides to stop offensive operations. Pakistan played a dirty game by accepting the appeal on one hand and launched attacks on important features, on the other hand which were either vacated due to weather conditions or otherwise. It was duplicity of Pakistan that important posts like Pandu, Bedori etc. were vacated due to bad weather, after the declaration of ceasefire but all were occupied by Pakistan, in connivance with senior British military officers. Indian government and its army was helpless as they were still under the shield of Mountbatten and his worthy generals, who had sway over the operations. Though the losses of major features mentioned above was great,

Sketch 5: Jammu and Kashmir after Cease Fire in 1949

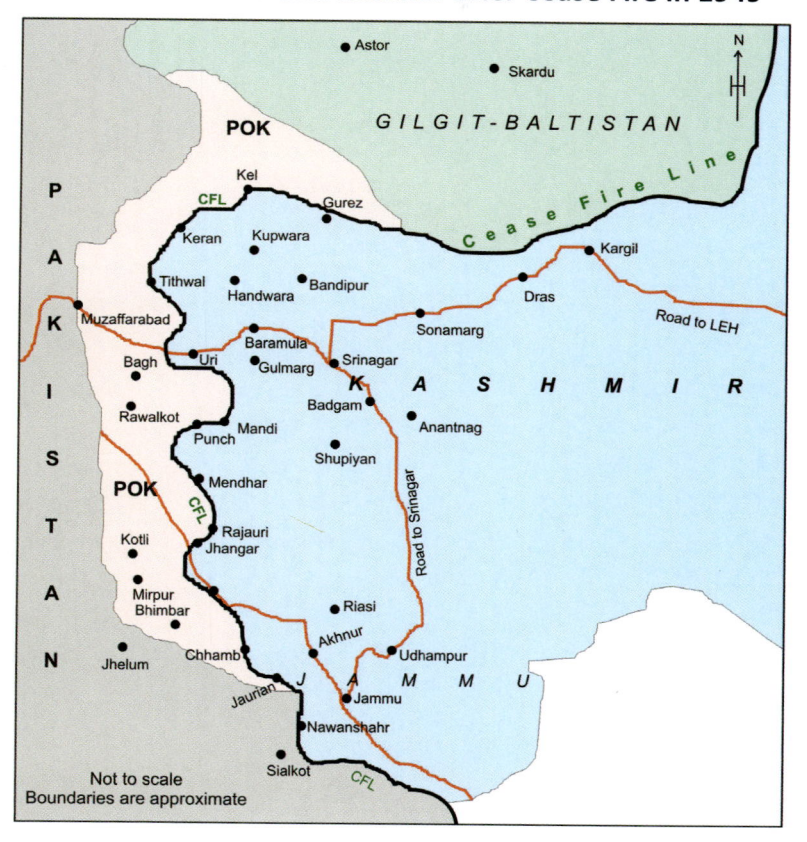

the slipping of the Uri-Punch road from our hands, was most notable miss. Had it been in our hands, by now it would have changed the texture of the problems of Jammu and Kashmir and warded off the desire of Pakistan to infiltrate and disturb every now and then. (See Sketch 5 and 6)

Looters at Village Peta Hir

There is an incident connected with our Regiment, which in recent years has got an undue mentioning about in 7 SIKH. There is one village known as Peta Hir west of Kupwara where the Hindu and Sikh families had assembled for safety in view of the looters and plunderers roaming around fully armed. Old 7 SIKH (now 5 SIKH) which was operating in the area learnt about killing and looting of non-Muslims. They were all surrounded by the unit, some who resisted were killed and the remaining were captured. It was Maj Sampuran Singh's company, who dealt with these freebooters. Reportedly there were no casualties of the battalion.

Empathizing Britain

Britain was empathizing with Pakistan and its army. Britain in fact was involved from the day one. It became absolutely and abundantly clear, when in an interview given to Brig AR Siddiqui, Maj Gen Akbar Khan, who commanded the raiders under the pseudonym of "General Tariq" stated:-

> "A few days after the partition, I was asked by Mian Iftikharuddin on behalf of Prime Minister Liaquat Ali Khan to prepare a plan of action for Kashmir... I was called to a meeting with Liaquat Ali Khan at Lahore, where the plan was adopted, responsibilities allotted and orders issued."

Maj Gen OS Kalkat in his book "Far Flung Frontiers" has very vividly brought out that while he was still in Pakistan, on a staff appt during the time of partition, he personally and by default came across a highly sensitive document called "Operation Gulmarg," which contained the Pakistani plan for invasion and capture of Jammu and Kashmir in 1947 and it was signed by the then C-in-C of Pakistan Army, Gen Gracy. Mustering of transport, therefore to convey such a large force of raiders from Peshawar and other areas could not have been possible without the knowledge of British civil officials and Governor of NWFP, Mr. Cunningham. Pakistan had to finally admit to the United Nations that their regular troops were fighting in Jammu and Kashmir.

Nehru and Mountbatten

Nehru was very wise, intelligent and farsighted man. Nobody could understand the British, better than him. He could read every move of theirs. Had he not been there, the British could have created some more problems like that of Kashmir, Hyderabad, Junagarh, Bhopal and other places. He had to go out of his way to establish good relations with Mountbatten, for serving the cause of the country. It is easy to comment and say that he did not realise the situation, but it will come out as non-serious thinking and interpretation if you go to the genesis of problem. He had to toe Mountbatten's line, for saving the integrity of the country. He had to keep Mountbatten in good humour to avoid any other sudden damage. He accepted that there could be some mistakes but the interest of the country, was never out of his mind. It is now that the things are perceived little differently. In his days he was most popular both with Kashmiris and English men besides Indians, of course. Some say, that Jawahar Lal Nehru, went out

Sketch 6: State of Jammu and Kashmir

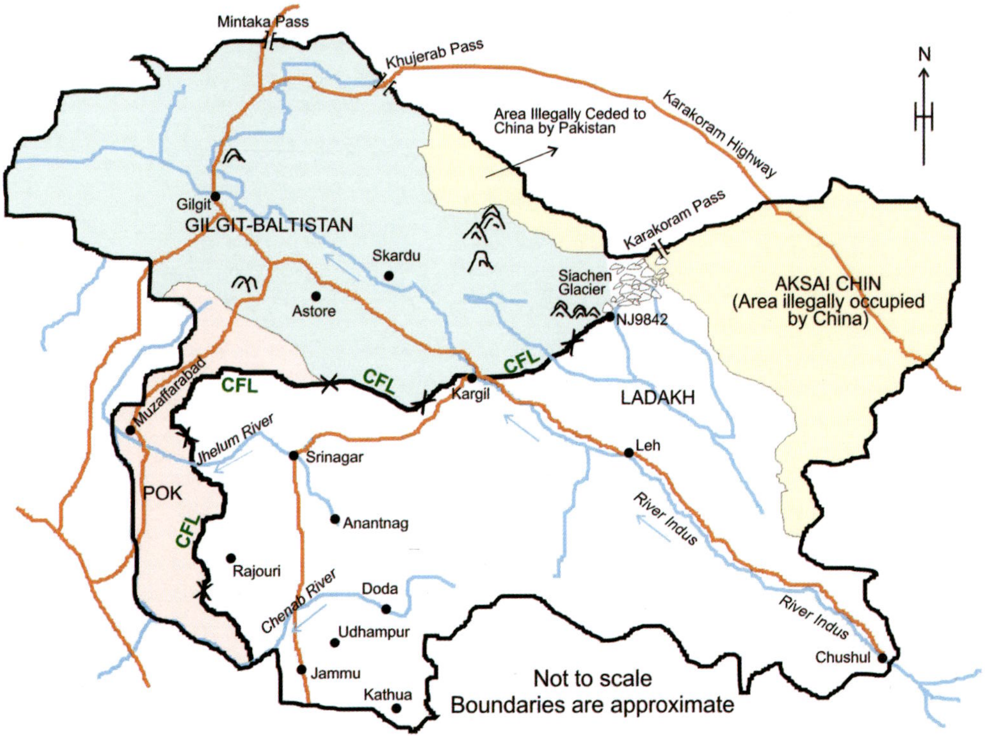

of the way to get Mountbatten appointed as Governor General of India. Had Mountbatten not been there, as Governor General of India, there would have not been any stipulation regarding the referring of the matter of J&K to the people, on the Instrument of Accession of the State to the Union of India. This matter would have ended then only. Well it is matter of further debate and research and it seems to have some weight.

7
TESTING OF METTLE AND MIGHT AT RANN OF KUTCHH

"History is a catalogue of mistakes, It is our duty to profit by them"
—Liddell Hart

Background

In Pakistan, there was a considerable pressure on government from the home constituency, to take advantage of India's embarrassment by China in 1962. But there was another pressure on Field Marshal Ayub Khan and he was advised not to venture at this hour. Instead, he was further advised to show gestures, which would allay India's fears. It was from both, USA and USSR – part of their own game plan in the international affairs.

A Chance in Thousand Years

The campaign to put squeeze on India was led by Mr ZA Bhutto, who was a minister at that time. He, when asked about his views on such a venture, quipped *"A chance in thousand years."* Even long before that he had been stoking public opinion in Pakistan for liberation of Kashmir, by force of arms. He at that time, decried, even the US military assistance and clamoured for

Pakistan's withdrawal from the military pact which was signed in 1954.

Foreign Powers

Ayub Khan was a different man as compared to Bhutto. He had the military system of working and was not as cunning as Bhutto, though ambitious, he was. He in his meeting, which he held after the action by China against India and having been warned by other countries, not to do anything which can be a cause for embarrassment for India, had emphasised to his own constituency that *"Security of Pakistan was not to be jeopardised for the sake of Kashmir, and such a war over Kashmir, Pakistan could not fight without foreign assistance."* He was quite clear that both USSR and USA at that particular time, policy wise, were coinciding with India. He was also fairly aware that he could not beat Nehru in international affairs. In fact every leader in Pakistan except Mr. ZA Bhutto, who was eccentric, huffy by nature and crazy about Kashmir, had realised that to demolish India would not be possible and that simple. In fact Ayub Khan himself was against Bhutto, but could not remove him because of situational compulsions. It is interesting to note that Bhutto, stupidly used to call Ayub as "Daddy" and tried to behave like his 'overzealous son'. Ayub Khan knew it but he had already given his trust to Bhutto. Bhutto was not a balanced man, was very keen to show to Pakistan that he and his family were the servants of Islam and well-wishers of Pakistan. The background, from ancestral side was that of a Hindu, he wanted to prove that he was a staunch Muslim and a true nationalist. Bhutto was not a seasoned politician and an astute political analyzer. Had he not been there at the scene in those crucial years, it can be safely assumed, that India-Pakistan relations could have taken some shape by now.

India and Non-alignment

In 1965, fighting took place between India and Pakistan in Rann of Kutchh, a coastal border region between Bombay and Karachi. It is desolate barren area which is devoid of any attraction except few grazing areas. India had not paid any operational attention towards this. Pakistan tried, in fact moved into this area for grabbing it. However, India's new assertion towards non-alignment policy had not been doing well with the western countries and particularly with UK and USA. It had antagonised them and they, both, again drifted away from India and had begun to provide the moral and material support to Pakistan. It was due to this reason that they helped Pakistan to become a member of both SEATO and CENTO. Resultantly, Pakistan became a beneficiary of billion dollars worth military hardware from 1955 onwards. From the donors side, it was mainly for the purpose of containment of communist expansionism. However, this hope of theirs was belied by Pakistan's structuring armoured division at Kharian and establishing other main bases for training and raising new units of army. Pakistan even did not try to hide this fact knowing and realizing that India somehow will come to know about it, and the western powers will not really mind it.

India had realised that partition of the country was a reality and wanted to go ahead with its developmental plans, which was so very important for inclusive growth. Economic growth was the basis for everything and to be militarily sound too, country cannot progress without steadily growing economically. India made so many diplomatic moves to normalise the relations with Pakistan but success could not be achieved. When India signed the Indus Water Treaty in 1960, it was presumed that Pakistan will understand the need of its people and develop the dry landscape into a green one. But no, she used it for constructing Ichhogil Canal – a water obstacle for military use and took the Indian gesture as a weakness.

New Weaponry for Pakistan Army

Every move by Pakistan was aimed at annexation of Jammu and Kashmir or part of it and it was always uppermost in the minds of Pakistani military leaders. With the acquisition of sophisticated Patton tanks, armament and other pieces of flashy military hardware from USA and other friendly countries, Pakistan felt that it was strong enough to wrest Kashmir by force. Despite the debacle in 1962, India had not started the modernisation of its armed forces and that made Ayub Khan take an opportunity to test his newly acquired weaponry. Ayub Khan, himself chose the area of Kutchh measuring about 9,000 sq. miles, all wasteland, to check India's reflexes. It was suitable from their logistic point of view also.

Rann of Kutchh used to be part of State of Kutchh before partition, which was now a part of India. Logically Pakistan had no right at all whatsoever over it. In early 1963, when Kutchh border was being demarcated by joint survey of international border between India and Pakistan, it was unilaterally called off by Pakistan. When India expedited the survey itself in this area, Pakistan claimed about 3,500 sq. miles of Indian territory. India rejected it, as pre-partition documents clearly showed the whole Rann lying in the State of Kutchh, which was a part of India now. Pakistan started patrolling the area bordering Rann of Kutchh from January 1965 onwards and thereafter its Indus Rangers occupied Kanjarkot, an area within our boundary (See Sketch 7). On 9 April 1965 Pakistani 51 Para Brigade attacked Sardar Post, manned by two companies of CRPF, which withdrew after putting up stout resistance. This made Pakistan to escalate the tension and on 24 April 1965, it moved an infantry division opposite the Indian position and attacked Point 84, east of Kanjarkot supported by Patton tanks and heavy guns. These two posts managed to hold out whereupon Pakistanis attacked Biar Bet north of Dhara Nala on 25 April 1965 but without success and suffered heavy casualties. Indian Army accordingly started taking defence on the border. Pakistan noticed this and proposed to end the dispute. India accepted the offer but only on one condition that Pakistan must first vacate the area occupied by force. Pakistan refused to do. It was at this time that Prime Minister Lal Bahadur Shastri warned Pakistan in no uncertain terms that in the event of further intransigence, India would be free to choose the point at which to strike at Pakistan. He thus stated in the Lok Sabha.

> *"If Pakistan continues to discard reasons and persists in its aggressive activities, the Indian Army will decide its own strategy and the employment of its manpower and equipment in areas which it deems fit."*

Current of History-Theory

True to his words, he gave free hand to army after that. On 25 May 1965 an Indian patrol party was attacked near Biar Bet and on 15 June 1965 Pakistanis once again probed Sardar Post and Vigokot. At Sardar post nine Pakistanis were killed and an officer was captured. A ceasefire then was mutually agreed on 30 June 1965 and PsW were exchanged on 21 July 1965. India upheld that they had no territorial dispute, as whole of Rann of Kutchh was her. However, status quo as on 1 January 1965 was restored with certain minor adjustments. Point 84, Kanjarkot and Biar Bet

Sketch 7: RANN of Kutchh

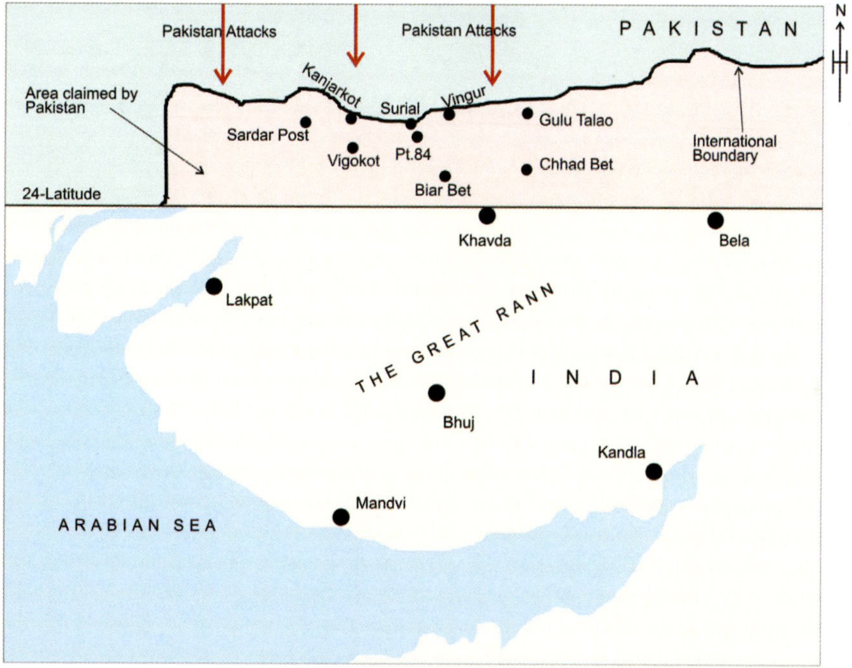

were restored to India, but India had to vacate Sardar Post and Vigokot and permitted Pakistan to patrol Surail–Kanjarkot track. Arbitration to this effect was suggested by Mr. Harold Wilson, Prime Minister of England. It was agreed that he could take a decision on the recommendations of the arbitration team which consisted of Mr. Morris James, Britain's High Commission in India, Mr. Johan Freeman, Britain's High Commission in Pakistan and the Indian Deputy Commissioner of the area. India accepted it as a internationally responsible country. In the discussion Pakistan put before the arbitration team, the so called "Current of History Theory." It stated that from about 6th century onwards, current of the history consisted of invasions by the rulers of Sindh, on the Kutchh main land. The Rann was crossed more often by Sindhis towards Kutchh area and not by Kutchis towards Sindh. This became the focal point of the Pakistani assertion that there was "current of history theory" the direction from Sindh to Kutchh, which could have not been without reason. It was thus construed as an element for the historic title in favour of Pakistan. PM Harold Wilson of England, had got, this done, by being the head of Common Wealth countries. It was completed by 7 July 1965 and area of about 320 sq. kilometers was awarded to Pakistan.

Escalation of Activities in Kargil Sector

Pakistan had suddenly got busy in Kashmir, her infantile obsession. Hardly two kilometers away from ceasefire line in Kargil sector, they commenced sporadic artillery (arty) raids on Indian posts along Kargil–Leh road, planting mines on the road and ambushing our convoys. They were successful in capturing two posts but were soon evicted. They had miscalculated the outcome and still had some doubts left. They started organizing, training and procuring more of new equipment from their supporter countries. The significance of Rann of Kutchh operations was the false sense of optimism, as superiority was created in the minds of Pakistani commanders concerning their ability of fighting a war against India, which certainly did create a mistaken euphoria for which Pakistan had to pay heavily and shortly afterwards.

Operation Ablaze

India immediately started "OP Ablaze" after sensing trouble from Pakistan, which involved move of troops to borders with West Pakistan, while the negotiations to end the dispute in Rann of Kutchh were still in progress. Pakistani troops on CFL in Jammu and Kashmir had been creating troubles. Pakistanis overlooking Srinagar–Leh road, tried to cut it off, which made the Indian Army to drive out Pakistanis from three posts of theirs. But later on, the captured posts were returned as a good gesture, after an agreement was reached on Rann of Kutchh.

In Pakistan, there was a general feeling in higher echelons of government and army that Indians are lethargic and Indian Government has no will to carry on fighting and as such Indian Army will not be able to do anything. They thought that they could do anything at any place with impunity. President Ayub Khan was fully convinced that Pakistan could attack India anywhere and India will not be able to contain it effectively. He felt that Indians lacked the will to fight and would not go in for war. Tactical results of its recent pursuits in Kutchh had been quite encouraging for them. They equipped units with new tanks and guns and thought that they will deliver as per their expectations. Altogether, after the new acquisitions and sensing its credibility Pakistan felt that the time was ripe for another adventure, like that of 1947-48.

Three things which Ayub Khan had considered for such venturesome exercise were:-

- Test conducted with new American weapons acquired by Pakistan.
- Steadfastness of her friends.
- India's capacity to resist or fight back.

"It was a role played by Bhutto and number of senior officers precipitating in the conflict of Kutchh and after."

This info was given in the Military Journal 1971, of Pakistan. It stated that Ayub Khan of his own, was hesitant but the hope to rekindle Kashmir and to keep it alive and thinking that a Hindu has not got stomach to fight, were the main criteria, inflamed by Bhutto for this misadventure.

Operational Analysis

- Pakistan could very successfully create another dispute about Kutchh and got it to be recognised by both the countries and where Britain as head of Commonwealth was also involved, which Pakistan and Britain both wanted it to be so.
- Pakistan tried to understand the nature and will of the Indian Government and its army and thought that India will not initiate war first, Indians will only react to a situation and that too in a milder way.
- Pakistan could test the utility and usage of new weapons, arms and equipment and had a limited success.
- Pakistan got a chance to understand the political situation

and steadfastness of her friends vis-à-vis opinion of world leaders in context of conflict with India. Awarding of 320 sq. kilometers area of India to Pakistan by Mr. Harold Wilson, based on the recommendations of two British nationals in the arbitration team, made India to firmly resolve that third party mediation will never be accepted. It is still sticking to it and knowing the history it should continue.

- Ayub Khan got a chance to endear himself to Pakistani people.

- He was successful in raising the morale of Pakistan army/defence services and placating of western countries with regards to its relations with India.

- Pakistan tested the new tactical concepts which were adopted as a result of training of large number of officers of rank of majors and captains in academies of USA.

- Pakistan was successful in making us to tie down troops in Kutchh and also in Ladakh mainly in Kargil area.

- Pakistan was successful in making us abandon our 'Sardar Post' in our own area and could get the right of patrolling on track Surail–Kanjarkot, awarded by arbitrators.

- Ayub Khan could establish himself as leader of Pakistan and got that legitimacy.

- Pakistan was successful in challenging the sanctity of International Border in Kutchh which made India to realise that Pakistan means mischief and has to be dealt with firmly.

8

INFILTRATION BY GUERRILLAS

"War cannot be divorced from politics for a single moment"
—Mao-Tse-Tung

Obsession – Kashmir

Jammu and Kashmir had become an integral part of India when Maharaja Hari Singh, the ruler of Jammu and Kashmir had signed the Instrument of Accession of his State to the Union of India, on 26 October 1947. Based on the legal, moral and constitutional provisions, which were laid down by the British Parliament, the decision to accede the state lay entirely with its ruler and no stipulations with reference to the will of people etc occurred in the minds or in the official documents concerned. It was not a unique document for Jammu and Kashmir, all other states numbering 562 and 11 Central British India provinces signed exactly the same type of Instrument.

The situation changed when Pakistan started an armed action by sending the tribal invaders in early October 1947, followed by regular troops later on. India referred the matter to the United Nations Commission for India and Pakistan and a ceasefire came into effect on 1 January 1949. As a result certain areas of Jammu and Kashmir were occupied by Pakistan which are still under her occupation.

Causes for Venturing Against India

Pakistan from the very beginning has developed never-ending obsession with the State of Jammu and Kashmir in general and Kashmir Valley and Punch basin in particular. Punch has been the north-western district of Kashmir region and as Pakistan is primary concerned with the annexation of Kashmir region, area of Punch is automatically drawn into it. All this is based on certain factors some of the important ones are listed below:-

- To divert the attention of the people of Pakistan from country's internal problems and misrule perpetuated by corrupt and unscrupulous politicians and dictators.

- To rally the support of other Muslim countries and Muslim population of the world and its own Islamic political parties.

- Kashmir can serve as an important access point to the Central Asian market and hence of significant strategic importance.

- Pakistan was supported wholeheartedly and almost openly by the Britain and USA and was armed accordingly. These were the powers who made it possible for it to retain some areas of Kashmir and complete area of Dardistan (Northern Areas as Pakistan calls it). Pakistan got emboldened and was regularly incited by such support.

- All water resources meant for Pakistan as per Indus Water Treaty 1960 either originate from Kashmir like Chenab,

Jhelum and Kishanganga (Pakistan calls in Neelam) or pass through Kashmir, like river Indus. Water being the life of human beings, Pakistan wants to ensure that it keeps getting it uninterrupted. Most of resources can be diverted to a great extent by India, if forced to do so, which can prove to be a disaster for Pakistan. Punch is of special interest because it is part of a particular drainage system and a large catchment area for Mangla Dam which is so very important for survival of Pakistan's agricultural economy, as given earlier.

Succorers of Pakistan

Pakistan was the brainchild of some self-seeking Indian Muslim politicians, who were suspicious of the domination of Hindu majority over Muslims. From day one, after partition, the relation of Pakistan with India had been bordering on hate, damning India and of course, on suspicions. Such rancorous nature of Pakistan towards maintaining mutual relations had been the cause of economic backwardness of both countries. Indian leaders knew it well but Pakistan's myopic view had always been coming in the way. Both countries were being exploited by the influential nations for their commercial and strategic interests. The intransigent and stubborn attitude of Pakistani authorities had not permitted the two countries to reach any agreement on any issue. Pakistan had only one agenda and that is being anti-India. Pakistan feels that normalisation of relations can go against the very concept of Pakistan. The people at the helms of affairs in Pakistan are trying to ensure that somehow the old generation of pre-partition days be out of scene, the new generation will be different and will lessen the problem of affinity and belongingness to erstwhile India. That way all issues old and new will become intractable and hence unamenable to any solution. It is also a fact that it is because of USA being its succorer, from the inception of Pakistan and more acutely after 1954, otherwise Pakistan could not have been a challenge of this magnitude to India's reasonableness. As a result Pakistan has developed an adverbial animus mindset and started suffering from parity syndrome which she tries to display on all available occasions, to global milieu. All efforts by India had gone for a fuss, kind courtesy western powers. All activities had become inimical to the interest of India and if at all, Pakistan promises positivity on some issues, it ultimately proves to be a façade. Pakistan really does not know what to do. She is misled by mercantile and hegemonically biased nature of its supporters, for their own interests who treat India differently. I may not be wrong if I say that

> "Philosophy of Pakistan is like that of a blind man in dark room, looking for a black cat which is not there"

Planning of Operation Gibraltar by Pakistan

Having sufficient background of hatred and suspicion on every move of India, Pakistan planned 1965 Operation which initially was named "Malta" to be conducted by an assortment of troops known as "Gibraltar Force." Later on to avoid the confusion, operation itself was named as "Gibraltar" and the force was known as Gibraltar Force. Failure to grab Kashmir in 1947-48, did not deter it and Pakistan went in for Kutchh operation in early 1965. But these two issues definitely left an impression on Pakistan that every operation will result in some gain for them as it happened in 1947-48, where she was able to control a large area of Jammu and Kashmir and in Kutchh operation also could secure some concessions of about 320 sq. kilometers of area by making it an issue. Pakistan did achieve a little area in Kutchh but not without the complete trust of British.

"Crisis Game" – Plan

The Institute of Defence Analysis in Washington conducted a 'crisis game' in early 1965 based on Kashmir scenario. The game concluded that Pakistan was likely to gain Kashmir or a larger part of it in 1965. One will not take much time to connect this whole issue with the American's thinking vis-a-vis Pakistan's intentions and launching of invasion. Pakistan had been talking of jihad in Kashmir for all these years and launching of Algerian type of struggle for self determination in Jammu and Kashmir, taking valley and Punch projection as main areas of such an operation. Military officers located in the area of responsibility of their 12 Infantry Division, had studied the Mao's text on guerrilla warfare in minute details and also the military-cum-political strategy. The basic struggle of the Algerian people, eventual withdrawal of France from North Africa, and Indonesia's confrontation against Malaysia influenced the thinking of Pak rulers. The failure of big powers like USA in Vietnam and Indonesia's success in keeping the British forces in South East Asia fully stretched showed the inherent strength of properly planned and well-led uprising against the outside forces. The short and successful encounter of the Pakistan army with the Indian forces in Rann of Kutchh further reinforced Ayub Khan's rising faith in its strength vis-à-vis India. Foreign office of Pakistan managed to persuade General Headquarters (GHQ) to produce a plan of action and thus came the birth of Operation Gibraltar. (See Sketch 8)

Effects of New Weaponry for Pakistan Army

Operation Gibraltar was launched by Pakistan in Jammu and Kashmir in August 1965 which was designed to instigate and engineer mass revolt followed by a *Coup d'grace* being delivered by the Pakistan Army. Its preparation started in May-June 1965. 19 Baluch an SSG unit, trained in guerilla warfare was stationed at Attock, where instructors in "irregular and sub-conventional warfare" belonging to various units, were assembled for imparting training to regular and irregular troops of 12 Infantry Division. This element of unconventional and irregular warfare training simply did not cross the minds of our intelligence agencies. After the training, they were attached to Azad Kashmir (AK) battalions of 12 Infantry Division. They recruited Rajakars the local people residing in their respective areas of responsibility of army units in POK. Muzahids and Jihadis were administered by AK battalions. They were forcibly recruited, trained and made to join.

This operation was launched for a finish and capture of J&K but primarily for conquest of Kashmir Valley and Punch Basin by Gibraltar Force. It comprised of 10,000 to 15,000 strong armed guerrillas and infiltrators disguised as locals wearing baggy trousers and shirts, being convenient for hiding their weapons. Info slowly started trickling in. Suddenly certain different aggressive pattern of firing on our posts were noticed. I was located at piquet 64 across Betar Nala almost opposite to their Post Chakias (we call it Pritam) on the down slope of own post 62. My company commander Capt Santosh Kumar and me were in company command post, where we were fired at with the Rocket Launcher (RL) at the time of our `Morning Stand To'. It was on 3 August 1965. Generally the following different patterns and use of new weapons were noticed in their activities in the first week of August 1965.

Sketch 8: Infiltration in Mandi Sub-sector

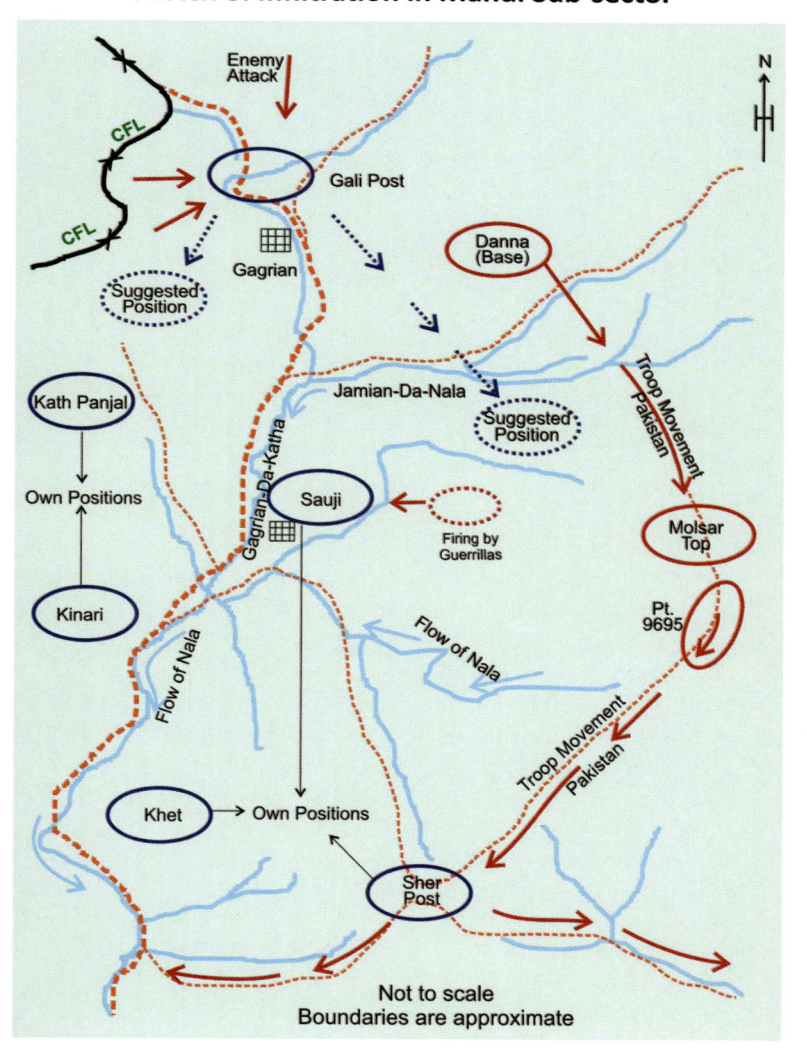

- Fixing the weapons at night by taking them at a convenient places ahead of their defences and fire at us, at the time of our Stand To. Our command post was hit at the loophole with RL.

- Mines were laid on the tracks, we used to follow for our daily maintenance from our base at Punch. New RL was used against the bunkers.

- 81 mm Mor was fired without any provocation during day time causing casualties.

- Accuracy at hitting the loophole made us to believe a change in weaponry like use of telescopic rifle and bigger machine gun.

These activities indicated the change in the behaviour of the enemy being from active to very active. Information (Info) also started coming in about the move of groups in far flung areas of Mandi Sub-sector, where our unit was responsible for holding four important posts at Kath Panjal, Kinari, Gali and telephone exchange at Khet.

In the meantime, info started coming to Higher Headquarters that Gen Mohammad Musa, C-in-C Pakistan Army had toured POK in May 1965 and held the conference of senior officers at Muzzafrabad. It also transpired that in front of an Indian post at Kargil, Chinese army officers were seen directing subversive activities on the road Srinagar – Leh, India's life line to its defences in Ladakh. 12 Infantry Division of Pakistan was getting ready for the offensive and training for some weeks was organised for selected persons at Muree, HQ of 12 Infantry Division, for last minute tips and bolstering of morale. 12 Infantry Division was commanded by a mediocre and informal person – Maj Gen Akhtar Hussain Malik not a person of high calibre, industrious alright but lacking initiative and push.

Launching of Enemy Columns

Eight columns were created for launching the invasion. Each column/force had four to six companies and each company had 116 men, making a total about 5,558 personnel besides other paraphernalia attached with them. Each sector was commanded by a Brigadier. Each company was commanded by a Maj or senior Capt of regular army. Each company had about 66 irregulars of Muzahids, Razakars, Police and Constabulary Armed Force etc. and 40 regular troops of the Pakistan army. The training at Irregular Warfare School had been given to all for six weeks, in infiltration, sabotage, subversion and political assassinations. Even FM Ayub Khan addressed the force commanders at Muree in second week of July 1965. On 1 August 1965 Maj Gen Akhtar Hussain Malik, divisional commander 12 Infantry Division of Pakistan met the company commanders at Kotli in POK after the recce parties had already gone and launched on their mission, invasion of Jammu and Kashmir, second in 18 years. This invasion was different from the previous one of 1947-48. This time there were no more tribesmen for looting, plundering and womanising. They were all well-organised trained men who were given the training by experts including the Chinese instructors in guerrilla warfare and tactics. They were armed with modern weapons including double LMGs in a section .50 BMG, 81 mm Mors, 83 mm RL, Telescope Rifles and Mini Transmitters etc. They were issued with high altitude clothing and each individual was given some Indian currency. All of them carried 5-7 days cooked ration, biscuits and nuts. The leaders carried with them the propaganda material like Proclamation of War of Liberation, which was to be distributed to the civilian population, (See Appendix B). On 3 August first group crossed CFL at all the important places. They moved in group of 2-3 men at a time and regrouped after crossing over to Indian side at the pre-selected points.

Punch-Mandi-Rajouri area was known as No. 2 Sector. This sector was commanded by Brig Rafiq and the force known as Salahuddin Force. The other names of the (forces) columns were Tariq, Khalid, Babar, Qasim, Nusrat and Ghazni, all named after Muslim warriors or so-called crusaders of yester years. The aim behind such names was to incite and motivate their Muslim troops using religion as a factor. Salahuddin Force had the following troops under command.

(a) (i) 4 AK Bn

    (ii) 6 AK Bn

    (iii) 7 AK Bn

(b) Composite Field Battery – 4 x 25 Pdr and 4 x 3.7 How, later reinforced by 4 x 25 Pdr, 4 x 5.5 mm machine guns.

(c) Muzahid   16 Companies

(d) Civil Armed Force   4 Companies

(e) Police   4 Platoons

Salahuddin Force crossed CFL on 30 July 1965. It had completed the dumping of stores in "Bases" by 4-5 August 1965. This element moved into Betar and Mandi Sub-sectors of Punch held by 93 Infantry Brigade. Own posts were fired at with fresh vigor, with .50 BMG and 83mm RLs. It was on 5 August 1965, NK Surjit Singh, Signal Platoon was injured in the AP mines planted on a track which was regularly used by troops for maintenance of post from our base at Punch. In the evening, at the time of "Stand To" Sep Gurnam Singh was badly injured by a BMG burst fired at the loop-hole of the bunker by having it fixed before. Same way they used their RLs fixed at a leisure time, by taking it ahead of their defences and fired at our posts. The enemy in Betar Sub-sector had the advantage of sitting at a higher features and could observe our activities as we were on lower slope. We also realised this shift in their behaviour in firing. We changed, our pattern of occupation of trenches during Stand To, as there was no point standing in a bunker or trench, which could be a fixed target, previously aimed, to be fired, at the time of Stand To.

Guerrillas in Pre-selected Basis

Reliable info started coming in from various sources, about infiltration of armed Pakistani Guerrillas from across the CFL. The alert was sounded about their activities and troops were warned to be ready for any eventuality. Brig Zora Singh, Commander 93 Infantry Brigade got the info of heavy concentration of enemy in front of Gali Post (602) jointly held by 7 SIKH and CRPF and under command 7 SIKH. He reached there on 5 August 1965. He got the info from all available sources and was sure that Pakistan was up to something. 2/Lt Dewinder Singh, 7 SIKH was the post commander at Gali post who informed commander that some element in civilian clothes have been reported to have come from Kopra side and had gone on the "Bases" on higher reaches north of Gali post. Brig Zora Singh met the villagers of Gagrian village and was given the same info. He appreciated the situation and from there only, he ordered Commanding Officer 7 SIKH,

Lt Col Bhagat Singh to immediately move to Sauji and establish his tactical HQ there. 7 SIKH was ordered to handover the defences of Betar Sub-sector to other units and immediately move these troops to Mandi Sub-sector. By 6-7 August 1965 more info of enemy movements on Molsar Ridge and their heading towards Mandi Town much inside on our side of CFL flowed in and thus the dye was cast for another round with the Pakistanis.

The complete details of the infiltration campaign of invaders in the entire State of Jammu and Kashmir is given as Appendix C for easy understanding of all the events.

9
DEFENCE AT SAUJI

"War is unfolding of miscalculations" —Barbara Touchman

Beginning of Hostilities

The hostilities broke out in the first week of August 1965, when the infiltrators crossed the CFL and headed for various pre-selected places in Mandi Valley. Brig Zora Singh Commander 93 Infantry Brigade, alongwith Lt Col Shabeg Singh, CO 3/11 GR and Brigade DAA & QMG, Maj Daljit Singh, on getting the info from his sources, reached Gali post on 5 August 1965. Gali was the farthest and an isolated post at the finger tip of Mandi Sub-sector. It was located on lower ground on a track junction and was meant to serve as a check post only. The commander however ordered that it should be maintained and not to be withdrawn, in case of enemy's advance on the axis. Gali was not a place for fighting a defensive battle. It was felt that it was a rash and impulsive decision, taken on the spot without making any other adjustment of nearby posts, meaning thereby that the previous task of its moving back, after the establishing of contact by the enemy, was changed to making it permanent defences. No thought was given as to how the effective Mor, Arty or Air support will be given, besides ensuring security of route of maintenance and route of withdrawal. For a lay infantry officer it looked palpably odd.

7 SIKH in Mandi Valley

Before the commencement of hostilities, 7 SIKH was deployed in two areas of Punch Sector. Half of the Bn was deployed in Betar Sub-sector on the posts namely 62, 64 Alfi and Jhula all on west of Punch town whereas other half was deployed in Mandi Sub-sector on posts, namely Kinari, Kath Panjal, Khet and Gali, with Bn HQ at Punch. On getting the info of the enemy's ingress in 1965, Cdr 93 Inf Bde ordered CO 7 SIKH to deploy the whole Bn in Mandi Sub-sector. The preparation for move from Betar Sub-sector started on 6-7 August and it was completed by 10 August. The relieved companies were concentrated at Punch. On 9 August, the enemy ventured to attack the Police post at Mandi town. Two companies relieved from Betar Sub-sector were rushed to Mandi Sub-sector. They cleared Mandi and surrounding areas on 11 and 12 August to the much relief of senior commanders. Lt Col Bhagat Singh Commanding Officer, 7 SIKH reached Sauji on 6 August and established his Tactical Headquarters. Sauji is a roundish, independent feature west of Molsar Top which dominates the former by fire and observation. There is, however a little depression in between and for attacking it, the enemy is required to climb it. It is not like rolling down. 'C' Company less a platoon, commanded by 2/Lt Hardial Singh had reached Sauji on 6 August with the Commanding Officer and organised the defences quickly. One platoon of 'C' Company was already at Gali ahead of Sauji commanded by 2/Lt Dewinder Singh. CRPF had one Company in this sector with Company HQ at Sauji and platoon each at Kinari, Kath Panjal, Gali and Khet augmenting the strength of the infantry battalion i.e. 7 SIKH then occupying these posts. (See Sketch 9) Before the commencement of hostilities, there was no other element of army at Sauji and it was exclusively held by a platoon plus the Company Headquarters of CRPF with their other paraphernalia.

'D' Company 7 SIKH was occupying Kinari and Kath Panjal with Company Headquarter at Kinari and it was commanded by Maj Jagdev Singh. 'A' and 'B' Companies, on having been relieved from Betar Sub-sector were brought to general area Sekhlu and astride road for clearing Mandi Town and heights dominating from east and west.

Redeployment of Own Troops

The infiltrators after having crossed the CFL from Kopra side (POK) dispersed in the area. One column of Salahuddin Force went towards Budhal, Rajouri and Kandi. It was commanded by one Maj Mansa Khan of Pakistani regular unit. Its sub column known as Mann column engaged Gali post on 7 August and other sub column of this, reached Mandi on 9 August and attacked the police post, killed the SHO and looted the weapons and established itself on eastern heights dominating Mandi town.

For the purpose of eliminating the enemy from Mandi town and around, 'A' and 'B' Companies, 7 SIKH were first launched for clearing the ridges on eastern and western side of Mandi town. At this particular moment the whole Bn was grossly involved with infiltrators. No 5 Platoon of 'B' company was dealing with them at Kalai Bridge, A and 'B' Companies were launching attack for throwing the enemy out of Mandi town complex, Sauji with limited strength was facing heavy concentration of enemy's BMGs, 81 mm Mor, 83 mm RL and telescopic rifle fire from Molsar Top whereas Gali was repulsing attack after attack – really testing time for the tenacity of the Bn.

After clearing the ridges, Mandi town was wrested from the infiltrators on 12 August. On 13 August, the companies were relieved by 8 Grenadiers, enabling them to join the unit in

Sketch 9: Defences at Sauji

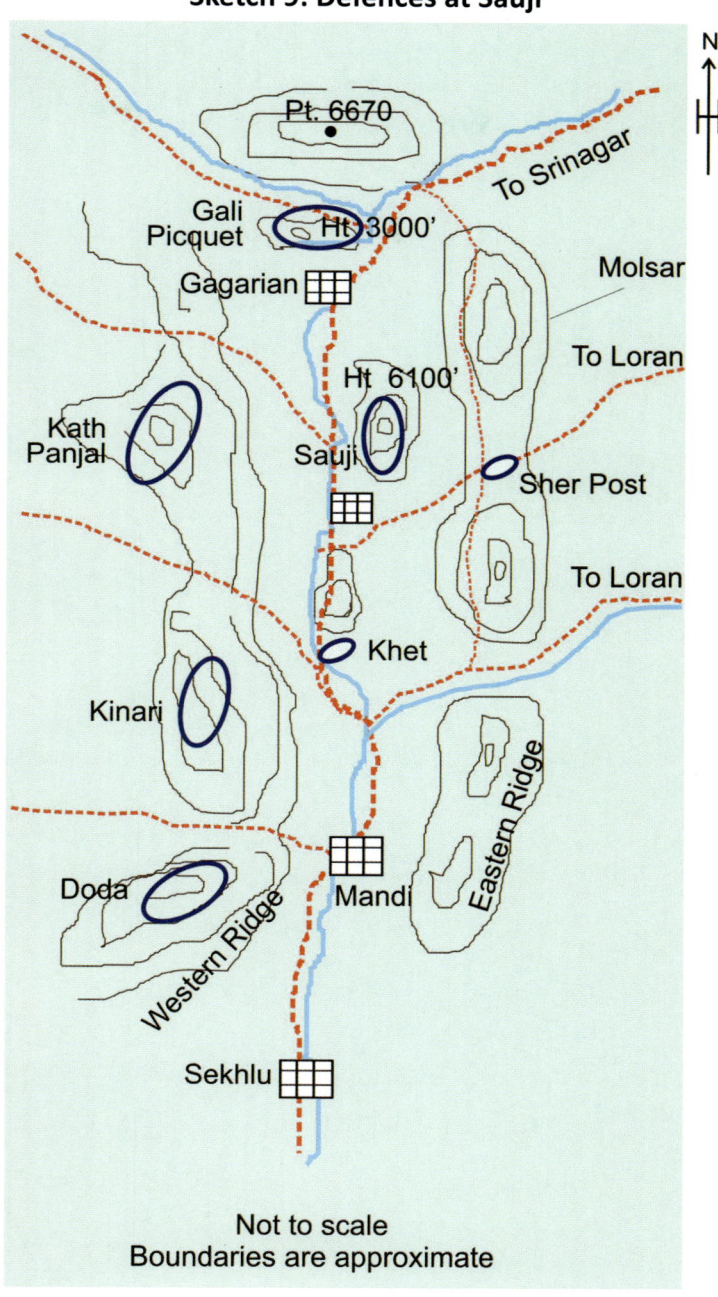

general area Sauji. 'A' Company was moved to Kinari to relieve 'D' Company. As a result 'D' Company reached Sauji on night 14/15 August. 'B' Company less a platoon reached Sauji on 13 August. One platoon of 'B' Company was at Kalai Bridge, an important joint in the area, which was a key target for the enemy.

On 16 August, the strength of own troops at Sauji was 'D' Company, 'B' Company less a platoon, 'C' Company less a platoon and the Battalian Headquarters. The enemy had occupied the Molsar Ridge just east of Sauji as early as on 5 August and had resorted to continuous firing, sitting on a higher feature, causing casualties. Maj Jagdev Singh was one of the senior company commanders and was specially called at Sauji along with his 'D' Company. He was given the task of eliminating the enemy from the Molsar Ridge dominating Sauji. On night 17/18 an operation was planned and 'B' Company less a platoon was placed as its reserve. Both the companies moved and covered up a small distance, when the operation was called off, for the reasons best known to senior commanders We, to my mind missed the opportunity. For the unit to miss an opportunity is a bad omen. One should take the help of courage and common sense and must manoeuvre of which there is no substitute. There is no other binding force towards unity of action. All Indian troops and specially Sikh troops, will excuse almost any stupidity but excessive timidity is simply unforgivable to them. A Sikh jawan by nature is an outgoing, aggressive and action-oriented.

It is easy to say that flexibility is important and should be resorted to, but it certainly hides our incompetence, confusion and unwillingness to face danger. Self preservation will always strike a jarring gong, which should not be permitted to prevail upon any commander. Hidden valor is as bad as cowardice.

Molsar Ridge Becomes Active

Molsar Top, a high feature on Molsar Ridge east of Sauji was occupied by the infiltrators and it was their administrative base. They extensively used .50 BMG, RL, LMGs and telescopic rifles and caused couple of casualties at Sauji, which was lower than Molsar Top and all the movements on Sauji were visible from there. The postponing of the planned operation was because of scanty info about the strength of the enemy. As BMG was the main weapon, along with RLs & LMGs, it was presumed, rather visualised that it could be, minimum a company plus and hence to launch operation based on such info or assumption could lead to difficulties. That was the point CO 7 SIKH was mentally occupied with. For throwing out one company of the enemy you require large body of troops and that was not available at Sauji. But probing should have been resorted to and calculated risk which cannot be called as rashness in any case, should have been taken. In tactics action is the governing rule of war. Factually the proof of battle is action. We should have acted. If we feel of not risking anything, we are risking everything. Our going and capturing would have committed the troops at Molsar Top after action and that was not thought appropriate by the Commanding Officer, I suppose. (See Sketch 9)

'A' Company was moved to Kinari after the Mandi attack. It had been there for only about a couple of days, moved to Rajauri and Capt Sansar Singh 'A' Company commander joined them there. Only 'D' Company, consequently moved back to Kinari. Sauji was left with 'B' Company less a platoon and 'C' company less a platoon alongwith Battalion Headquarters, Mor Platoon less a section was also concentrated at Sauji only.

On 22 August the author along with 2/Lt SS Sandhu was

sitting in his bunker on the eastern side facing Molsar Top, when 2/Lt Ravel Singh and 2/Lt Hardial Singh also came, for discussing the next night's patrolling programme, as ordered by Maj KG Belliappa 2IC, 7 SIKH. After couple of minutes, .50 BMG started firing from the lower slopes of the Molsar Top, towards us. One long burst hit the parapet and inner side of the bunker. One bullet after hitting the parapet got ricocheted and hit 2/Lt SS Sandhu on the chest and through the ribs went inside and got struck there. There was no bleeding outwardly. He seemed okay for sometime but eventually had to be evacuated to Punch. 2/Lt Ravel Singh a bold and strong willed person, with robust health took him to Sekhlu covering a distance of about 15 kilometers, braving through the enemy infested area. 2/Lt SS Sandhu was taken to hospital at Punch, where he unfortunately died on night 24/25 August. In him, we lost a very brave and intelligent officer. That way we lost three as killed and couple of others injured, while holding the defences at Sauji.

2/Lt SS Sandhu with Inspector S Singh of CRPF and Sub Jagir Singh 'C' Company on the FDLs

Clearing of Sauji – Mandi Area

Sauji was finally vacated by 7 SIKH, after own forces in Uri Sector had made substantial gains toward Haji Pir and the battle had spread to Punjab front. The infiltrators soon felt the heat and getting a shocking defeat at number of places started running back across the CFL. 'B' Company was moved out and was tasked to raid Kabar Ki Dheri, where as 'C' Company was tasked to establish a new post on Molsar ridge just north of Mandi town on a track junction. There 'C' Company had a chance encounter. Though the company suffered five dead but enemy was never seen after that incident around this area. That was the last action the unit fought in Mandi Valley.

Our Officer's Mess Cook house was visible from Molsar heights. The enemy sitting at lower slops of Molsar ridge had visualised that this bunker is an important place as couple of activities were taking place and boys were coming out quit often. Mess cook L/Nk Bhagat Ram came out for some job. He was fired at with RL and he fell down. Enemy then fired with the BMG and he was killed instantly. He had to be buried as there was no way of cremating him. His body was exhumed after couple of months and cremated as per the wishes of his family members who were called by the battalion and had arrived from the village for last rites.

Administration at Sauji

Sauji at one stage on around 16-20 August had enough of strength and was rather over-crowded. Enemy was most active and the movements of the troops were duly restricted. There was always fear of maintenance columns being ambushed. We were put on hard scale of rations. Dropping by 'Dakota' was arranged, but it could not drop the supplies, due to non-availability of suitable dropping zone. As there was every possibility of rations being dropped in the enemy dominated area, it was asked to fly back. The rations were somehow arranged with the efforts of jawans and porters only. But the morale of troops was always high. They could manage among themselves with whatever was available. They all were active, jovial and moving, even when the enemy was consistently firing from Molsar top. There were strict orders for not unnecessarily exposing outside the bunkers and communication trenches. One afternoon, I was called by the Commanding Officer. There I found my jawan (helper) injured and bleeding. Commanding Office asked me why did not I control the boys of my platoon, they are unnecessarily getting injured. I asked the jawan what had happened and he smilingly said Sir, I was coming with a glass of tea for you.

Battalion HQ at Sauji

Establishing the tactical headquarters of the unit at Sauji was a well thought of plan of Commander 93 Infantry Brigade. It gave the much needed moral support and depth to all the posts around. Enemy was surprised, when it found a formidable feature in the middle of the area occupied by a much larger force of about of two companies in addition to a company HQ of CRPF. They had established their Administrative Base at Molsar Top and started dominating Molsar Ridge and the premise that they could deal with the elements of CRPF at Sauji without any resistance as the same was then not equipped and tasked like an infantry battalion. This baulked enemy's entire plan vis-a-vis Mandi Valley. Sauji in such a situation would have fallen had it not been occupied by 7 SIKH and that could have created very serious situation. Without this the scenario of the operation could have been different.

10
CAPTURE OF MANDI

"Attack inspires soldier. It adds to his power, rouses his self reliance and confuses the enemy" —FM A Graf

Enemy Guerrillas and Irregulars

Pakistan once again, after 1947-48 operations, ventured for annexing Jammu and Kashmir by force, in August 1965. It dispatched its, so called "Gibraltar Force" in the form of Guerrillas and Irregulars, having elements of various regular armed organisations integrated with them for the purpose. They were dressed in Kurta–Pyjamas, Salwar–Kameez and carrying loi (shawls) etc. for merging with the population. Their garments were loose, so that the weapons could be hidden easily. The aim was to create disturbances in J&K and specially in the Valley, and Punch, both Muslim dominated areas and part of the Kashmir region, cause damages to the important installations and carry out assassinations of political and military leaders and incite the people of Jammu and Kashmir to raise banner of revolt against Government of India and the civil establishment in the state. Once that was achieved, they could establish a Revolutionary Council in Srinagar and then the proper operations by regular army could be launched from north-west or west of Punch town and as also in other areas of Kashmir Valley.

Accordingly, in our Sub-sector they had dumped rations and ammunition in higher reaches of mountains north of Indian Post Gali (602). Pakistani troops started this exercise in the last week of July 1965. Gali is a place on the track junction where from, the tracks lead to Chor Panjal Pass, Kopra and Jarni Gali, all being on Pir Panjal Range. The Pakistani troops started entering Jammu and Kashmir in the first week of August 1965, mainly from Kopra side (in POK). They were in small groups of seven to ten men and were dispatched independently for carrying out independent operations. The upper areas were not occupied by regular army of India, though occasionally patrols were sent for domination and getting the info, if any.

The author with Lt Ravel Singh after the Battle of Mandi

Mandi Town under Enemy

One enemy column came and engaged Gali post and another group occupied the ridge connecting Molsar with Mandi town in Punch. Their move was fast as there was no opposition on the ridge routes they followed. This complete area from Gali to Mandi and then to Kalai Bridge was in the operational responsibility of 7 SIKH. The enemy occupied the feature dominating Mandi town, from east. They ventured to go to Mandi town, attacked the Police post and looted their weapons. Info had started coming in about their entry in Mandi Sector on 2/3 August 1965 and as a result Commanding Officer, 7 SIKH, Lt Col Bhagat Singh had reached Sauji on 6 August 1965. Own sources from Khet informed that trained infiltrators and intruders, attacked Mandi, 23 kilometers from Punch Town on 9 August 1965 at 0930 hrs. The Police Sub Station was their first target. The Station House Officer was killed in action. Head Constable Mukand Ram engaged the raiders in close and hand to hand fight. He lynched one of them and snatched his sten gun and with that only, he fired at the infiltrators and extricated his men to a safer place. The guerrillas then assembled and went to the dominating feature on east of the town, where they had established a post. (See Sketch 10)

Deployment of Own Troops

Mandi a small town is, however a local trade centre for meeting the basic needs of the people. It is located on a flattish piece of ground at the confluence of Gagarian Nala and Dali Nar. It is about 23 kilometers from Punch in north-easterly direction, on the track Sekhlu to Sauji and to Gagarian (Gali Post). The enemy column had reached general area around Mandi on 6-7 August.

Sketch 10: Battle of Mandi

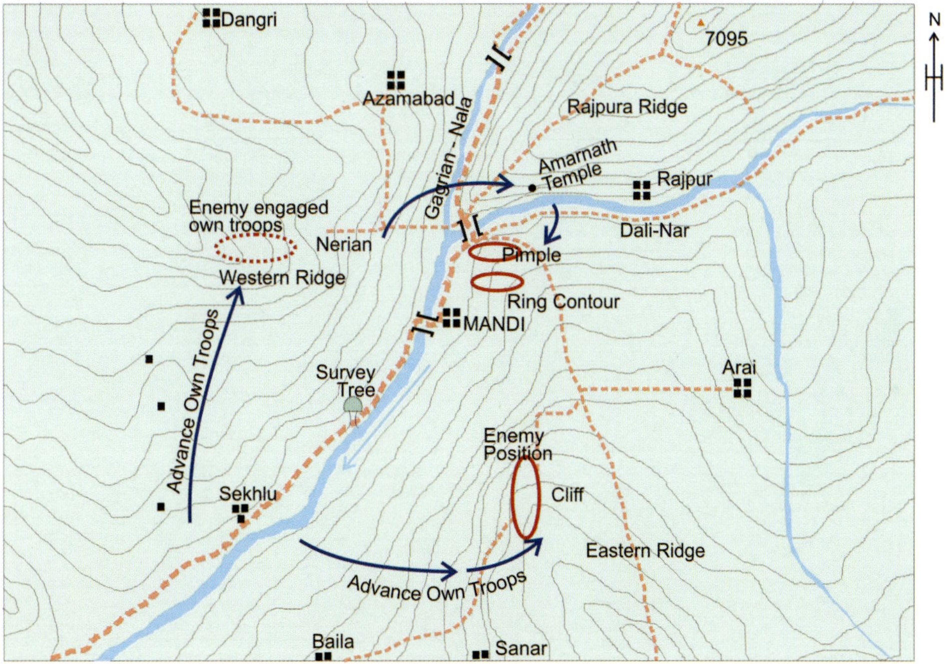

'A' and 'B' Companies of 7 SIKH were ordered to be relieved from Betar Sub-sector, for launching in Mandi Sub-sector. 'C' Company less a platoon, had reached Sauji with Commanding Officer, on 6 August. Platoon ex 'C' company with 2/Lt Dewinder Singh was already located at Gali with elements of CRPF. 'D' Company was at Kath Panjal and Kinari, with element at Khet. The enemy activities were gradually reported from all areas in Punch Sector. The strength, weapons and modus operandi of Pakistanis was still not known, except that they were dressed in civvies in various colour combinations. The die was thus finally cast, for dealing with the Pakistanis.

'A' and 'B' Companies concentrated in the unit Base at Punch on 8-9 August. Both companies were launched in Mandi Valley for operation on 10 August. On 11 August, the companies moved from Sekhlu for clearing the Eastern and Western ridges astride Sekhlu-Mandi-Gali track. 'A' Company under 2/Lt SS Sandhu moved on Eastern Ridge and 'B' Company started combing and advancing towards north on the Western Ridge, under 2/Lt SS Ahlawat. The troops were in high morale and had enough experience of operating in this active area, for the last two years. Battalion was popular in the area and people of all hues were happy to have a Sikh battalion in their area. Lt Col Bhagat Singh, Commanding Officer 7 SIKH, had very good relations with the important civilian people and his knowledge of area, people, terrain and weather etc. stood him and us all in good stead. Sikh troops due to their ancestry and history, in normal parlance are not afraid of Pakistanis. They always felt that, given a level field, a "Khalsa" will beat a Pakistani, outright. Here in Punch/Mandi Sub-sector, they were equally confident of dealing with Pakistanis effectively.

Pakistanis had thought that:-

- Muslim population will cooperate with them in their venture.
- They could play havoc with civilians like raiders of 1947-48, if they did not cooperate.
- Carry out sabotage, disrupt communications and kidnap and kill important personages.
- They were composed of various groups for ease of merging and conversing with the civil people.

Mandi town is located about 20 kilometers, towards own side of CFL from north i.e. from Gali side. As mentioned earlier, it is located on elongated feature astride a track leading to Sauji and onwards to Gagarian village (Gali Post). On the western side, own posts of Doda, Kath Panjal and Kinari are there for dominating CFL of Haji Pir Bulge (Pakistanis call it Bedori Bulge). They selected the Eastern Ridge for operation for affecting Kalai Bridge area and Punch-Rajouri route, following the Molsar Ridge, which being very much away from CFL, was not occupied by own troops.

Task Force and its Composition

On 11 August, both companies that i.e. A & B, 7 SIKH commenced the operations at about 0800 hrs. 'A' company moved towards Eastern Ridge and started climbing after crossing Sekhlu nala. 'B' company commenced its move on Western Ridge. The task force comprising of 'A' and 'B' Companies was commanded by Maj KG Belliappa, 2IC 7 SIKH. It is of interest to note that at this point of time, HQ 52 Mtn Bde with 8 Grenadiers was under move to reach Sekhlu for carrying our clearing operations against the infiltration in Mandi Valley. It reached Sekhlu on 11 August in the evening and was commanded by Brig RD Hira. It was necessitiated due to the report of large number of infiltrators having come in this area, which was approx. 30 kilometers by 10 kilometers from Sekhu to Gali. The situation was taken as very alarming at higher HQs.

(a) **Commander**   Maj KG Belliappa, 21C 7 SIKH Assisted by Maj RK Sharma

    HQ   Sekhlu
    Int Officer   2/Lt M S Punia

(b) **'A' Company**
Company Commander   2/Lt S S Sandhu
No. 1 Platoon Commander   Sub Bharpur Singh
No. 2 Platoon Commander   Sub Bikkar Singh
No. 3 Platoon Commander   Sub Gurdip Singh

(c) **'B' Company**
Company Commander   Maj RK Sharma, who assisted HQ Task Force
No. 4 Platoon Commander   2/Lt SS Ahlawat
No. 6 Platoon Commander   Sub Surjit Singh
*****No. 5 Platoon**   Under Sub Jagir Singh was dispatched for the security of Kalai Bridge

(d) **Mor Position**   Sekhlu
    Mor Platoon Commander   2/Lt Ravel Singh

(e) **MMG Det**   One det with each company.

2/Lt SS Sandhu was commanding 'A' Company. 'B' Company commander Maj RK Sharma, was kept at Task Force HQ at Sekhlu and as a result, 'B' Company comprising of two platoons was commanded by 2/Lt SS Ahlawat, in addition to his being, platoon commander of 4 Platoon.

Conduct of Operations

"Percept is instruction written in the sand. The tide flows over it and the record is gone. Example is graven on the rock and the lesson is not soon lost."

Sense of responsibility will make even a timid, brave and the men will follow him. One has to see that as a leader, one has to pull up, push, guide and lead if the situation so demands and be an example to others. There is no other way to deal with the task of leading.

'A' Company was asked for clearing the Eastern Ridge, dominating Mandi town, keep advancing and descend down at the confluence of nala junction, in north of Mandi town. By this time and specially after the episode of attack on Police Post at Mandi, the composition of the Pakistani troops operating around was known a bit. It was confirmed that they were irregulars operating as guerrillas, in small groups of 7-10 men. But still the total strength on the feature and their weaponry was unknown.

'A' Company crossed Sekhlu Nala at about 0600 hrs, on 11 August and started climbing the Eastern Ridge. The troops were moving in single file, most of the time due to the restrictions imposed by the terrain configuration. They had hardly covered a distance of about 700-800 yards, across Sekhlu Nala, on the ridge when they came under the machine gun fire (See Sketch 10). 2/Lt SS Sandhu, was a brave officer with pleasing and polished manners. He was from 'B' Company but in this action, he commanded 'A' Company. A very bold officer who, in this move was at head of the pack. The move of the company was halted. The company was organised for assault but there were no reserves. The strength of the enemy was estimated to be a company based on the premise that, if it is machine gun fire, it will be about company strength or less. However, the troops took up position and started studying the situation and in the meantime Mor platoon commander 2/Lt Ravel Singh let loose the Mor fire on the enemy. The fire was very effective and enemy withdrew along the ridge. Company moved another 500-600 yards, after taking a little detour but could not make much progress and suffered one killed and one seriously wounded. Sep Pritam Singh was killed, when he charged the enemy machine gun, while Sep Prem Singh suffered a direct hit of RL. Company was ordered to stay put there only for the night 11-12 August. One platoon under 2/Lt SS Sandhu was sent to area Cliff to clear it at night and firm in there only, if possible. It could not make much headway due to BMG fire of the enemy. Company was ordered to concentrate at Sekhlu by 0800 hrs on 12 August for further orders.

Arrival of HQ 52 Mountain Brigade and a Unit

'B' Company was tasked to clear the Western Ridge on the east of own post Doda, occupied by 3 RAJ RIF. The move had commenced at about 0800 hrs on 11 August, simultaneously with 'A' company. The Western Ridge was cleared by about 1600 hrs on 11 August. The company was ordered to descend down to lower slopes. While company was moving down towards Nerian and Mandi town, it came under a very heavy machine gun fire, from Ring Contour and Pimple on the Eastern Ridge. Own MMG crew started engaging Ring Contour and Pimple. But own MMG position was fired at by the BMG of the infiltrators, wounding two members of the crew. Here a very big bullet was "noticed," fired by the intruders, which was different from old MMG bullet. It was then known that the enemy had acquired a new Machine Gun i.e. .50 Browning Machine Gun. Both boys were evacuated being seriously wounded. The company was ordered to be firmed in there only. HQ 52 Mountain Brigade with 8 Grenadiers had reached Sekhlu on 11 August in the evening and Task Force comprising of A&B companies with supporting weapons commanded by Maj KG Belliappa at Mandi was placed under command 52 Mountain Brigade, for capturing Mandi and clearing surrounding areas.

On 12 August at about 0500 hrs, orders were received for taking 'B' company down to area Survey Tree, just about one and half kilometer behind Mandi town, towards Sekhlu. 'B' Company under 2/Lt SS Ahlawat reached Survey Tree at about 0800 hrs. Company of 8 Grenadiers commanded by Maj Dilawar Singh Sangwan had been sent to Mandi town, securing firm base for launching operations on Eastern Ridge by the task force of 7 SIKH. 2/Lt SS Ahlawat was told to report to Brig RD Hira, Commander 52 Mountain Brigade, where Maj KG Belliappa and Maj RK Sharma were also present. Commander 52 Mountain Brigade shot his briefing-cum-orders something like this:-

"What is your name?

I am Ahlawat Sir.

How many men have you got?

Sixty-six including two JCOs and me Sir.

You see these two features call them Pimple and Ring contour?

Right Sir.

You are to capture these two features with your two platoons, I will be pounding these two features till you tell me to stop, on your reaching very close by.

Right Sir.

Company of 8 Grenadiers is already in Mandi town and have secured your firm base.

Right Sir.

Any doubt about anything?

No doubt Sir.

Thank you, you can start off."

What a brief and crisp order. Typical of a bold field commander.

B Company was addressed by Maj KG Belliappa and objectives were explained. 6 Platoon under Sub Surjeet Singh was to capture Pimple and 4 platoon under 2/Lt SS Ahlawat to act as *immediate* reserve. Section MMG was reorganised and Mor platoon commander was briefed and tasked accordingly. 'A' Company was kept reserve to 'B' Company. Both the objectives were engaged with Bty each of 25 Pdr and 120 mm Mors. H hour given for phase I was 1031 hrs, in broad day light, on 12 August 1965. Phase II was to be launched after securing Pimple in Phase I.

Capture of Pimple

'B' company started for the objectives at about 0900 hrs on 12 August. The order of march was, 4 platoon leading, followed by 6 platoon. Some element of the enemy who had come down from the Eastern Ridge to the town of Mandi, started running back over the slopes, upwards. They were fired upon with 3" Mors led by 2/Lt Ravel Singh who played havoc with them, till he was asked to stop. He was a well-trained and enthusiastic officer, who was ready for such operations. He ensured that the target was dealt with adequately and was available at all times.

The company quickly passed through the Mandi town, which, as already said was secured by Company of 8 Grenadiers. Everything was on fast mode. 'B' Company reached the base of Pimple and the arty and 3" Mor fire was shifted on to Ring Contour and higher side, where enemy had his strongly held "Base." The platoons were organised at FUP for the assault. No 6 platoon commanded by Sub Surjit Singh which was to assault Pimple, started moving upwards in a sort of extended formation. Arty and 3" Mor fire was stopped and the section commanders were ordered to be firmly in control of their sections. The platoon kept on moving silently. The enemy kept on firing while running upwards towards Ring Contour but it was plunging fire and did not affect. When the troops reached about 100 yards of Pimple, the *jaikara* was raised for the assault. "*Bole So Nihal Sat Sri Akal*" which ranted the Mandi Hills. Sub Surjit Singh, a very simple and sincere JCO moved the troops on to the top. The enemy kept on firing from a distance while running upwards towards Ring Contour. The enemy had vacated Pimple leaving behind broken pieces of arms, ammunition and packed rations, which was enjoyed later by the jawans. There were no permanent bunkers, places were dug behind the boulders and rocks and temporary shelters were made. No. 6 platoon established itself on Pimple and organised to face as the enemy was nearby on Ring Contour and the fire was coming from there.

Sub Surjit Singh played his role well. He was otherwise considered to be a "so-so" in the unit and not counted in a lot of "hi-fi." But he led the platoon in a bold manner, taking everybody with him. True character pierces through in moments of crisis.

Capture of Ring Contour

Ring Contour was dominating the main bazar of Mandi town. The enemy had established himself well on Ring Contour. BMG and 81 mm Mors of enemy were making the move of own troops, on the track to Sauji, Gali and towards Loran, difficult. The enemy elements at Pimple had also come to Ring Contour and it seemed that the enemy was in strength there. It was earlier reported by civilians and also observed from stiff opposition faced by 'A' Company, on 11 August, that enemy had organised on this main feature, covered with jungle beyond and upwards of Cliff area. From the preparation of defences at Pimple and the opposition faced by No. 6 platoon, it became little clear that the enemy was not a lot of regular troops, destined to give a pitched battle, but an assortment of guerrillas and irregulars. Their aim seemed to stall the move of own troops in the area and dominate it, by operating in mobile columns. But the situation was still not very clear as to what this all, was about.

However, they had strong base at Ring Contour and the strength was reportedly about two sections armed with .50 BMGs, RL and telescopic rifles. They were equipped with mini transmitters and were seen using by the civilians on 9 August when the Police Post at Mandi was attacked and looted. A large number of them could not understand the local language as reported by civilians and in appearance they looked like Pathans and Baluchis.

No. 4 platoon moved towards Ring Contour in dispersed extended formation. To avoid the detection and direct firing on own troops, the movement was through the rocky complex and it was a steep climb. The enemy was firing towards Pimple but the move of No. 4 platoon was not seen, by them. Arty and Mor fire was going on and enemy's head was kept down. When we cleared the steep climb and reached a relatively easy ground for movement, the top was visible. The troops immediately formed the assault line and attack was launched. It was day time attack. The enemy was firing from the top, the troops started halting and running for cover. The situation was becoming difficult as every move was visible to the enemy. 2/Lt SS Ahlawat started exhorting the troops and pushing them upwards. He himself moved ahead from the right and threw grenade on the enemy. The troops were made to leave cover and move towards top, fastest under effective LMG fire cover, provided by Sep Gurmel Singh. NK Lal Singh and Sep Gurmel Singh kept on firing intensely on the BMG position, which was also silenced. The move upward became possible. Another lot of two good NCOs NK Harnek Singh and NK Gurdial Singh took the enemy from left. NK Harnek Singh fired 2" Mor and kept on pushing his men too, towards the objective. The platoon commander visualising the developing situation well, reached the top from

2/Lt SS Sandhu who led 'A' Company in the Battle of Mandi

right with NK Lal Singh and Sep Gurmel Singh and immediately fired on the enemy. NK Harnek Singh and NK Gurdial Singh joined them from the left. The enemy after causing delay and suffering casualties, withdrew towards south-east, leaving behind two dead. It took over 30 minutes to deal, evict then defeat the enemy and capture Ring Contour. The enemy left behind ammunition, clothing and two dead bodies with their personal weapons. Both these Pakistan intruders were Baluchis from 19 SSG, which is their elite organisation as was revealed later on. They could have taken their wounded with them. Mandi town was secured and both features, Pimple and Ring Contours were in our hands and the movement beyond Mandi was thus made possible. Both platoons firmed in and stayed there for the night, Next day i.e. on 13 August both platoons were relieved by 8 Grenadiers. Both Companies were assembled at nala junction north of Mandi town and then 'B' Company moved to join Battalion Tac HQ at Sauji, to be again under command 93 Infantry Brigade. Our Task Force HQ, two sections of Mor platoon and MMG section also moved with 'B' company to Sauji.

Restoring of Situation in Mandi Town

The task force did a commendable job in capturing the important town of Mandi and dominating heights, which made the usage of track to forward areas possible. It was a day attack and move was difficult and dangerous. 2/Lt S S Ahlawat led them well without caring for his personal safety. NK Lal Singh, NK Harnek Singh, Sep Gurmel Singh and NK Gurdial Singh went into action with determination and courage.

Brig RD Hira came to the companies assembled at nala junction and congratulated all. He was briefed by 2/Lt S S Ahlawat as to how our troops were able to inflict casualties, evict and beat the enemy at Mandi. He, himself was a man of measured words. He spoke to our troops something like this-

> "I congratulate you all for the excellent work you people have done in the capture of Mandi Town. I never had any doubt about the capabilities of a Sikh Soldier. I have already talked to Division Commander and Army Commander about your contribution. I will apprise your Commanding Officer also, of the same."

He made a special mention of 2/Lt SS Ahlawat who was instrumental in timely clearing of Mandi town. He showered praises on 2/Lt Ravel Singh and his Mor platoon for having done a splendid job, in supporting the troops during ops. He met and gave Shabash to NK Lal Singh, NK Harnek Singh and Sep Gurmel Singh and also to those, who had been evacuated, being wounded.

He thanked Maj KG Belliappa for all the cooperation. 'B' Company after this along with 2/Lt SS Sandhu 2/Lt SS Ahlawat and Mor platoon started for Sauji where as 'A' Company under 2/Lt MS Punia was ordered to go to Kath Panjal and Kinari for relieving 'D' coy for operations to be carried out in and around Sauji.

About the Mandi operaions, the Western Command "War Despatches" recorded something like this.

> "Further South in PUNCH Sector, 1 Madras cleared point 4007 killing 12 wounding 16 infiltrators. This was followed by capture of Mandi by Task Force of 7 SIKH under 52 Mountain Brigade. And with that the first ray of light brightened, otherwise dismal situation prevailing in Punch Sector, where all semblance of command and control was rapidly slipping

through the fingers of local Brigade Commander, for want of initiative and offensive spirit." (See Appendix D & E)

Operational Analysis

"What we have to learn to do we learn by doing. There is no other short cut." Capture of Mandi town and it surrounding heights, by Task Force 7 SIKH, under command 52 Mountain Brigade, was a glorious feat. It gave the first taste of victory over the enemy and raised the morale of the troops. It finally blocked the open movements of the enemy, who was otherwise emboldened of his entry, deep into Indian territory of Punch in north-western Kashmir. This operation can be called as a turning point because had Mandi not been cleared and the enemy was allowed to be firmed in, it could have completed the northern pincer, to cut off Punch and there would have been a direct threat to Kalai Bridge. The enemy on the southern pincer however was successful in occupying OP Hill Complex, which created a real danger to Kalai Bridge and Khanater Gali besides immobilizing Balnoi and Mendhar areas. Operationally it can be analysed as:

- It was almost clear that the enemy troops were mobile but strong, well-knit, well-determined and well-equipped.

- New weapons were noticed during the encounters, .50 BMG, 83 mm RL and mini transmitters were seen for the first time and all these were very effective.

- Good and cordial relations with the civilians based on respect, welfare and help paid rich dividends and some of them gave info voluntarily and timely.

- Companies should have adequate reserves of trained

persons for duties in specialist platoons for the 3" Mor and MMG. In case of necessity, these can be used. 'B' Company faced the crunch when two MMG crews were injured, very seriously.

- The unbothered, awkward, uninterested, incorrigible, rogues and superseded who are bane for every senior during peace, do excel in operations at times. Such people have ego problem. NK Lal Singh, who was superseded, was the main architect in silencing the enemy BMG on Ring Contour. This aspect is worth exploiting in operations at company and battalion level.

- Own supporting weapons should always be given priorities. Own Mor platoon was available to us till the last minute. There was a distinct advantage of it.

- Reorganisation in such operations should be quick. During day time, it can be very costly. The enemy can cause maximum damage, even from a distance, as each individual can be spotted easily, more so when the enemy is retreating towards higher ground. First thing should be to secure the position firmly and be prepared to face counter attack.

- Whatever info is fed from any source must be passed down to each rifle man if possible. For days together the composition, strength and modus operandi of infiltrators was not known; which delayed the operations against them. At higher HQ, the scheme of things are known earlier kind courtesy various intelligence agencies at their disposal. But it was not properly disseminated to battalions, companies and platoons. Composition and grouping of infiltrators was known much later.

Appendix – D

Maj Gen R D HIRA, *PVSM*, *MVC*
GOC

DO No 2531/1/PF
HEADQUARTERS
15 INFANTRY DIVISION
C/o 56 APO

23 March 1973

Dear Ahlawat,

    Thank you for your DO letter No 22648/PERS dated 10 Mar 73.

    The MANDI engagement has been recognised and since two Companys of 7 SIKH did take part during this battle on 11-12 Aug 65, your entitlement to claim MANDI as a battle honour is justified and valid.

    I would advise you to pursue the matter in accordance with SAO 27/S/72.

With my good wishes,

Yours sincerely,

Capt SS AHLAWAT
OC 'A' Coy
7 SIKH
C/O 99 APO

Appendix – E

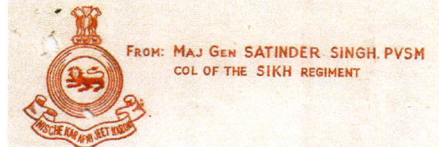

FROM: MAJ GEN SATINDER SINGH, PVSM
COL OF THE SIKH REGIMENT

D O No 02210/SDS(A)/NDC/SRC
NATIONAL DEFENCE COLLEGE
(MINISTRY OF DEFENCE)
6, TEES JANUARY MARG
NEW DELHI-11

/ May 73

My dear Sutra,

Thank you for your letter No 22648/W/P, dated 25 Apr 73.

I have forwarded to the Regimental Centre my approval for the Battle Honour recommended by your Commanding Officer.

I am afraid, as regards citations for officers and OR who took part in the Battle of MANDI, it is now too late to submit them. I feel that is no point taking up this case.

With regards Jakhi

Yours
Satinder

Major SS AHLAWAT
OC 'A' Company
7th Bn The Sikh Regiment
c/o 99 APO

- Quick and calculated risks should be taken against the enemy and more so against the fluid one. Delay can be costly. Brig RD Hira, Cdr 52 Mtn Bde was prompt and to the point. He took a very bold view of the whole thing and put both companies of 7 SIKH into attack with no loss of time and cleared Mandi, to the great relief of both Divisional and Army Commander besides commanding officer 7 SIKH sitting, at tactical HQ at Sauji. Impetuosity and audacity often achieve, what ordinary means fail to achieve.

- Day time attack is very risky and will not progress without the commanders being in the lead. 2/Lt SS Ahlawat, at one stage in attack on Ring Contour had to go ahead as a leading man, exhorting the men to move fast. To take the troops to the enemy position could be a herculean task, in day time. Only a man of men who has established firm relationship with the men based on respect, firm handling and effective command would lead them properly. No man is a leader until his appt as a leader is ratified in the minds and hearts of his men. Sikh troops will seldom let down a well-meaning commander.

- Fire and move, is the only desirable way to go ahead. The enemy's head must be kept down. Actions are won by superiority and intensity of fire.

- Combination of approaches used by Brig RD Hira, in launching two companies, from two directions on Eastern Ridge, really, confused the enemy who ran away leaving the dead behind, at Ring Contour.

- Unconventional approach to operations adopted by the enemy and his complete modus operandi once known must be explained to the troops at the earliest. Getting ready to face an organised and stereotype set up of the enemy like platoon and company and facing the irregular or a mixed amalgam not capable of holding ground are two different factors and do affect the minds of men in appreciating correct tactical situation.

- There is no need to hit the head against the wall, when other alternatives are available. When 'A' Company came under fire on the Eastern Ridge moving from its southern tip upwards and could not make a head way, that approach was not pursued and instead, 'B' Company was immediately launched from the northern end of the same ridge. Flexibility is an essential criterion of warfare.

- In war immediate and wilful obedience of orders is crucial. For the obedience in face of the enemy and besides the enemy, in the midst of danger of varied and unforeseen circumstances, of a menacing unknown dimension, add to the problems. Training, officer-men relationship and fair play pays handsomely.

Honours and Awards

The task force, of 7 SIKH, 93 Infantry Brigade had cleared the surrounding heights and captured Mandi Town in Punch Sector, J&K. The task force commander was Maj KG Belliappa 2IC 7 SIKH and this particular operation was fought by it having been placed under command 52 Mountain Brigade. On completion of task, 'B' Company along with 2/Lt SS Sandhu and 2/Lt SS Ahlawat were released to join the Battalion Tac HQ at Sauji and reached there by evening of 13 August. After that 52 Mountain Brigade moved away and the relevance and importance of this action was totally forgotten and ignored. Had Gali Post not abandoned only next day i.e. on night 14/15 August, recognition could have come through, for action of 'A' and 'B' Companies and individuals. The unit afterwards remained very heavily committed till 3 November 1965, the day Battle of OP Hill was fought. The commanding officer then got posted out immediately after and the whole chemistry got changed under the new dispensation. However the names had been forwarded by Maj KG Belliappa to Lt Col Bhagat Singh immediately after the operation, as approved by Brig RD Hira, but somehow the issue got buried under the weight of circumstances. These were :

1. 2/Lt SS Ahlawat   Offg 'B' Company Commander
2. Sep Nachhattar Singh   'B' Company
3. Sep Karam Singh   MMG Section
4. NK Lal Singh   'B' Company
5. NK Harnek Singh   'B' Company
6. Sep Gurmel Singh   'B' Company
7. Sep Pritam Singh   'A' Company

Casualties

Own   Killed-1 (One)
           Wounded-6 (Six)

Enemy Killed-2 (Two)
           Wounded – Not known

11
BATTLE OF GALI

"Duty, above all the consequences, and often at the crisis of difficulty, commands us to throw them overboard. It commands us to look neither to the right, nor to the left but straight onwards. Hence every act of duty is an act of faith. It is performed in the assurance that God will take care of the consequences."
—A De Vere

Post in a Bowl

Gali, as the name indicates is a place on ridge line, for passing from one side to the other. It is lower in the middle and is a bottleneck, usually having two important shoulders. But Gali Piquet or Post (602) referred here is little different (See Sketch 11). Behind a nala junction, where bigger nala has taken a left turn, there is a small mound, which is higher on the west and tapers down a little toward east, touching the flat piece of ground, over which passes an important track, leading to Chor Panjal Pass on the Pir Panjal Range. Slightly ahead towards north-west, another track takes off which turns left and leads to Kopra in POK. Therefore, it is basically a track junction to go to the above mentioned places. However, it is named as Gali which is a misnomer. Southern side of the mound is a sheer cliff. The mound is practically enclosed

Sketch 11: Battle of Gali Post

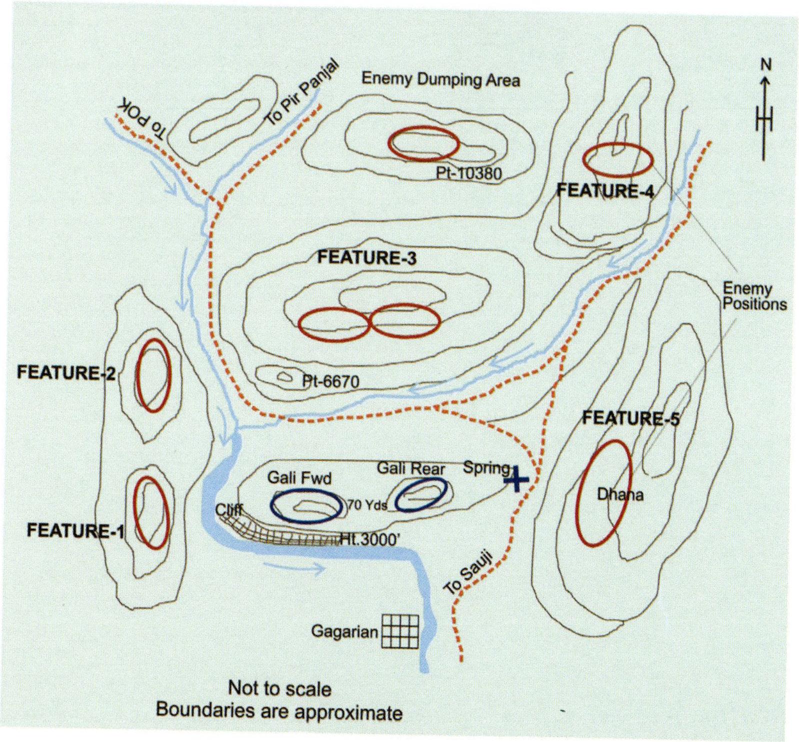

by a big nala from three sides on which was located, own post known as Gali Piquet (602). It has dominating features in north, east and west and as such we can therefore conveniently call it, as post in a bowl.

In the south of Gali Piquet in the open space, there is a big village known as Gagarian. It is on the northern extreme of the Mandi Valley at the foothills of Pir Panjal Range. Two very important tracks pass through it, one to Jarni Gali and the other to Chor Panjal Pass, both on the Pir Panjal Range. "Gagarian" is about midway between Punch in Mandi valley and Ferozpur in Kashmir Valley. Track to village Ferozpur leads from Gali to Chor Panjal Pass, runs along Ferozpur Nala to Ferozpur Pass and then to the village and in this, lies its importance

Nk Shangara Singh, one of the heroes of Battle of Gali Post killed in action at Gali

for military operations by and against Pakistan. Gali is therefore very important from intelligence and security point of view. Akbar Khan was the Numberdar in year 1965 who had his influence in the area around and could be useful in getting info about the enemy, if invested properly and contacted by the experts. There were other small villages ahead and around Gagarian, and as such, it was difficult to keep an eye on them all. Also people keep moving with their cattle from one place to the other and in that case keeping close watch becomes more acute. Such distant but important places were often required to be kept under constant surveillance.

As a Police Check Post

Gali post was established way back in 1950 and it was invariably occupied by Police or CRPF and known and served as Check Post. Before the commencement of 1965 operation, it was occupied by a platoon of CRPF and a platoon of regular army with a detachment of 3" Mors and a section of MMGs of respective Infantry units, deployed in Mandi Valley. In July-August, 7 SIKH was occupying it with other three posts in this Sector, i.e. Kath Panjal, Kinari (604) and Khet (605). At the time of outbreak of the hostilities in August 1965, there were two platoons at Gali, one of 7 SIKH and other of CRPF. Overall post commander was 2/Lt Dewinder Singh, 7 SIKH. Normal patrolling and laying of ambushes etc. was resorted to, for domination of the important tracks and having an eye on the activities of smugglers, cattle lifters and enemy agents, and enemy venturing for exploits from across the CFL.

Developing into Defended Locality

Gali Post (602) was established on a small mound, approximately 3,000 feet high, which was about 150 meters by 40 meters. Though it looked like a mound, as it was enclaved by a nala from three sides, it could neither be made into a defended locality, nor it could be called a piquet in the real sense of the term. Defences made were not of permanent nature but were temporary, constructed of CGI sheets and 'ballies'. Once 7 SIKH reached there, Lt Col Bhagat Singh, its Commanding Officer who knew the area very well, got it done up a little, but still it was not in the shape and form of being called a defended locality. It was simply a "Check Post" for checking smuggling, cattle lifting etc. as discussed earlier. There were no minefields or wire obstacles around. Simple perimeter fence was existing. Troops had "on weapon scale of ammunition." Telephone line was unreliable and radio set was the only means of communication which also could be easily jammed. Its task was to dominate the tracks leading to and from the area. It was on a finger tip in respect of other posts, beyond the range of our arty and not tactically sited as said earlier. It was without any mutual support of any nature. Even during peace time for performing of assigned tasks, accepting responsibilities and discharging duties, it should have been sited on a feature of tactical advantage, otherwise it invited destruction of men, and material, during sudden outbreak of hostilities.

On 1 August, 7 SIKH had a depleted platoon i.e. one officer and 17 other rank and one platoon of CRPF, with one Sub Inspector (equal to a JCO) and 27 constables. On 3 August, just before the infiltration or we can say, when the infiltration was stealthily taking place, one platoon with one officer and 27 other rank ex-7 MADRAS reinforced the post. Earlier the post was not designed to fight a battle to the "last man last round," but was to withdraw after giving the required info and causing little delay, if required. As the post was in little elongated fashion, established on the mound it was temporarily divided into two portions known as Forward Post and the Rear Post. With the coming in of one more platoon on 3 August, the post was organised by 2/Lt Dewinder Singh as under:-

Forward Post 1 Officer, 17 ORs – 7 SIKH
1 Officer, 12 ORs – 7 MADRAS

Rear Post 1 JCO, 15 ORs – 7 MADRAS
1 Sub Inspector, 27 Constables – CRPF

The route of maintenance for own troops was from Punch-Sekhlu-Mandi-Khet and to Gali, based on coolies and at times on troop labour, if necessitated.

Infiltration

The whole Gibraltar Force of Pakistanis was divided into eight task forces as said earlier. It was launched in the first week of August 1965. In this area main group or task force, which was given the responsibility was named as Salahuddin column/force. A group from this force, known as "Mann Column" branched off for Gali for carrying out operations in Mandi Valley. It was of about two companies plus, of strength and made its presence felt on 7 August, when it concentrated in force against Gali picquet at Danna Hill on north-east of own post. The strategic aim of the enemy was to cut off Punch salient by capturing Kalai Bridge – severing communication with Punch and making a way for two-pronged deep infiltration on a massive scale via Mandi Valley in the north and Mendhar Valley in the south to establish a link at Kalai Bridge on Road Rajouri – Punch. Once that was achieved, the conventional attack on Punch from north or north west would have been launched. It has already been mentioned that large number of groups of infiltrators had crossed into own side of CFL on or around 1 August and they were to go to pre-selected locations. In general area Gali Post, they had come and occupied their "Base" at Dhanaa. Some from the Base at Dhanna and others directly from across the CFL were led to the features 1,2,3, and 4 (See Sketch 11). The enemy groups were self-contained. The concentration area for the bigger enemy force was in general area around Point 10380 just north of Gali Post. Beside the columns and groups operating around Gali and Mandi Valley, a large number of infiltrators had bypassed Gali and established base at Molsar Top and Loran. Within a very short span of time, their activities dominated the Mandi Valley and particularly Mandi town and affecting the movements on the main track-Punch-Mandi-Gali, as far as 7 SIKH was concerned and hence affected.

Importance of Gali Post

The infiltrators were a sort of combination of Pathans, Baluchis, SSG elements, Razakars and Mujahids etc. putting on civilian type baggy and loose dresses. They were divided into groups of 7-10 members, each group carrying one each of .50 BMG, RL, telescopic rifle and mini transmitter, all newly acquired items of equipment by Pakistan from USA and other friendly countries. Section 81 mm Mors was one with their company's strength column. On all the features surrounding Gali Post, the groups were accordingly armed. 81 mm Mor was located on Feature 4. Basically, these guerrilla groups were not to launch conventional attack but if felt necessary attack and destroy the post and evict Indian troops from Gali, so that they could carry out subversion of civilians and establish their own control in these areas firmly and quickly.

The case of Gali Post had assumed greater importance in the mind of Commander 93 Infantry Brigade, when he, based on info, got this post reinforced by another platoon on 3 August making to a company strength as mentioned earlier. It then automatically warranted a change in the task. As defensive position, it was tactically weak and if still desired to be held under all circumstances, then it required other parts of equipment and stores also to be made up, which was not done. Mere strength equipped with rifles and LMGs would not have compensated for other standing requirements. Enemy thought of eliminating it (Gali) in the first instance as it was a hindrance in his moves and dominance for Mandi town and beyond. The enemy could have calibrated his actions as per earlier info about troops on Gali vis-a-vis time and space available to them.

Own Intelligence Agencies and Enemy

There was no intelligence agency, worth the name operating in general area Gali. The dumping of stores by enemy had commenced in last week of July 1965 and prior to that their recce parties would have come and done the required job. Nothing was reported at least to 7 SIKH. 2/Lt Dewinder Singh had taken over as Post Commander on 29 July 1965 and virtually had no time to cultivate the sources and get on to his task properly. It however goes to the credit of Brig. Zora Singh Commander 93 Infantry Brigade, who having got an air of enemy's activities through his own sources got a platoon of 7 MADRAS to be in position at Gali on 3 August, virtually making it to a company post. On 5 August he himself visited Gali Post. He met few civilians. He informed 2/Lt Dewinder Singh about the activities of the enemy and likelihood of some adventure. He ordered him to prepare the

Lt Col Dewinder Singh (then 2/Lt) Checkmated the Gibraltars at Gali Post, giving a thrilling account of himself, later got wounded in Operation Phanne-Shah

post properly and stay put under all circumstances. 2/Lt Dewinder Singh brought to his notice, various deficiencies on the post. He told him that there were neither any wire obstacles nor any minefield around the post. He said that with the existing state of affairs and more so, its location being in a bowl, he would find it difficult to withstand the deliberate attacks for long. Commander, however was of the firm view that Gali must be held at all costs and that was the reason, he said, for his giving another platoon to Gali post on 3 August. He said that he would look into the other requirements and do something soon to overcome that. Thus, the die was cast for battle to be fought at Gali, a post established on a nala track junction, virtually having no defence potential and with no support from any side and of any kind, ignoring all the previous considerations and accordingly assigning it the previous task. *"A plan, which does not stand to reason, defies logic, devoid of any rationale and admits no modification cannot be called a good plan."*

Commander 93 Infantry Brigade somehow gave the impression that these people were simply irregulars and will not be able to put up a well determined attack.

Commencement of Hostilities

2/Lt Dewinder Singh was a committed, intelligent, well determined and straightforward soldier, who always was very respectful and followed orders truthfully. He had relieved Sub Sant Singh of 'C' Company 7 SIKH only on 29 July 1965 as post commander. He did not have much time to settle down and prepare the defences to face the enemy effectively. There was much to be desired at Gali but the basic issue of "located in a bowl" and not tactically sited was irking him the most. This was the biggest handicap, he had to start with and cope up. It is fatal to enter any war without the wherewithal and preparation to win it. To win a war quickly takes long and deliberate preparations, which 2/Lt Dewinder Singh had not been able to accomplish. But being disciplined and obedient officer, he knew it well and did his best in that very short time available to him. *War educates senses, calls into action, the will perfects physical constitution, brings men into such swift and close collision in critical moments that man measures man.*

Composition of Force at Gali Post

On 7 August 1965, the day the contact with the intruding enemy column was established our strength at Gali was:-

(a) **Post Commander** – 2/Lt Dewinder Singh, 7 SIKH

(b) **Strength**

Forward Post	Rear Post
1 Officer, 18 ORs – 7 SIKH	1 JCO, 27 ORs–7 SIKH
1 Officer, 27 ORs- 7 MADRAS	1 Sub-Inspector, 27 Constable – CRPF

(c) **Supporting Weapons**   Section MMGs – 7 SIKH
Detachment 3" Mor – 7 MADRAS

(d) **Minefield & Wire Obstacles**   Nil

(e) **Arty & other Support including mutual from other posts**   Nil

On 7 August, 2/Lt Dewinder Singh was informed by the civilians that a large enemy force of about 400-500 persons, dressed in civil clothes, mostly in Kurta-Pyjama had entered our area and had gone to the jungle-clad mountains of village Danna and around. 2/Lt Dewinder Singh sent a group of trusted civilians to area Danna to confirm the news. They came back and confirmed that a column of enemy was there. They had established their camp or 'Base' there. Info about their moving out to other heights, surrounding Gali, however, could not be known at that moment. Own post was hastily readied to face the enemy's challenge. Booby traps were laid at the selected places, trenching tools and ammunition were put at respective places and 2" Mors, 3" Mors, LMGs and MMGs were put in their pits and emplacements. Lt Col Bhagat Singh, who had come a day earlier at Sauji (601) was informed and apprised of the latest situation. He advised 2/Lt Dewinder Singh to prepare the post for all eventualities. Lt Col Bhagat Singh discussed the situation with Brig Zora Singh Commander 93 Infantry Brigade, who asked him to get the post readied and ordered that it would not be vacated. His convictions were very firm. The way the developments took place, 2/Lt Dewinder Singh became apprehensive of launching of offensive by enemy, at any moment.

First Series of Attacks

By 2300 hrs on 7 August, the enemy had occupied the heights surrounding Gali Post and sited its RLs on top of Pt. 6670 in the north and western tip of the feature Danna near the main track leading to Chor Panjal Pass. It had quietly happened and the post could not be aware of all this. They came to know only when enemy opened up with all his weapons, at about 0020 hrs on 8 August, from all the surrounding heights, marked as features 1,2,3,4 and 5 on the Sketch. Complete post comprising of Forward Post and Rear Post was engaged. However the main concentration of fire was on the Forward Post. The enemy used the para bombs to see the target and engaged it. 81 mm Mor fire came from feature 4 and was effective. It looked to be a serious effort on the part of the enemy. The post, as expected, was mentally ready to deal with the enemy. Normal to heavy to very heavy fire from enemy's MMGs, LMGs and RLs was brought on the post. It is also added here that another column of the enemy had reached at Molsar Top on 5-6 August and had started engaging Sauji for tying down the troops there.

The first formal attack came at about 0100 hrs on 8 August. It was mainly directed towards, Forward Post. During this time Rear Post was kept under heavy firing and move outside the post was not possible. The enemy then came near the fence, created noise and attacked Forward Post. Most of the enemy men were halted outside, but one group came in, through a breach in the fence from north-western side. The enemy rushed towards the trenches firing with their weapons, creating noise. All jawans, specially, Sep Sher Singh and Sep Darshan Singh fired at them very effectively. The enemy having been fired upon immediately retreated, carrying dead and wounded. But both of our own jawans mentioned above were also wounded seriously. The enemy attack failed. Sub Sunder Rajan of 7 MADRAS was wounded with the enemy BMG fire at Rear Post. The enemy gathered courage and came and attacked again at 0200 hrs, then around 0300 hrs and finally at about 0400 hrs, somewhat new technique. Own troops were very well-determined and did not permit the enemy to enter and all the attacks were beaten back. Regarding this attack the War Dispatches of Western Command record like this:

> "Night 7/8 August, number of clashes were reported. The most serious of them took place at Gali (602), the gateway into the Mandi Valley. Here the Pakistanis launched four vicious attacks in a determined effort to overrun the post. But 7 SIKH who were in occupation of this piquet repulsed all these assaults inflicting severe casualties."

From this action of night 7/8 August 1965, the following observations could be made about the enemy:-

- New machine gun .50 BMG was used for firing on our post. Its fire was effective and it had a bigger bullet, as collected and seen by own jawans.
- RL used by the enemy was of new type, which hit our bunkers almost accurately and for effect.
- Loopholes of all bunkers were fired at to ensure that we leave the bunkers and stand outside and then suffer casualties with their 81 mm Mor, RL and that of Machine Guns.
- The enemy's attacking troops were not a cohesive, resolute and determined unit. They fired from a distance, created noise and fell back, suffering casualties, every time.

.50 BMG firing continued till 0830 hrs on 8 August. Exact positions of enemy were identified and 3" Mor fire was brought on them. BMG at Feature 2 was silenced and there was no firing from that BMG for whole day of 8 August.

Views of Commander 93 Infantry Brigade

Commander 93 Infantry Brigade was apprised of the situation by Lt Col Bhagat Singh. Brig Zora Singh was firm on his decision and suggested that no alternative position to be occupied, when so advised. He ordered Lt Col Bhagat to dispatch another platoon from Sauji to Gali because the platoon ex-7 MADRAS at Gali was being withdrawn. By evening of 8 August, our platoon had reached Gali and replaced the platoon ex 7 MADRAS, who headed for their unit. The strength at Gali, however remained almost the same i.e. 2 platoons of 7 SIKH and a platoon of CRPF. Now the immediate worry for the post commander and CO 7 SIKH was not of the strength but of:-

- Defence potential of the picquet
- Defence preparedness of the picquet
- Lack of mutual support
- State of ammunition on the post as it was not being replenished being almost cut off. It enforced the strict control on the troops for use of ammunition.
- Maintenance of the post against the devastating and demonstrating fire, besides being isolated and almost sieged.

On 8 August, during day time, the firing of the enemy continued unabated. There was difficulty in preparing food and fetching water specially for Forward Post, but somehow the day was managed. Every move on the post was drawing enemy fire as the enemy could observe, sitting on heights all around. Enemy's BMG at Feature 1 and 4 were also silenced with own 3" Mor, but our positions on the post, were totally exposed.

On 9 August, the intensity of the enemy fire on Gali increased substantially. Own Mor and MMG fire was brought on the enemy positions and this ding dong battle and heavy exchange of firing from both sides continued. The state of ammunition was causing anxiety as it was being expended without being replenished and the administration on the post had slackened a bit. The men could not have proper food, bath and rest.

Reinforcing a Success or a Failure

Lt Col Bhagat Singh discussed the situation again with Brigade Commander. He in addition also brought out that he did not have any troops worth the name except his Protection Section and a platoon of 'C' Company at Bn HQ at Sauji and required own platoon sent to Gali, back to Sauji as it was taken out from Sauji, and Gali be strengthened from other sources. Commander agreed and told Lt Col Bhagat Singh that on 10 August, platoon ex-7 MADRAS will reach Gali and 7 SIKH platoon could be withdrawn to be relocated at Sauji, as desired. The action were completed in time. Lt Col Bhagat Singh suggested to the Brigade commander that as the move and task of the infiltrators was becoming clearer, the post at Gali, having a company strength can be brought either to Molsar Ridge or Nawan just due south-west of Gali and north side of Kath Panjal and the infiltrators could be dealt with by our own strong mobile columns from these locations. Commander did not entertain this suggestion and finally told him that Gali will not be vacated, withdrawn or relocated. *"Reinforce a success and not the failure,"* – the old maxim was stubbornly ignored, which did require due reconsideration. Own troops on isolated Gali post were not in a position to go out and attack the enemy on surrounding features. The post was being observed and kept under constant fire by the enemy. 10 August was also routine tough day. Any way some water was procured and some sort of meal was arranged by the men on stoves in the trenches. Two "dry days" of 8 August and 9 August had started having a telling effect on jawans and that little seriousness could be noticed on every one's face.

On 11 August, the enemy started with new vigour. It ensured that all living accommodation and visible bunkers were continuously kept under very heavy and devastating fire with BMG, Mors and RLs mainly from north and south-west directions. 2/Lt K Rao, 7 MADRAS was seriously wounded with BMG fire at about 1200 hrs. By 1300 hrs two jawans had been killed and five jawans were wounded while doing up the defences. Irony was that own troops could not go out to deal with the enemy. The enemy was sitting tight on all surrounding heights, however could not come near us for assault after having seen the results on 7/8 August. Situation in any case was becoming difficult and grim, day by day. It was not permitting any alternative. *"Whatever was enforced, was more imputed (attributed) to him (Commander) who exacts than to him (Dewinder) who performs."* 2/Lt Dewinder Singh talked to almost everyone and exhorted to do their best. Pep talk by a well-meaning commander at such a time does play an invigorating role.

Second Series of Attacks

On night 12/13 August, the enemy again made a plan to attack. First the enemy engaged the post as usual. At about 2300 hrs the attack was launched. Sep Surjeet Singh and Mohan Singh fired and killed all three enemy men who came nearby but themselves too succumbed to the injuries sustained due to ensuring enemy fire. Later on Sepoy Rao of 7 MADRAS took the toll of two of the enemy while approaching towards him, but being injured he also fell due to heavy bleeding. On the Rear Post Sep Dharam Singh, L/NK (Cook) Dhoom Singh, Sep Sadhu Singh, Sep Tulsa Singh and L/NK Narender Singh were wounded but successfully repulsed the enemy attack once again. About 15 enemy men were killed by our jawans in this fierce attack of the enemy. Lt Col Bhagat Singh was informed of the latest situation who managed some arty fire which had come at 2345 hrs and pounded the features around. It was very much desired. The beating of this attack gave another jolt to the enemy. The enemy was thrown back due dogged determination and resolve of 2/Lt Dewinder Singh and his men. The War Dispatches, record about this action, in these words:-

> *"The enemy's fierce attack on Gali Piquet on night 7/8 August 1965, had been followed by a lull in launching attacks to be broken on the day, when infiltrators made an all out bid to capture the post on 13 August 1965. The piquet Garrison, marooned since 7 August 1965, refused to yield ground and repelled assaults with severe casualties on the enemy. It was evident however, that the depleted force, unless speedily reinforced would not withstand for long and further attacks in strength."*

Changing Scenario

The situation at Gali had slowly become precarious. "Mann Column" was faced with a stiff opposition by the band of 2/Lt Dewinder Singh, but at a heavy cost due terrain restrictions and tactical miscalculations. The post was reduced to rubbles by enemy's BMGs, RLs and 81 mm Mors. Ammunition was being expended without any replacement and jawans were without food, water, shelter and sleep. Large number of them were wounded and some killed. Enemy looked firm in liquidating the post and as such new plan for facing them was ordained. The situation however was grim and the stark challenge to face the enemy lay ahead. Enemy tested tenacity of our soldiers and had to bite the dust in the attacks on night 7/8 August and again on night 12/13 August. The situation had, however, changed much, since then but still jawans were not much worried as far as fighting stamina of Pakistanis was concerned. The isolation and domination by deadly newly acquired weapons, however had changed the situation altogether which had brought the post to ruins. The administration had almost crumbled and jawans were facing acute problems.

Fiercest Battle Ensued

The enemy again started assault on the Gali Post. At about 1300 hrs, on 13 August, heavy BMG fire came mainly on Forward Post. For about an hour, there was no respite. As mentioned earlier there was no place for taking shelter except trenches. At about 1345 hrs, the enemy attacked the Forward Post with fresh fury, with about a company strength converging from all directions. They were heard saying *"Sikho bhag jao, nahi to tumhe maar denge"* (you Sikhs run away, otherwise you will be killed). They were mainly Punjabis, Pathans and Baluchis, who this time followed mainly the difficult approach from southwest, negotiating the difficult cliff. There was nothing in form of minefield and wire obstacles etc. to stop them and the Pakistanis had identified command post, MMG bunker, 3" Mor pit and LMG bunkers and thus rushed inside. One group of about three men rushed towards command post. The leading enemy was killed by 2/Lt Dewinder Singh whereas the other two halted and hid themselves. 2/Lt Dewinder Singh had his courage intact which had a trickle down effect on men and they stayed put and fought bravely. Another group of three enemy men ran towards LMG bunker, which was manned by Sep Ram Singh. He fired at them with a cool head and killed one and wounded the other, who managed to run back. Third threw a grenade at Sep Jagrup who got wounded. Sep Ram Singh, a real brave heart, who had been seriously wounded with grenade succumbed to his injuries. The enemy ran through the post towards east and escaped leaving his dead inside the post. 2/Lt Dewinder Singh reorganised the post and faced two more assaults at 1600 hrs and 1740 hrs, but enemy could not throw out own troops. About 20-25 bodies of the enemy were lying there around and inside the perimeter. To evict a Sikh soldier had become a nightmare but also a prestige issue for Pakistanis. But alas, gradually our jawans were becoming victims of dicey circumstances. At the last light, enemy tried his luck once again, and came from all sides. Two were killed by L/NK Amarjeet Singh, signal operator with his sten gun, but he was also wounded when they fired upon him. One group ran towards MMG bunker, where NK Shangara Singh a very robust and dependable NCO was waiting anxiously. When they came nearby, he challenged in chaste Punjabi and killed two of them but himself also got seriously injured and died after sometime there only. His body and of the two enemy men, who were killed by him were lying in the same pit. *What a coincidence, what a fate to accompany the enemy in the last journey together, what a heroic dead, what a devotion to duty, what an example of cool courage and determination – very rare and worth admiration.*

Destruction of Post

By now the post had been totally destroyed and large number of weapons damaged, the enemy was beaten back several times, but there is a limit to everything. Own troops were also broken down due fatigue, hunger and other administrative problems. The post had really become difficult place to stay anymore. Around 30 bodies of enemy men were lying right in front but own troops also suffered 12 killed and over two dozens very seriously wounded, with many more with minor injuries, for which a Khalsa would never bother about or report. It was proved beyond doubt that in one to one and on equal plane, a Pakistani is no match to an Indian soldier and specially a Sikh soldier – the bedrock of the Indian infantry. Realizing the situation becoming grave, planning for withdrawal was thought of. The strength was gradually collected at the Rear Post and wounded were lifted and helped, rear guard nominated, Sub Jagir Singh of 'C' Coy, brave soldier being at the tail end. Thus 2/Lt Dewinder Singh after having fought with efficiency and alacrity finally left Gali with a sense of remorse as well as satisfaction, after fighting a crucial action for eight days. He definitely measured up to the expectations. Own troops carried nothing else except their "own body" escorted by the "personal weapon."

On this, War Dispatches of Western Command records:-

"In Punch area, the gallant defenders of Gali Piquet now severely depleted in strength and administratively isolated for a week, abandoned the post in the early hours of morning. They had put a brave fight in a tactical situation of great disadvantage, the post lay in the bowl dominated by heights held by overwhelming hordes of infiltrators. The piquet had been unable to draw any water or cook food, since 8 August 1965."

There was no way to salvage and carry or dispose off the

dead bodies and broken and damaged weapons. We had to leave them there only. During the mopping up operations, skeletons were collected by 2/Lt Ravel Singh on 5 October, 1965 and the last rites were performed on that 'Mound' which remind us:-

> "*Go and tell the Sikhs of Seventh,*
> *Thou who passeth by*
> *carrying out their orders,*
> *most faithfully, here we lie."*

Gali post was held with determination and courage for eight days. The devastating fire effect of newly acquired weapons by Pakistan did have effect on our jawans. Total destruction of the post had made the position untenable. The enemy was though determined to make us vacate the post, he had no courage to evict us till last. And enemy suffered very heavy casualties. Thirty dead bodies were lying right in front of our jawans, in and outside the perimeter. In round calculations in any attack the defender suffers less casualties than attacker and based on various studies carried out, the ratio normally comes out to one to four-five. Enemy thus could have suffered about 50-60 dead and minimum double its number wounded.

Critical Appreciation

- Bare Check Post

   The battle fought by 2/Lt Dewinder Singh and his gallant boys of 7 SIKH along with the element of 7 MADRAS and CRPF at Gali Piquet (602) was a remarkable feat of doggedness of an Indian soldier and very high standard of discipline, devotion to duty and motivation. A Sikh soldier has a psychological superiority over a Pakistani, but sitting on a post surrounded and overlooked from all sides by the enemy who is resorting to heavy firing from all newly acquired sophisticated weapons and causing damages to bunkers and shelters, without any effective reciprocation, was a cause of dismay and frustration. To make him fight in a god forsaken bowl without any defence potential, arty support, communication and administrative back up on a "Bare Check Post" achieving no strategic or tactical aim was a...

- Inflexibility

There was no requirement of experiencing crucification. The post should have been withdrawn after needful was done. About a hundred highly trained A class soldiers were tied up for nothing. Even in holding, it could have served no purpose. It was neither a commanding position nor it could check the move of mobile enemy columns. Equally adamant seemed the enemy, hitting his head, time and again against this wall of faith. Bypassing it, the enemy could have done better, I suppose, as it was mainly a Guerrilla operation, known later on.

It can be very conveniently said that not very many commanders take bold and innovative decisions for fear of earning bad name of vacating a post and giving flexibility a chance. It takes 20 years to make a soldier out of a youth and it takes a minute to get him destroyed, if handled without care. To lose such a valuable quality and commodity in war without any useful gains will cause unlimited hardships to the organisation. It certainly did give an impression that the wise counsel was not heard, no properly administered course was adopted and the troops were left to defend themselves, carrying their lives on their hands and wishing for the grace of God in their hearts.

- Lack of Offensive Action

    Offensive action is always the essence of measuring up with the enemy. Without initiative and aggressive posturing with bold and resolute actions, resorting only to defensive moves is sure to cause you defeat and destruction. In case of Gali, the role to be played by the post, during hostilities, got mixed up due to personal views of Commander 93 Infantry Brigade. Where in reality, the post should been withdrawn after getting the correct info about the enemy, instead it was made to fight the battle, taking it to its logical end does not seem to be convincing, for reasons of in defensibility of the feature and against previously considered plan and rehearsed practice.

- Non-recognition of Efforts

    And unfortunately the supreme sacrifices made by own men, were ignored and were not even processed to be recognised. Alas, the pragmatic view of the heroic deeds of 2/Lt Dewinder Singh, L/NK Amarjit Singh, Sep Rao 7 MADRAS, Sep Ram Singh, Nk Shangara Singh and others should have been taken. The men fought like tigers and did what the outstanding uniformed men are required, to, lay down their lives in performance of their duties. There was no justification for washing off their role, so unthoughtfully, and unfaithfully. Such an action on the part of men, even if it eventually ends in abandoning, should not be ignored to my way of looking at it. It is so heartening to note that the troops obeyed so faithfully and kept on laying down their lives till last, knowing in full measure that it was futile to fight and hold on, at such an odd place. Such an action could be taught in the Schools of Instructions bringing out as to how a battle is fought at a disadvantageous location and the well-trained unit/sub-unit conducts itself in such circumstances. The actions fought by our men of 4 SIKH at Saragarhi and 3 SIKH at Chakdara post in 1897 were graciously acknowledged and awarded by British, though at both the places, the posts were overrun. We must take out a leaf from such historical chronicles which contribute immensely in the study of warfare and recognition of heroic deeds.

12

ENGAGEMENT AT MOLSAR RIDGE

"A defensive attitude of mind can, at best, avert defeat, it cannot achieve decisive results."
—Lt Gen Harbakhsh Singh, VrC

Importance of Molsar Ridge

By the third week of August 1965, the situation in Jammu and Kashmir along the routes of ingress of infiltrators into the Mandi Valley was becoming clearer, by each passing day. The maintenance and administrative bases of Pakistanis and the routes they followed had been mostly identified on ground and the Indian Army had commenced offensive operations in almost all sectors. In the Mandi Valley, the Mandi town was wrested from their control by the Task Force of 7 SIKH on 12 August 1965. Gali Post (602) had given heroic account of itself and had caused a most desirable delay of eight days to the advancing columns of the enemy, who thought to have a free run. Sauji was firmly held by 7 SIKH inspite of intermittent but devastating and concentrated fire from Molsar feature held by enemy with strong administrative base. Initially the enemy was noticed operating on Molsar and Mandi Ridges all along, but that was restricted after the capture of Mandi town.

Element of 'C' Company fell back from Gali to Sauji and the strength of the troops on various posts in Mandi Valley was readjusted. 'D' Company moved to Kinari and relieved 'A' company which a little later went to Rajouri. 'B' Company less platoon with 2/Lt SS Ahlawat was moved to Kinari for carrying out offensive actions there. 'C' Company under 2/Lt Hardial Singh was tasked to establish a new post at track junction, on the southern bump of Molsar Ridge to block the move of the enemy into Mandi-Sekhlu-Kalai Bridge and beyond from Loran side. It was named as "Sher Post." It was supposed to dominate the surrounding areas by aggressive patrolling. (See Sketch 12)

In the Uri Sector in Kashmir Valley, the plans of capture of Bedori, Kiran, Pir Kanthi and Haji Pir Pass were being made after cracking the outer crust. Punjab front was opened, by the Indian Army and these developments had terrific effects on the morale of the infiltrators, who by that time had not been able to consolidate any substantial gains at any place. They were hunted down at most of the places. Their activities subsided a little bit and Indian troops, as usual were confident enough to deal with them. 7 SIKH was also in its element to face the enemy boldly in Mandi Valley.

Enemy at Molsar Top

Molsar Ridge takes off from Loran Nala-Sauji Nala junction, just north of Mandi town near Amarnath temple and leads northwards, culminating into a rocky crop, the Molsar Top, east of Sauji (See Sketch 8). This ridge is quite long and higher than Sauji and the enemy could dominate the area around by fire and observation. It is a formidable feature. An important administrative base was established on it on 5-6 August, 1965 which served as a launching

Sketch 12: Engagment at Molsar

pad for various sub-columns. By third week of August 1965, it had become quite clear that the guerrillas operating in these areas were in strong groups, equipped with new weaponry. The maximum use of .50 BMG and RL was noticed by own troops at Gali and Sauji. The enemy did not come down to lower areas and could not hinder the move of own troops to the point of stopping them, though they were a disturbance, causing casualties at times.

Occupation of Sauji, immediately after getting the info of enemy's infiltration was an important development which changed the course of operation, the enemy could have carried out for control a of Mandi Valley. There used to be numerous movements to and from Sauji being the Battalion HQ which confined the enemy to the Molsar ridge only.

Enemy's Pattern of Operations

7 SIKH, a lone unit, in Mandi Valley was deployed on five posts with Bn HQ at Sauji. The enemy had established its 'Bases' on the upper reaches of Gali, Molsar Top and Mandi Ridge. Its aim was to cause maximum damage to our installations and posts, dominate the valley and establish links with their column trying to come from south through Mehdhar, at Kalai Bridge. It was an audacious plan. The enemy was mainly moving along the ridge routes and thus dominating them. It was more active on east of Mandi River in general areas of Molsar, Loran and Mandi. Once the strength was augmented with the arrival of companies from Betar Sub-sector, the enemy's movements were checked quite a bit, especially in lower areas. The movement of the enemy were for:-

- Reinforcing the columns operating in Mandi Valley.
- Shifting of its troops and leaders to and from Loran side.
- In the later stages, for readjustment in the other sectors.
- For keeping contacts with the civilian population by the commanders for inciting and instigating them against Indian Government machinery.
- Ex-filtration.

CO, 7 SIKH, had studied the situation and was not unnecessarily overawed about their activities. However, he was careful about safety of his troops and was not willing to commit them without palpable results and gains. The other important reasons for not committing the troops were:-

- Paucity of troops vis-a-vis area of operations.
- Requirement of troops at posts to avoid any misadventure by the enemy.
- Domination of area by patrols and mobile columns.
- Enemy not occupying permanent positions.
- To keep maximum reserves for optimum utilisation as on required basis.

Establishing of Sher Post

There were reports of the enemy using the track junction quite often for launching of troops to and from Loran. Commanding Officer 7 SIKH appreciated the situation and decided that it was important to keep the movements of the enemy under check and establishing a post at track junction. It would serve the following purposes:-

- Security of maintenance columns
- Security of Khet post and telephone exchange.
- Checking of shifting of enemy troops and commanders.
- Check movements along Molsar ridge-Mandi ridge – Loran or Kalai side.
- Carrying out limited offensive action.

In view of the points given above, the domination of the Molsar Ridge had become a necessity for own maintenance, control and operations in Mandi Valley and consequently blocking and eliminating the enemy menace from the Loran area and vice-versa. About a week before, a group of `F' Force of Pakistani had reportedly strengthened the already located amalgam and the activities were increased.

On 25 August, Lt Col Bhagat Singh moved 'C' Company with 2/Lt Hardial Singh and senior JCO Sub Sant Singh, with a task to establish Sher Post on track junction, on the bump, on the southern side of the Molsar Ridge (See Sketch 12). As mentioned earlier after establishing the post, the company started moving out for domination of area. As the move of enemy in groups were often reported along this ridge, 'C' Company sent out a strong fighting patrol of a platoon strength on 28 August at 2200 hrs towards north along the Molsar ridge. It was a rocky and jungle covered area and it was raining. It was at about 0100 hrs on 29 August, when strong enemy column bumped into our patrol. Our platoon took no time to engage the enemy and caused heavy damage. In the ensuing fire and move, we lost five jawans, whereas the enemy started withdrawing north-wards taking away the wounded and dead. The patrol was under a tremendous mental pressure to follow them and could have caused more damage but was drastically depleted in strength with five killed and 13 seriously wounded. No reserves were there to make the immediate pursuing possible. The patrol stayed put there only to avoid another possible engagement enroute while moving, back to post and came back next morning after day light, after duly salvaging the situation.

The determined offensive action by 'C' Company at Molsar Ridge brought the movement of enemy in the general area Mandi to an absolute halt. No activity of the enemy was reported after this pursuit, from that area, courageously led by 2/Lt Hardial Singh and well-executed by the brave jawans of 'C' Company. Not even the withdrawing columns of enemy tried this route. They went in ones and twos via northern jungles to cross back to POK.

> *"Courage is the first of human qualities because that guarantees all the others"*

Thus complete Mandi Valley was gallantly held by a lone unit, 7 SIKH, but for that, unit had to pay a heavy price. On 29 August, Haji Pir Pass in Uri Sector was captured and as it was on a main route of infiltration of the intruders, had demoralising effect on the enemy columns operating own side of CFL. The reports of their exfiltration started trickling in fast. It was our last operation in Mandi Sector in 1965 War. The unit was then relieved and concentrated at Punch for further operations.

Clearing of Mandi Valley

Mandi Valley was cleared of all enemy forces by 29-30

August. Whole month of August 1965 was really a committed one for the battalion, where slow and slogging match for control and domination of the area took place very often. After couple of tough fights, where our troops excelled, enemy was eliminated. Mandi Valley was restored to civil administration.

13
RAID AT KABAR-KI-DHERI

"War is like love, it always finds a way" —B Bracht

Enemy's Modus Operandi

During certain encounters in Betar Sub-sector in Punch in J&K, in the initial stages of war in 1965 and then in the Mandi Valley, we experienced that the enemy was fighting the unconventional way. The Operation Gibraltar was based primarily on this concept. The enemy did dare for arranging mobile columns and launching them in some sectors, for reinforcement or conducting operations though their success depended on lot of other factors. The enemy could vacate or thin out a post at a short notice, if a situation so demanded and occupy again.

Planning of Raid

There was a heavy pressure on Pakistan for mustering troops to face the Indian Army's advance both from Uri and Punch for the link up. The out-flanking or bypassing was an other threat. They were worried about and more so in this sector. In view of this general feeling, it was expected that "Kabar-Ki-Dheri" might have thinned out or vacated momentarily for facing the threat to their other posts in general area Haji Pir dominating Uri-Punch

Road, meaning thereby augmenting strength at Raja, Rani or other posts. This was the reason that this action was planned to exploit the situation. Kabar-Ki-Dheri was a Pakistani post across CFL north west of Mandi town in Punch sector. It was reportedly occupied by a platoon. It was located north of our own post Doda, on the other side of CFL in Haji Pir bulge of POK (See Sketch 13). It is an elongated feature and over 9,000 feet high. One company can be easily deployed on this. It can be approached from Doda. But it was the most likely approach. From own post Kinari or from Mandi town also it can be approached but the going would be tough. There were thick jungles around and cover for movement was available even during day.

Haji Pir had been captured and the attack on Raja and Rani posts of enemy in Punch Sector was planned on night 1/2 September 1965. 3 DOGRA was to capture Raja in Phase-I and Rani was to be captured by 2 SIKH in Phase-II. The attack was to be launched and H hour was after midnight. By that date, the nuisance of infiltrators in Mandi area had been dealt with effectively by 7 SIKH. Most of them had been liquidated by taking bold and sustained moves. Successful capturing of Raja and Rani, would provide road link between Uri and Punch. In Punch sector in front of our post 405, across CFL there is Pt 7702 which is called Chand Tekri by Pakis. It has got two bumps, the rear one provides depth to the front one. We call the front one as Raja and rear one as Rani. "Rani" Post of enemy was also referred as Chand Tekri at places in our official communications.

Mission

In view of the Indian Army's advance from Uri and capturing of Haji Pir Pass had enough of reasons for Pakistanis to see that their most important posts, Raja and Rani will be dealt with soon or late. There were reports that they are in the process of strengthening them and as such had created strong mobile columns at various posts which could be launched to the threatened area. It was the result of training of their officers in the American Academies that Pakistanis were following religiously. The area around Kabar-Ki-Dheri was not active. There was every possibility of momentarily shifting of these troops to Raja and Rani for strengthening. That was the reason that a raid was planned at Kabar-Ki-Dheri for exploiting this situation.

Composition of Team

Raiding team, consisting of 1 Officer, 2 JCOs and 42 ORs of 'B' Company 7 SIKH commanded by 2/Lt SS Ahlawat was chosen. It was to conduct an exploratory raid on the enemy post "Kabar-Ki-Dheri" about which the info was scarce. It was not really a proverbial raid in its strict terms in which, other issues like launching, carrying out the mission and extrication etc. is planned with the help of the other groups, agencies and organisations. It was to be carried out by the raiding team itself, with no other support of any kind except the arty fire, which was made available for the raid, however no arty OP accompanied the raiding team. It was like a protective patrol, the difference was that if situation was favourable, the enemy was to be dealt with at the post itself, otherwise, after causing extensive damages from a very close range, raiding team would fall back. The enemy post was reportedly occupied by a platoon of regular Pakistani troops, but accurate and latest info was not available. This action was linked with capture of Raja and Rani, in the sense that troops from Kabar-Ki-Dheri should not be released for strengthening defences at Raja and Rani as the attack on these posts was very

Sketch 13: Raid on Kabar-ki-Dheri

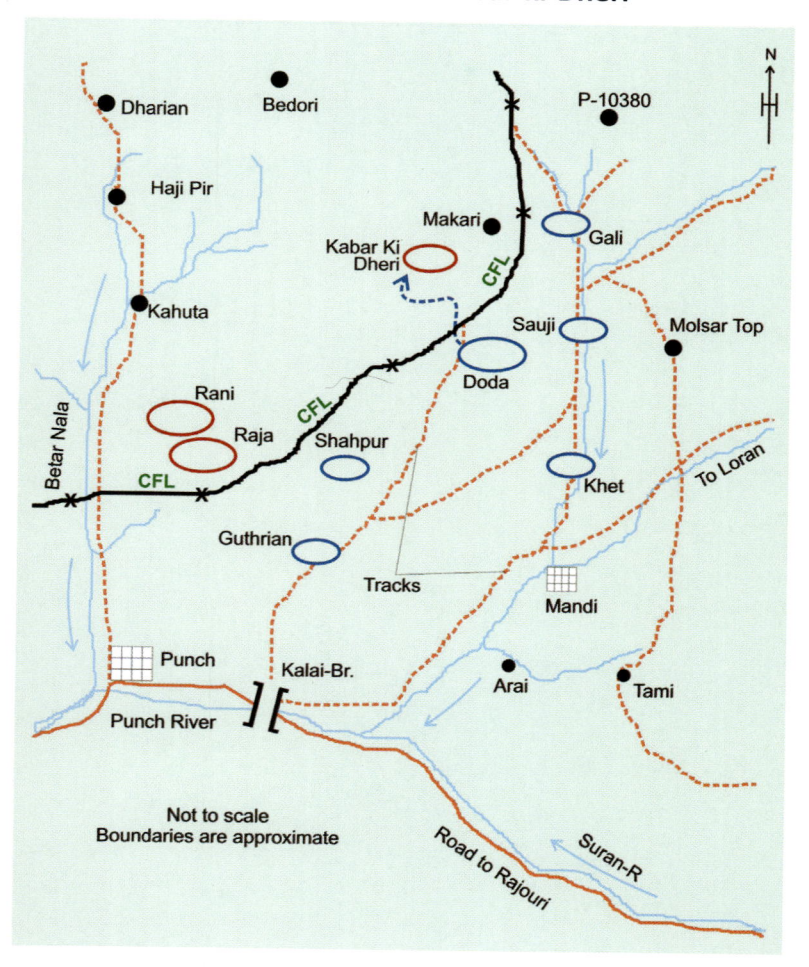

much expected by Pakistanis also as said earlier. Actions to be taken were:-

- Raiding Team, would move and close in with the enemy post and fire with all available weapons on the post.

- The enemy post will be fired at and the reaction observed by the raiding team. If there was very little or no fire of automatic weapons from the enemy, the raiding team will go and occupy the post. If the enemy is present and retaliates with automatics, then he is to be given a proper crunch of all available weapons from a close distance, cause maximum damage and fall back to own position. Raiding team will try and identify weapon pits, troops dispositions on the ground and the strength of enemy troops present, if possible.

- The enemy post will be fired upon effectively and maximum damage ensured.

Conduct

The raiding team left Doda post at about 1830 hrs on 1 September for Kabar-Ki-Dheri. An unlikely approach, from the eastern side, cutting across the nalas and ravines, covered with thick jungles was followed. It was a tough going, in the pitch dark night and took lot of time. The enemy post for finally tackling however was approached from the western side. It was at about 0200 hrs, we reached near the post. By this time the post had been given heavy arty crunches. We could very hazily see the bunkers and shelters. Para flares were fired, surprise lost, enemy position seen and the post was fired upon heavily. 2" Mor bombs were fired along with firing of LMGs and other weapons. The enemy retaliated with LMGs, 2" Mor and MMG fire. We could hear the yelling and shouting of the enemy. We opened with all weapons, and carried on for about 8-10 minutes. Then we went down towards east and started back for Doda. We reached back own post Doda at about 0730 hrs on 2 September. It was seen that the enemy had not vacated the post, which was intact as before.

Operational Analysis

"If we let things terrify us, life will not be worth living. It is ought to be the other way."

This operation was planned, for causing maximum damage and just to keep the enemy guessing and tying them down there when Raja and Rani were being tackled. In this sector, the enemy's regular posts were intact and had not been attacked by the Indian Army. Only the infiltrators were fought with and their designs were defeated. Most of them had disappeared without achieving any worthwhile result. Raja and Rani posts of the enemy were being tackled the same night and this was a Major offensive against the Pakistanis after capture of Haji Pir. It had its own importance for entire Western Command. The action against Kabar-Ki-Dheri was linked with this offensive and as such, it was having its own advantages as well as limitations. Some of the major achievements of this operation were:-

- It was to tie down the enemy's strength at its respective places, so that enemy could not move the troops from here for augmenting strength at Raja and Rani. It could have been occupied, if found lightly held or vacated that could have served as launching pad for further operations in Haji Pir Bulge or deeper areas.

- It gave a shock to the enemy along with causing casualties and damages, in a sudden and surprising heavy fire of the infantry weapons from a close range, after having been given an effective dose of arty fire. Heavy arty crunch had caused extensive damage as reported by civilians. It was later cleared by 3 Raj Rif after the Uri-Punch link-up.

- To raid a post, occupied by a platoon requires sufficient strength for covering, assault and supporting groups, besides being extricated successfully after the action. No other troops were earmarked for the action. It was therefore a probing and damaging mission and taking a chance.

- It was certainly a morale booster for own troops but as it was planned in haste and as a diversionary move it could only serve a limited purpose of tying them down besides, of course causing casualties with arty and infantry weapons.

- In the circumstances then prevailing it was the best option, being of exploratory in nature.

Conclusion

Offensive action is the essence of any action. The enemy's move can be checked by offensive moves by our troops. Such offensive actions do instill confidence in men and help developing aggressive nature for soldiers. It is better to meet the danger than to wait for it. The enemy should not be permitted to dominate own areas. It is also to be borne in mind that one should never, so entirely, avoid danger, as to appear irresolute and cowardly, but at the same time, we should avoid exposing ourselves to palpable danger, than which, nothing can be more foolish, if no worthwhile purpose is served.

14
OPERATION – PHANNE-SHAH

"History is likely to be taken left-handedly, if written by those, who were not involved in the event and it will be interesting only when it is strictly true" —LD Cecil

Changed Scenario

The operations in the Mandi Valley in Punch Sector, in Jammu and Kashmir in 1965 Indo-Pak War, against infiltrators came to halt, after the capture of Haji Pir Pass in Uri Sector by 1 PARA and Raja and Rani (Chand Tekri) posts of the enemy in Punch Sector by 2 SIKH and 3 DOGRA respectively. The situation was thus reversed. The enemy had come, to cut off and capture the Punch bulge and create mayhem in J&K but he had to give Haji Pir bulge in the bargain which was under their occupation since 1947-48. The infiltrators, who were supposed to be "trained and talented" had started exfiltrating fast. Large number of them were killed and some were captured in encounters with Indian troops. 7 SIKH had played a key role commendably blocking their moves and defeating them in their aims, in Mandi Sub-sector of Punch Distt., J&K. However, the unit suffered number of casualties in defeating enemy's designs. In Punch Sector, the Uri-Punch road via Haji Pir pass was still dominated by Pakistanis, in area, near Punch town west of the road, across Betar Nala. In this sector, unless the western side was captured by the Indian Army, the convoys could not use this road linking Punch with Uri comfortably. This was very important to be captured and as such the plans were made to move into it, eliminate the enemy and dominate the road so that move on the road was possible. The areas which were to be captured were, the northern ridge of the feature known as Lahori Shah on which exists Pakistan Post Pritam and the areas north of this, across Palangi Nala, which also dominates the said road (See Sketch 14).

Earmarking for Offensive Action

Pakistani post "Chakias" is called by us as Pritam. This post was captured by Brig Pritam Singh in 1947-48 operations and was in our hands for quiet sometime. Later it was captured by Pakistanis and since then it is in their hands. It not only dominates the Road-Punch-Uri but also the complete Punch town and surrounding areas. Its importance for us and them is of immense value in terms of defence of the area. The planning for capture of these above mentioned features was made at the HQ 93 Infantry Brigade. 7 SIKH was assembled and located at Rakha Haveli, at the base of spur leading to own Post-62 near Gulpur, facing

2/Lt RS Cheema who was present in all actions fought by the unit

Pritam. The unit less 'A' Company had just been relieved from Mandi Sub-sector, where they were seriously involved with the infiltrators, who were equipped with new weapons received from US and practising new theory of unconventional fighting. The unit did deserve this rest of few days, after heavy commitment and suffering casualties. After that both units i.e. 3/11 GR and 7 SIKH were tasked for the capture of features on the north and south of Palangi Nala respectively, both on the western side of the Road Uri-Punch.

Reece of the area was ordered. A patrol party of 3 RAJ RIF was sent in the area where 7 SIKH was to go for operation. The patrol party came back and informed that there was no enemy on the feature extending northwards from Pritam toward Palangi Nala i.e. feature Lahori Shah. Lt Col Bhagat Singh commanding officer 7 SIKH, wanted to send another patrol from 7 SIKH for confirmation of the info given by patrol party of 3 RAJ RIF. For understanding the area himself and for tasking the patrol, accordingly he took 2/Lt SS Ahlawat with him and went ahead of own post-Malti (408) towards Betar Nala. The enemy area was observed from the nearest place, on the bank of Betar Nala. Some movements of men were noticed in area Ring Contour. It was on 16 September 1965.

Launching of Fighting Patrol

On night 17/18 September, a fighting patrol comprising of 1 officer, 2 JCOs and 23 ORs of 'B' Company under the command of 2/Lt SS Ahlawat, fully equipped with arms and ammunition was sent to the enemy area to ascertain:-

- Is the enemy there?

Sketch 14: Operation Phanne-Shah

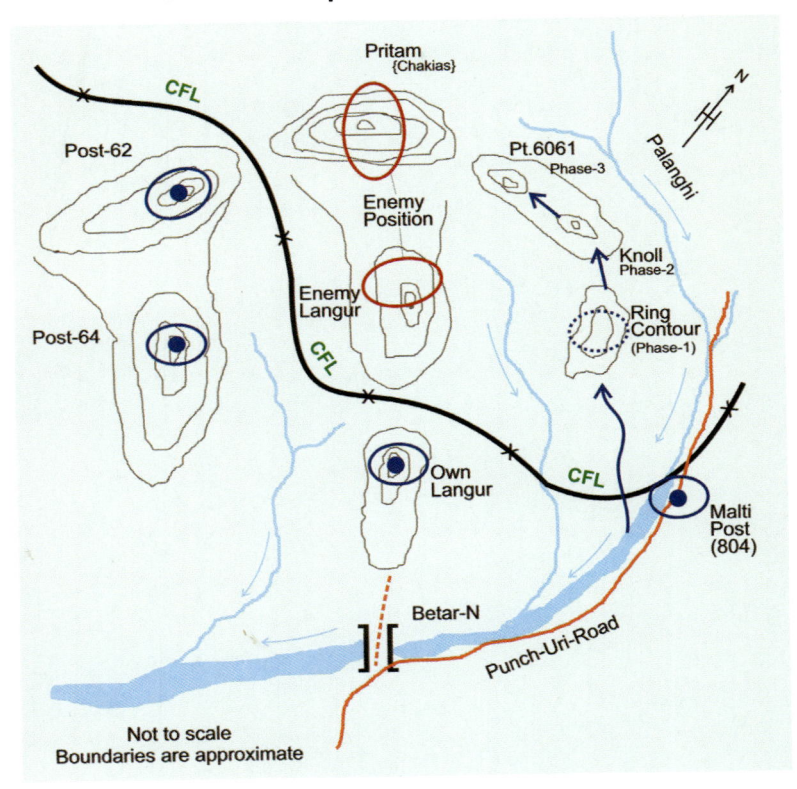

- If so, what are the dispositions on the ground?
- What Supporting weapons are held by the enemy?
- The info will be got by firing and fighting and observing the places, from where the enemy fire would have come and with what weapons. For doing that own troops will fire the ammunition belt fitted with tracer rounds. In fact in those days tracer rounds were filled in the ammunition belts of automatic weapons, of both the armies, a practice in vogue since Second World War.

The patrol left own area at about 1800 hrs on 17 August and crossed Betar Nala and entered into Pakistan occupied territory. The officer had observed the area very well the previous day and he made the troops move upwards, steadily but stealthily. At about 0130 hrs, the Patrol Second in Command suggested that since they had gone very deep and should not go forward to avoid trapping by the enemy. 2/Lt SS Ahlawat, a young officer had been given the specific tasks by Commanding Officer who had quite a faith in him and there was no question of going back without info. He pressed on and asked the junior leader to follow and help boys to move fast. At about 0210 hrs, leading scout NK Gain Singh, a physically fit and robust NCO informed that there was some movement of men around in a shelter. He then saw them and he said, 'Sahib jaldi aage aao, dushman hai'. It so happened that enemy had sensed it, the two men came out of a small shelter and he saw and grabbed them, with the help of Lance Hav Kaur Singh, who was not far behind. We all then pounced upon them, as we all were so close by and dragged them down. These two men were Razakars in mazri dress and were staying on the lower slopes of the feature Ring Contour. Razakars were the local people of the that specific area who were recruited, trained, maintained and armed by Pakistan Army. They used to be the extension of the troops on the nearby posts and were to give early warning of the enemy troops entering their area, besides augmenting the strength at the posts.

The Enemy's Reaction

2/Lt SS Ahlawat spoke to Commanding Officer on radio set and informed of the progress. Commanding officer who was already waiting for the info and was through with the patrol, all the time, advised that the patrol should come down a little and then open fire with tracer rounds in between on the suspected positions and observe the fire, flashes and reactions of the enemy. Fire of all the weapons was opened. The enemy fired in response and then the patrol started back after ascertaining the enemy's disposition. The enemy did not dare to follow, but when the patrol was crossing Betar Nala for coming to own side of CFL, the enemy opened up with MMG, as the men were seen better in the background of water. Six jawans were injured but no one very seriously. Firing seemed to be from a little far away place. At Malti, the Commanding Officer was already there. He met these two enemy men who were both Razakars and then was briefed by the patrol leader on the tasks given. The patrol reached Rakh Haveli after handing over two Razakars to Brigade HQ for debriefing and further necessary action. The time taken by this platoon size patrol, from Malti to reach Ring Contour to do the needful and coming back was about seven and half hours.

Planning and Conduct of a Battalion Attack

7 SIKH earmarked for attack on Pir Lahori Shah started its planning. The feature comprised of Ring Contour, Knoll and Point

6061 and all were to be cleared and occupied by morning of 22 September 1965. Important issue, connected with date was that the ceasefire was announced by India and Pakistan and was to be effective from 0800 hrs on 22 September 1965. It would be pertinent to note that such declarations do have effect on the operations and general psychology of men going for the battle. Complacency does set in. Anyway, briefing was given by the Commanding Officer on a set of tarpaulins and the area was shown from general area around Malti post. Close recce by all the junior leaders was not carried out, due to the restrictions of the terrain and enemy dominating the features across Betar Nala. It is mentioned here that 'A' Company had gone to Rajouri for the protection of Divisional Headquarters and also for carrying out operations in general area around and the other three Companies which were to attack also had depleted strength, having suffered heavy causalities in Mandi Valley operations. The total strength was 270 all inclusive.

Enemy Dispositions and Plan for Attack

The feature comprising of Ring Contour, Knoll and Point 6061 was described by Commanding Officer. Troops to tasks were earmarked and the objectives were allocated to the Companies. The plan of attack was as under:-

- Ring Contour was likely to be held by about section plus as an out-post of Pritam post for early warning. It was to be captured by 'C' Company commanded by 2/Lt Hardial Singh. Reserve for this was 'D' Company commanded by Maj Jagdev Singh. H hour given was 0030 hrs 22 September.

- Knoll, was likely to be held by platoon less a section, again a temporary arrangement for giving early warning and causing delay for attack on Pritam. 'D' Company was to attack with 'B' Company as reserve. H hour was immediately after the success signal by 'C' Company.

- Pt 6061, being nearest to Pritam Post, was likely to be held by a platoon. The track to Pakistani Langoor Post, passed through base of Pt. 6061. It was to be captured by 'B' Company with 'D' Company as reserve. H hour was the success signal by "D' Company after capturing Knoll. 'B' Company was commanded by Maj RK Sharma and 2/Lt SS Ahlawat and 2/Lt Dewinder Singh were platoon commanders. Once, all the features would have been captured and secured, then enemy's Langur post on the spur east of Pt. 6061 was to be tackled, as planned by the Commanding Officer based on the progress of the operation. The total strength of our battalion was over two companies actual strength. It was a rainy season and Betar Nala, could come in spate anytime, depending upon the rain in the catchment areas. The two Razakars who were captured and brought by the patrol on night September 17/18, 1965 were taken alongwith and given to 'C' Company as "guides." The order of move was 'C' Company, Battalion HQs, 'D' Company followed by 'B' Company. The unit moved from Malti, at last light and reached Betar Nala, at about 2000 hrs, on 21 September. It had rained heavily on the upper ridges towards north and Betar Nala was in spate. It could not be immediately crossed. The unit wasted over four hours there, which were so crucial. Men and mules with the ammunition were struck up. It was creating anxiety and was becoming a cause of great concern. Commanding Officer was perturbed. Somehow the men crossed Betar Nala and started climbing.

The Crossing Site

The Battalion HQs comprising of Commanding Officer, Lt Col Bhagat Singh, Maj KG Belliappa Second in Command, Capt Surjeet Singh the adjutant, 2/Lt DK Kapur signal officer and 2/Lt RS Cheema as intelligence officer was behind 'C' Company. A point to mention here, is the move of the Adjutant, with the battalion in attack. Teachings do not subscribe to that. He is supposed to remain in the office and ensure passing of messages and other requirements to be noted for the unit, involved in the fighting. How did he manage to go with the attacking troops leaving his office at such a critical moment and how was he allowed by Commanding Officer, so meticulous and stickler for norms, is question still not understood. The most plausible reason could be that the attack was taken lightly by Senior Commanders, in view of the announcement of ceasefire, to be effective from the next day. Two Razakars who were captured from the same area and were on the rolls of Pakistan Army, were taken as guides which also speaks of casual attitude prevailing around, in unit and at Brigade HQs. How such a rosy picture was painted to Commanding Officer, 7 SIKH, who otherwise, could not have taken that situation so lightly. As I know of him, he always meant business, moved very carefully and had an acute sense of duty, security and responsibility.

Crowding of Ring Contour

'C' Company, the leading company, delayed by almost Five hours assembled across the Betar Nala and moved fast. They reached Ring Contour by 0530 hrs on 22 September and gave a success signal at about 0630 hrs. Minor opposition of Razakars was there, which was brushed aside. 'D' Company reached soon after but did not go for Knoll which was their objective and plonked themselves on Ring Contour only. Soon after, the Battalion Headquarters came and that too found a place for themselves on the Ring Contour only. There was no enemy fire or enemy men at that time on the Knoll. Had 'D' Company moved, it could have occupied their own objective and enough dispersion of troops would have been achieved. Then it became broad day light. A ruthless Commanding Officer could not have permitted any one to do so. It was a big mistake. Probably everyone was day dreaming about the ceasefire to be effective at 0800 hrs on 22 September and that could be the reason for not moving for Knoll. There was no other sensible reason, for not going in for the objective, and more so when there was no enemy. It is very rightly said that.

> *"When your time calls you to live or die, do both like a field commander"*

'B' Company also had to stay on the lower slopes of Ring Contour, due to space restrictions. As a result of combination of lot of factors such as delay in crossing of Betar Nala, heavy rain, and Companies not moving for their objectives, Ring Contour became heavily crowded. The enemy had come to know about it. We were visible from Langur post of Pakistanis, as we could not hide ourselves, feature being small and number of men being more.

The operation seemed to have been planned in haste, without going into the nitty-gritty of the problems. It was a general impression that the enemy was not there on these features in strength. The whole issue was taken very lightly by higher formations too. The battalion was not solely responsible for the info and other inputs for operations. It was the Brigade HQs and other senior HQs in the chain who fed all info to the battalion and planned the operation, as clarified earlier. It is a well-known fact that no operation, in the context of the Indian Army is planned exclusively at executioner's level without the tacit approval and express orders of minimum two immediate superior HQs and commanders, may be three up for a bigger operation.

Capt Surjit Singh was killed in Operation Phanne-Shah while being with the forward most troops

Non-occupation of Knoll and Pt 6061

By seeing our troops not moving ahead, enemy took advantage, enemy OP party came to Knoll camouflaged themselves well and started shelling the feature. We were on lower and flattish ground. Unfortunately, Capt Surjit Singh who was with forward troops, was killed with the first rain of fire. Very bad omen, the Adjutant of the Battalion, became the first casualty. The enemy fire intensified manifold but their troops did not dare to come nearby. Pakistanis also did not have much strength to spare. Maj Gen Shaukat Riza (Pak Army) has mentioned in his book.

"Pakistan Army in 1965 War" that the post was reinforced by 20 Punjab of Pakistan which reached at Chakias (Pritam) at about 1100 hrs. After the arrival of this battalion, the situation became comfortable with them otherwise they themselves were worried on this development. Had they had the troops they could have launched counter offensive earlier only, but could not do so due to paucity of troop and lack of courage. We were unlucky that we could not occupy, Knoll for such a long time, which was vacant till late on 22 September. Another point which indicates towards the subdued performance of the unit in moving fast and occupying the feature was the absence of certain pushing and senior officers being away on various courses and duties. Had these officers been with the battalion, it would have definitely made the difference for influencing the thinking of the commanding officer on various issues and performance of the unit. Maj Tirlochan Singh, Capt NS Koak, Capt Sansar Singh, Capt Darya Singh and 2/Lt MS Punia were all very capable, dependable and popular officers and their absence was definitely felt. Good officers are the backbone of the unit and the performance of the unit does get an effect. Capt Sansar Singh was away with 'A' Company to Rajouri as mentioned earlier, whereas all others were on various courses of instructions. Had they been there, the command and control would have been tightened and corrective measures could have been taken. I am sure all being the men of accomplishment, would have wasted no time and taken their sub-units on the objectives, which would have saved the situation. Later in the Battle of OP Hill Maj Tirlochan Singh, Capt Sansar Singh and 2/Lt Ravel Singh, 2/Lt SK Singh and 2/Lt MS Punia were basically the officers whose presence and style of command made all the difference and the unit came out with resounding success. When it comes to getting the things done we do need certain architects, brick layers can be arranged. It can be contended that all these officers were popular in the unit and troops knew that they were the men of action.

Lack of Arty Support

We could not get enough arty support, while sitting on that bare feature, Lahori Shah right in front of the enemy. Arty OP was there, who also became a casualty with the enemy shelling at Ring Contour. Though lately, little bit of own arty fire was arranged, the enemy posts were, however in the permanent defences and were not really affected. Own Mor platoon started taking shoots and engaged the enemy. Unfortunately, a shell landed on the Mor position, itself where own Mor were knocked out and crew suffered heavy casualties. MMGs too could not be taken up and were sitting on a lower ground, not their fault, as all were mixed up and sitting down at Ring Contour, doing nothing. Seriousness did dawn on the faces of all commanders, but it was very late.

Plastering of Area by Pak Arty

Pakistanis had arranged, the fire of their complete Corps Arty and started plastering the feature where we in a large number had concentrated. Casualties started increasing. 'D' Company commander, Maj Jagdev Singh, was hit by a splinter suffering injuries. He then started asking the Commanding Officer to be evacuated to Punch. Commanding Officer, was really in a fix. His Adjutant was killed, his senior most company commander needed evacuation. Out of three, only one objective and that too the lowest one was captured and Brigade Commander was very unhappy. With the advancing of the time of the watch, the Pakistani Arty increased the intensity of the fire. By about

1600 hrs very large number of our men were injured and about 15 killed. Dr (Capt) AK Singh was the RMO of the unit. The casualties were mounting with the advent of time. Dr AK Singh did a commendable job and attended all, and saved as much as he could. His role was really of savior. When everyone was tucked in the pits and holes, he was moving from trench to trench and attending and dressing everyone's wounds.

The Only Choice

For an infantry battalion, it was unfortunate that it was sitting idle and not involved with enemy infantry at all whatsoever, but facing arty shells. There was no choice. Seeing all this and deducing, what would happen if we stayed put there only, Maj KG Belliappa 2IC 7 SIKH talked to Commander 93 Infantry Brigade who asked the battalion to come down after the last light, but only if we could not stay. The morale of the men was affected due to their helplessness and the situation being precarious. A Sikh soldier would have achieved a great deal against his equal enemy, but there was no role for him. We missed a chance of occupying both Knoll and Pt 6061. I have my doubts, even stay at pt 6061 would have been easy without effective arty cover. The platoon sitting in defences on Pakistani Langur also could

Maj Santosh Kumar (then Capt) remained throughout with the battalion and commanded 'D' Company in OP Hill

have been a big hindrance if not given a devastating arty crunch by own arty. As the stores had not reached, any move upwards from Betar Nala was ordered to be stopped, to avoid further congestion on Ring Contour. Amn and picks and shovels were also in short supply having been left behind. Trenching tools were not carried by the men and specially officers and JCOs and we suffered maximum casualties, because we did not do the digging/could not do that. Just before last light, the wounded including Maj Jagdev Singh, 2/Lt RS Cheema 2/Lt Hardial Singh and 2/Lt Dewinder Singh and large number of wounded men started moving down and by last light, most of the men were feeling the heat of the situation and started moving downwards voluntarily alongwith the wounded. Move had totally become disorganised and could be more disastrous had the enemy followed. No drills by way of thinning out, lay back position, flank protection and detailment of rear guard etc. were followed. To be frank we were not in a position to assert ourselves. The enemy was equally frightened and thought that this unit might attack Pritam Post after last light. They also thought this could be a diversionary move and attack might come from Post 62 side. They did not move and stayed put firmly at Pritam Post only. I noticed our men moving disheartenedly and grudgingly cursing the planning for attack and lack of arty support. Some of the men had reached by 2000 hrs across Betar Nala towards own side. I along with Capt Santosh could reach the area, short of Malti where ADS was located at about 0300 hrs. Thus the unit had suffered mentally and physically besides being lowly moraled.

"Wealth lost – something lost
Honour lost – much lost
Courage lost – all lost"

Occupation of Own Langur

On 23 September, the battalion was collected and semblance of order was restored. It was then ordered to move and establish the post at own Langur. It was till then not occupied by us, though it was on our side of CFL. It is a step downwards of Pakistani Langur, towards our side and had it been occupied by Pakistanis, it could have been a big hindrance for general area Jhula Bridge on Betar Nala and the road linking Malti with Punch. 'B' Company under 2/Lt SS Ahlawat quickly moved and occupied it and then developed into proper post. It was on 23 September 1965 and the ceasefire had come into effect, actually on that day.

Hard Times

This fine unit beat an ignominious retreat in face of intensive arty crunches and did suffer a sense of guilt as was unable to do anything. It was most impalatable thing to digest. To have fought and lost would have been better than this. The saving grace and that too for our own consumption only was, that it was not against an enemy infantry but against the enemy's Corps Arty for which this unit was neither equipped nor properly supported. But we were to blame for our own lapses. Had we moved as per the time schedule and gone for all the three objectives or atleast gone upto Knoll, irrespective of the consequences, dispersion would have saved us from the casualties and chaos. Had we gone for all the objectives in time and dug in, it would have been very difficult for Pakistanis to throw us out. They were really not so determined in attacks as experienced in earlier actions. Post 62 being on the shoulder and 7 SIKH occupying Lahori Shah could have made Pakistani Langur itself to abandon the post.

The dead bodies could not be carried and were left there only, which were handed over to us on 23 September 1965, through the UN efforts. The unit suffered due to poor study of weather and terain, inept planning, accepting the task at such a short time with two companies strength, poor leadership provided by officers and imbalanced and casual higher directions, besides rain and delay in crossing Betar Nala. Had we crossed it well in time, it would have given us substantial gains. Due to heavy rains on the upper reaches, the Betar Nala was in spate and could not be crossed at scheduled timings and caused a delay of over five hours. Pakistanis did not come nearby at any place and no casualty was caused by the enemy infantry weapons including machine guns. All casualties, we suffered were caused by the arty fire only.

Operational Analysis

From Operation Phanne-Shah, some of very important lessons can be learnt:-

- There seemed a lack of planning at higher levels. Fighting patrol led by 2/Lt SS Ahlawat came back on 18 September 1965 only after doing the needful. The Battalion attack was planned immediately after for night 21/22 September. Detailed recce therefore could not be carried out by leaders at all levels. Aspect of foresight seemed to have been ignored. Deliberate and detailed planning was not done.

- The objective was shown from a distance of two-three kilometers. The details were explained on the drawing made on tarpaulin. The difficulties for crossing the nala in spate and negotiating the terrain were really not understood/visualised by the leaders as well as men.

- The main cause, for what all had happened, was the easy and relax atmosphere prevailing all around due to the declaration of ceasefire date. Most of them, thought that firing will stop at 0800 hrs on 22 September 1965, which did not happen. Pakistanis just did not bother about and carried on blasting with devastating arty fire.

- There was miscalculation about the time to be taken by the battalion to reach its objectives. When own fighting patrol had taken almost seven and half hours to reach to Ring Contour and back, only two days earlier how could the battalion less a company could reach within the same timings. It takes roughly four times, as compared to a patrol, by a battalion to reach the same spot in normal circumstances.

- This feature was very important for Pakistanis and for us too. The importance grew more for Pakistanis, after the fall of Haji Pir Pass and Raja-Rani posts. This should have been dealt with all the sincerity and common sense at our command preferably in two phases, by two or three battalions, one establishing a firm base across Betar Nala and the others launching attack from the firm base, with over whelming arty support.

- Sending a battalion with three companies of depleted strength, for an important feature and capturing three objectives irrespective of whether these were held in strength or not, without any reserve was not a wise decision. It was due to lack of higher directions of war. Someone in the chain willed it that way but the will does not operate in vacuum. It should not have been imposed if it could not stand to reason. The things in war are not done in a way because someone wills it, they are done because they are doable. The limits for the commander in battle are defined by circumstances. What he asks his units/sub-units, must be consistent with the possibilities of the situation. Commanding Officer 7 SIKH was misinformed, miscalculate or misled, it seems.

- Crossing of Betar Nala, should not have been from the same one point for whole battalion. Two more crossing points upstream, could have saved time, gain speed and offer independent moves. It will always be necessary to shape operations on estimates of weather as this is always changing. One cannot take the experience of one try with the following one. The tactical and administrative mobility will be severely affected with the change of weather.

- Two Razakars, who were brought by the patrol on 18 September 1965 were not taken seriously. They infact were treated as guides. They disappeared, during the crossing only. They probably gave all info about the unit to the enemy. The enemy, accordingly reacted violently by pounding the feature with all its might.

- Arty support given to the battalion was not sufficient. Situation demanded that adequate, rather more than adequate resources should have been made available for this operation, being fought by over two companies strength, on an important and bare feature, with no reserves.

- Moving the Adjutant, with the battalion, in attack was not a correct decision.

- The absence of the certain senior officers was very much felt there. Had they been there the things could have been definitely different. Even 2/Lt SK Singh and 2/Lt Ravel Singh who were tied up with MMGs and Mors, respectively would have gone straight on the objective, had they been with the leading companies.

- There was a general surmise that unit will fight a very little opposition and then ceasefire will come into effect on the morning of 22 September 1965. This misplaced notion was the main cause of delay, destruction and chaos. Once an enemy is always a enemy. Pakistan will never stick to any rule of any game. We had not learnt the lessons from 1947-48 operation, where Pakistan had occupied large number of our posts like Pritam, Bedori and many others after the ceasefire and of our vacating of certain other posts due to weather conditions.

- Trenching tools were not carried in sufficient quantity specially by senior NCOs, JCOs and officers. When the time came, they were seen running here and there for managing one. All casualties were due to arty fire as we were not dug in properly.

- Company tasked to capture Knoll made a big mistake of not going in for its objective, which caused doom for the whole battalion. The sub-unit should have been made to move for the objective, by the Commanding Officer. If not that the following one should have been sent. Had they moved, the following element also would have moved and the delay could have been lessened and situation saved. It is rightly said:-

"Of all our losses, those delay does cause, are most and heaviest. By it we lose power and often, alas, the never dying soul."

- Majority of men are timid but cowards are those who let their timidity get the better of their manhood. It was reflected quite in clear with many of us in Operation Phanne-Shah. Situation was not controlled, which could have easily been, had we occupied our respective objectives and thus dispersed and then dug in. Promptness was no where resorted to. That included us all.

- Pakistanis having been battered at Haji Pir and Raja and Rani and losing everywhere in that sector did not have the courage to come and attack us even at such a position like Ring Contour which was much lower. In fact, in "Allaha" they were praying that we should go away. They came to know, our finally moving down but did not pursue us. It sufficed them that we go down otherwise they had no option except pounding it with Arty fire.

- Commanding officer is required to be consenting and gracious towards his officers, but not to be too familiar, not even with the selected ones, lest he subjected himself to a want of that respect, which is necessary to support a proper command. Commanding officer should have been ruthless to all and made them move to their respective objectives irrespective to their feared and anticipated casualties. Casualties will take place and they should not take precedence over the task allotted. War means fighting and fighting means killing, is as simple as that. It is not the rashness but the desire to do necessary resolute fighting where casualties will be there, one cannot avoid.

- It was the cardinal responsibility of Commander 93 Infantry Brigade to foresee, as to how and what kind of crisis his command could face. He should have carefully appreciated the capabilities of enemy arty fire vis-a-vis arty support provided to us.

- If the platoon or the company commanders are wounded but are in a position to stay put, they should not leave nor they should be permitted to roll down as happened with us. Moving away of commanders sends a very wrong signal. The moving of officers from the front lines really affected the whole battalion. And as the order for withdrawal had already been extracted from Commander 93 Infantry Brigade, there was no requirement of sending them earlier. The more helpless situation a leader finds his men in, it is his bounden duty to stay and share their fortune whether for good or ill.

- There should have been some manoeuvre by us. The fundamental characterisation of strategy of this is not the formal offensive but the initiative and action. The sitting and suffering lowered the moral of our brave jawans.

- One of the requisite studies for senior officers is the study of his juniors, which will serve him daily in battle or otherwise. As a commander, to get the right man in the right place is one of the questions of success or defeat.

- There was casual atmosphere prevailing before the move for attack. The men had managed liquor and most of them were carrying it, which was noticed at crossing site. Incidentally a jawan who was kept with ammunition at the lower side across Betar Nala could not move back with the battalion and stayed there only, having been drunk, to be captured by Pakistanis the next morning.

Home Truths

Operation Phanne-Shah was conceived by 15 Corps Commander and 25 Infantry Division Commander and given to 7 SIKH for execution through 93 Infantry Brigade. In view of the impending declaration of ceasefire after capturing of Haji Pir, it was planned like a closing ceremony of an event, where the winner enjoys taking everything on a easy mode. Nothing seemed to have been studied deeply. It was typical case which exposed the brinkmanship of foresight and serious planning. Enemy's arty capabilities vis-a-vis our resources were just not given a thought. Enemy's reaction to the developing situation was not visualised. Basic tenets of deliberate planning were not adhered to. It was further compounded by the Battalion and its Company Commanders in not paying any heed to weather in view of crossing of the nala and above all not capturing and occupying the assigned objectives. Everything gave an impression of complacency coupled with carelessness bordering unprofessionalism, which put the bravest of soldiers of the Indian Army into the jaws of death, misery and infamy.

15
BATTLE OF OP HILL

"Company Command is the most demanding job in the battle. The Company Commander as a combat leader is directly responsible for physical implementation of plan given to him. He very cautiously calculates available resources and manpower against enemy's will and strength and executes the action with wisdom, courage and on spot appreciation."

—John G Meyer

Situation

Ceasefire, to end the Indo-Pak War, actually became effective from 23 September 1965, though officially it should have been in place from 22 September as was conveyed earlier. Initially, in the first three weeks of August 1965, the Indian Army, in J&K, was searching for the infiltrators and dealing with them. Once the situation was stabilised and the role and mission of Gibratar Force became clear, the Indian Army started its offensive against enemy held defences across CFL in various sectors in J&K. By the beginning of fourth week of August 1965, the infiltrators had lost the initiative and after having been hounded and some of them getting killed, started exfiltrating fast across the CFL.

OP Hill Complex

In the Mendhar Sub-sector, the Pakistanis had occupied an area, which later came to be known as OP Hill Complex. It was very large area, thickly wooded with excellent defence potential, with couple of bumps and mounds. It was between two of our own posts KDL 636 and KDL 475. Its occupation by the Pakistanis was the part of the master plan of isolating Punch by linking Mendhar Valley with Mandi Valley via Kalai Bridge and Khanater Gali. This complex was occupied in strength by regular Pakistani troops alongwith the launching of infiltrators sometime between 13 to 22 August 1965 and developed into a formidable defences. Pakistanis however were first spotted in this area on 5 August. It was reported by 2 GARH RIF on 11 August in their Situation Report that enemy was observed duly holding this feature in permanent fashion. It is important to note that almost on the same dates, the enemy had established its `Base' on Molsar Top, east of Sauji as said earlier on 5 August and after capturing Mandi Town occupied Eastern Ridge dominating Mandi on 9 August. It was a part of a pincer move designed to cut off the Punch salient as said earlier (See Sketch 15) Simultaneously, the enemy actively dominated the elongated feature, south of Sune Gali and temporarily occupied by its fighting patrols to facilitate the move to OP Hill Complex from east. (See Sketch 16) The tracks passed through OP Hill complex

Sub Bikkar Singh who played crucial role in capture of OP Hill

and enemy made use of them. It was reportedly named as "Mall" by the enemy, as their troops could easily go from east to west and vice versa. It may carefully be noted that Op Hill Complex and OP Hill Top are two different areas and should be clearly understood. While Op Hill Complex was main feature and the objective for 120 Infantry Brigade comprising of 7 SIKH, 5 SIKH LI and 2 DOGRA, whereas OP Hill Top was one of the two objectives i.e. Jungle Hill and OP Hill Top, to be captured by 7 SIKH in Phase II of the operation. In other words, OP Hill Top was part of OP Hill Complex.

Ceasefire and After

On 23 September 1965 the day the cease fire came in effect the enemy became active having successfully established itself on OP Hill Complex and started engaging the movements of vehicles and troops of 120 Infantry Brigade in general areas of Mendhar and Balnoi. All efforts to get it vacated through UN Offices had failed. The importance of OP Hill Complex had thus increased manifold. How could enemy come and occupy, this area between two of our own posts and well within our area, was surprising. Things were certainly not in order, in 120 Infantry Brigade areas of responsibility and more so, in battalion defended area of 2 DOGRA and 11 J&K MILITIA, which ultimately necessitated the removal of Brigade Commander 120 Infantry Brigade and CO 2 DOGRA immediately and simultaneous shifting, of 11 J&K MILITIA from post 475 (Pt 5136). An attack to evict the enemy from OP Hill Complex was launched by 2 GARH RIF on night 6/7 October 1965 but it failed as the intensions, strength and the enemy preparations were not clearly known in this hastily conducted operation. The unit suffered heavy casualties and Pakistanis got emboldened. Some jawans of 2 GARH RIF were taken as PsW. After this action, it became quite clear that enemy meant business

Sketch 15: Haji Pir Bulge and Punch Salient

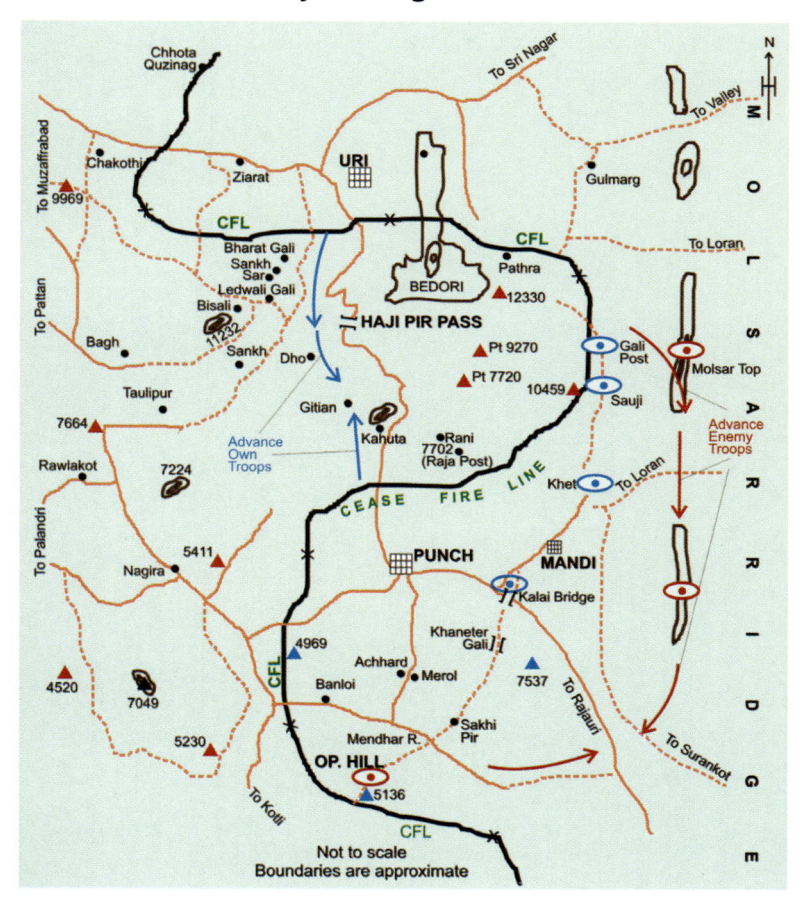

Sketch 16: Attack on OP Hill Complex

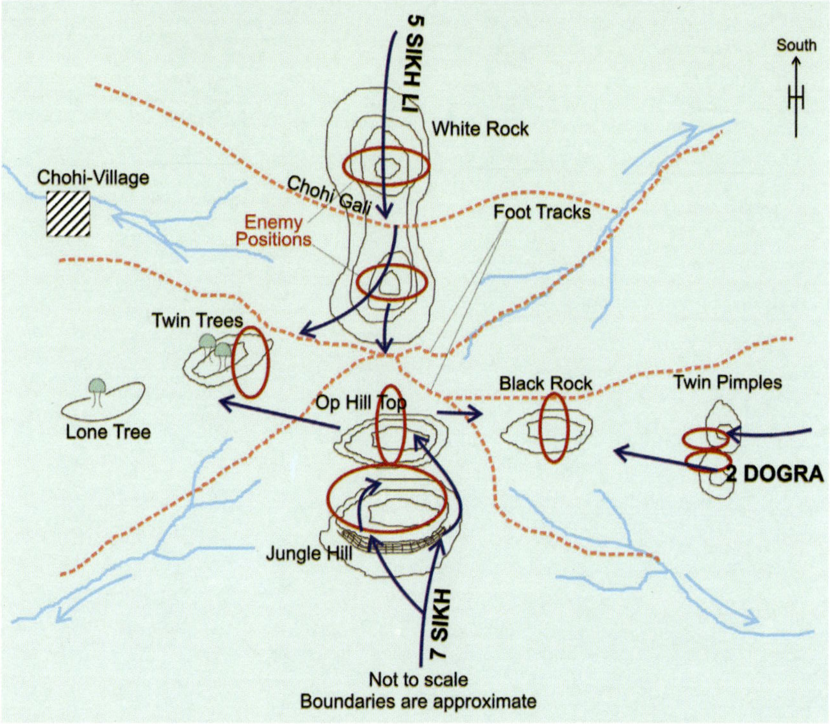

and on our part it required a deliberate and well-planned attack with violent execution for evicting them and capturing the OP Hill Complex at all costs.

Pakistan's Intensions and Designs

As mentioned earlier, the initial aim of the enemy was to link up Mendhar Valley in South with Mandi Valley in North via Kalai Bridge and Khanater Gali. The planning so envisaged, by involving infiltrators had petered out in Mandi Valley as Mandi town was wrested from them but they were successful in quietly occupying OP Hill Complex in Mendhar Valley. Now the enemy by occupying Op Hill Complex, could encircle post 475 at Point 5136 and capture it as it would have been surrounded by enemy from three sides i.e. east, north and south. The regular enemy troops of 21 PUNJAB and 10 AK Battalion directly supported by 14 arty guns of various calibres had occupied OP Hill Complex and the area around was used by infiltrators of Nusrat Force, which initially misled Indian Army authorities to believe that enemy troops moving on OP Hill Complex and around, were infiltrators only. Own troops were involved in various searches and trailing the intruders and enemy regular troop quickly and coolly occupied it. Its leaving like that and permanent occupation by Pakistan would have been a very big loss of territory. Road Balnoi-Mendhar would have been under enemy's direct observation and that would have created very serious operational and administrative problems for army and the civil government and population. Pakistan as a country will go in to grab any part of J&K, as it has got infantile obsession for it. With the mirror of history in front we should have been more vigilant and proactive in this so sensitive an area.

Local Intelligence

The civilian Muslim population of J&K is divided between India and Pakistan. Per force they have to play their role and tread their path very carefully. They really choose to "run with the hare and hunt with the hound." Civilian people all around in Mendhar and Balnoi areas to my mind knew what was happening. Our commanders at important levels initially failed in getting any sort of info, which could have been deduced even after having normal interaction with the civil population. 11 J&K MILITIA having local advantage should have played their role better. The result was, this very serious, dangerous and consuming development. Pakistanis had made full use of agents and civilians and probably got the complete info of our buildup and later the plan of attack on OP Hill Complex on 2/3 November 1965. Only time, was not known to them. It was later revealed by the PsW captured by 7 SIKH and also became clear from the way they fought a well coordinated battle and escaped almost unhurt, considering the magnitude of our efforts.

Tactical Advantages of OP Hill Complex

OP Hill Complex was very important from defence and domination point of view. Its tactical advantages therefore were:-

- Dominated the various heights on own side of CFL.
- Denied observation and access to own rear areas.
- Protected own line of communication.
- Provided commanding view of the enemy areas and movements.

Planning for Brigade Attack

Brig BS Ahluwalia took over as Commander 120 Infantry Brigade just before the Battle of OP Hill. Commanding Officer 2 DOGRA, was posted out just two days before the attack. 7 SIKH and 5 SIKH LI were loaned to 120 Infantry Brigade from 93 Infantry Brigade and 80 Infantry Brigade respectively. Brigade attack was finally planned for evicting the enemy and capturing the OP Hill Complex. Force allotted for the attack were as under:-

7 SIKH 5 SIKH LI 2 DOGRA	Assaulting Battalions
Company 11 KUMAON Company 2 GARH RIF	Stops
Company 2 SIKH Company 2 GARH RIF	Deployed in depth at Balnoi
7 Commando Platoons	Ex 93 Infantry Brigade Located at Acchard on Road Mendhar – Punch
Fire Support	23 Field Regiment 168 Field Regiment

Lt Gen Harbaksh Singh and OP Hill

The important redeeming feature of this development was the presence of Lt Gen Harbakhsh Singh, VrC as the Army Commander Western Command. He was very well conversant with everything, because from the 1947-48 operations till end of the war in 1965, he had mostly been associated with Western Command in one capacity or the other. And above all this, individually he was professionally an outstanding general of very high military repute. No one else could have been more suited for conducting this operation, than him. A very bold leader, conceived a very bold plan and used bold leaders for achieving sure success. He decidedly was a unique personality. Normally boldness is little less common in the higher ranks. Nearly all generals known to us, as mediocre, even vacillating had been noted for dash and determination as junior officers. But Lt Gen Habakhsh Singh stayed brave throughout. He was always seen as impetuous and audacious leader. He himself was the architect of OP Hill attack plan and he went to details of every small little issue. It was firmly engraved on his brain that:-

"To win a war quickly and surely, takes very thorough and deliberate planning"

Enemy – Dug Down

OP Hill Complex, as a whole is something like an inverted bowl, roundish in shape and flattish on top with few bumps. It had cliffs, on sides which were vertical in true sense and the rocky precipice on the fringes. However, it is elongated finally taking a turn towards east and tapers down. On the northern side, form where 7 SIKH was to move, the enemy had made bunkers which were not visible from a distance, due to roofs merging and levelling with the ground configuration and bunkers having been boxed in the vertical cliffs. These were flushed and merged with the natural background. If there was no fire by the enemy, one could find these bunkers only when reached right in its vicinity. The general lie of the ground upto the bunkers was rugged, uneven but was negotiable, and could provide some cover. But at the same time, the enemy had laid mines in conventional as well as non-conventional manner in a very cunning and deceptive style behind boulders, tree trunks etc. Laying of mines and wire obstacles seemed to have been done with utmost care and a sense of practicality (See Photo No. 1). Bunkers were made, with double layers of logs of thick girth of pine trees. These were all shell proof. Each bunker and trench was connected with the deep communication trench and move from one place to the other could take place undetected. All localities were through to each other on the latest mini transmitters. It was a very well-prepared position and the enemy had determined to give a deliberate fight before being thrown out. Dictation of the ground realities were given due consideration by them in minute possible details.

Attack by 2 GARH RIF

All approaches to the newly constructed enemy defences had to face the same type of mine field and wire obstacles. Arty DFs were very accurately registered as the enemy had studied and practically seen this area during their three months long occupation. The fire of all automatics was coordinated for maximum effect. Alternative positions for switching over of the troops, towards any area of threat, was intelligently catered for. Each locality was provided with additional 2 X .50 BMGs and one 83 mm RL and double the number of LMGs in one section. After the attack, launched by 2 GARH RIF on night 6/7 October 1965, which was not successful, the enemy got the idea that this complex would definitely be attacked. Moreover, few boys of 2 GARH RIF who were captured could have given certain other details, which made the enemy to go whole hog and prepared the defences as it did. Enemy knew that we could not leave the things like that, and thus decided to give us a well determined fight.

Enemy Dispositions and Own Plan of Attack

After the abortive attack by 2 GARH RIF and subsequent serious, but few engagements with the enemy, we were able to see through the designs of enemy for defending OP Hill Complex. 2 GARH RIF had learnt the hard way but had been able to ascertain the location of enemy troops to a large extent on the ground. They were the best to give the details of the Arty DFs around. From Intelligence and Field Security company, civilians and other sources, it was confirmed that the feature was occupied by regular troops. They had a distinct advantage of quickly cultivating the civilian informers, besides being familiar with the ground, climate, administrative problems encountered and the knowledge of tracks and negotiating rocks and difficult terrain. Gullible civilian people could be cajoled and attracted due to the family relationship and religious affiliations etc. for getting info.

The enemy had prepared the defences on the whole of OP Hill Complex feature covering all possible approaches. The enemy dispositions on the ground were believed to be like this:-

- Company at Twin Pimples and Black Rock.
- Company at Jungle Hill and OP Hill Top.
- Company at White Rock.
- Company at Twin Trees and Lone Tree.

To deal with the well entrenched enemy and ensure its eviction and annihilation, demanded sacrifices. Determination on the part of respective commanders was the only key. Haphazard tackling at this juncture could have led to disastrous consequences. Adequate arty support was made available and all issues were discussed threadbare. The units were well determined to

Photo No. 1: Enemy Info and Disposn

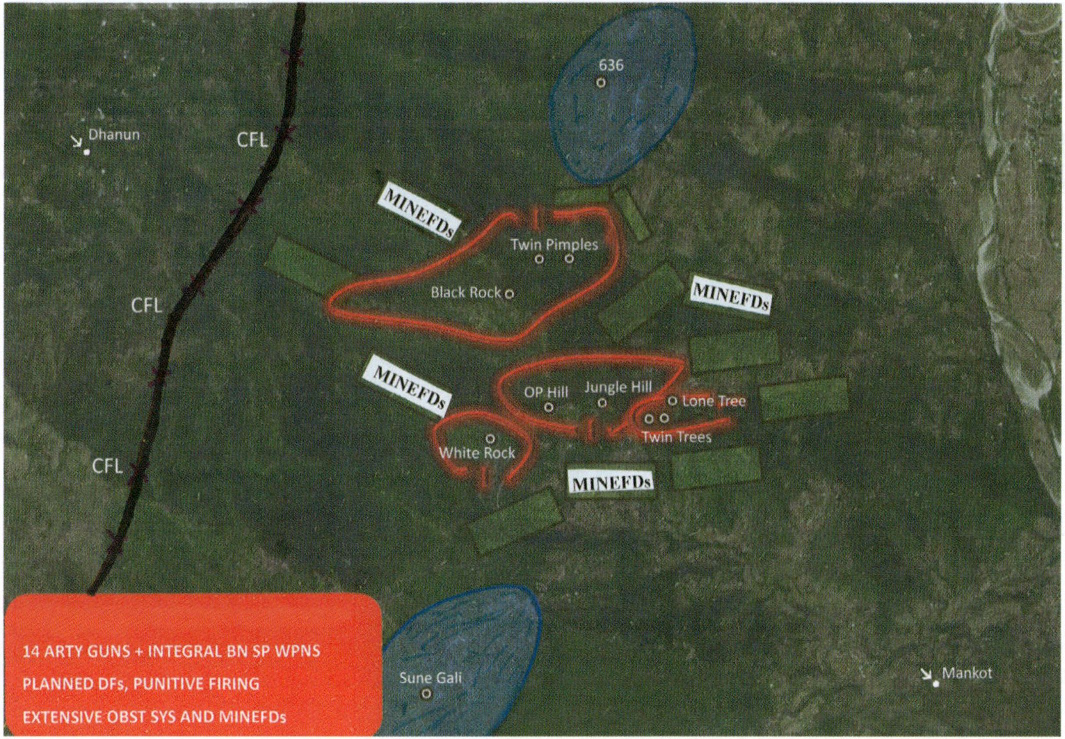

- Mankot
- MINEFDs
- Lone Tree
- Twin Trees
- MINEFDs
- 636
- Twin Pimples
- Jungle Hill
- Black Rock
- OP Hill
- White Rock
- MINEFDs
- MINEFDs
- Sune Gali
- CFL
- Dhanun
- CFL
- CFL

14 ARTY GUNS + INTEGRAL BN SP WPNS
PLANNED DFs, PUNITIVE FIRING
EXTENSIVE OBST SYS AND MINEFDs

Photo No. 2: Changed Sit after Pak Misadventure

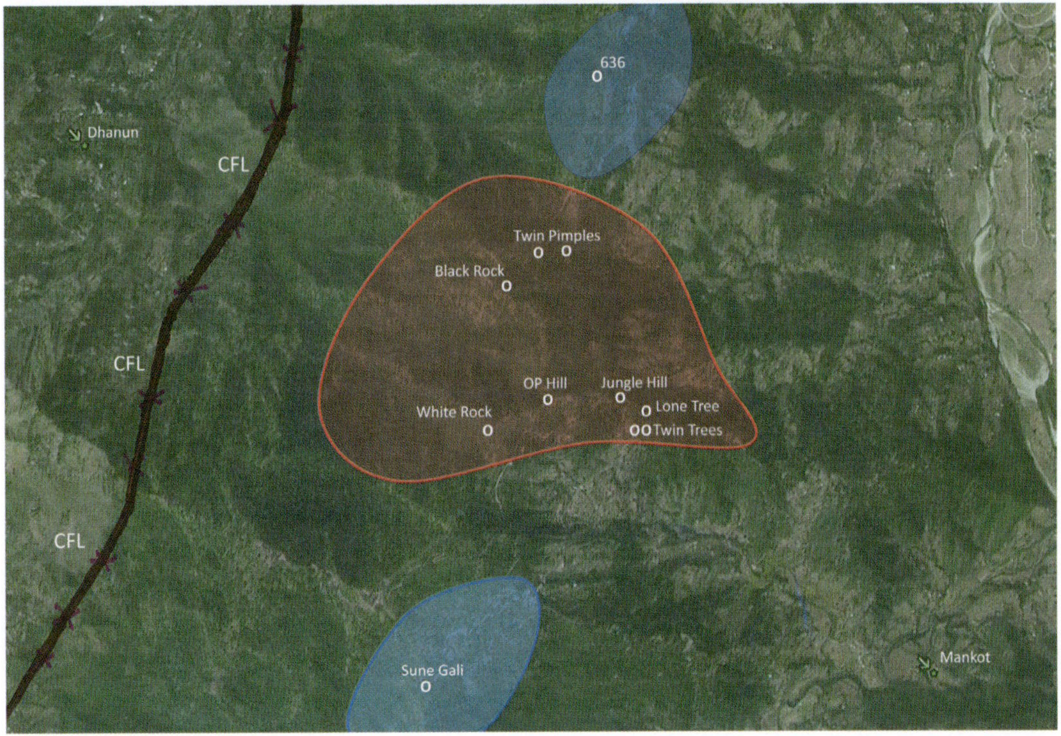

complete the task, the morale was high and assuring. Command structure including at higher levels was responsible, demanding and delivering. The plan of attack was:-

(a) **Phase I**   H hour 2200 hrs, 2 November 1965.

   2 DOGRA to capture Twin Pimples and Black Rock and 5 SIKH LI to capture White Rock.

(b) **Phase II**   On success of Phase I, 7 SIKH to capture Jungle Hill and OP Hill Top.

(c) **Phase III**   7 SIKH to Capture Twin Trees and Lone Tree

Addressing of Troops by Lt Col Bhagat Singh

Lt Col Bhagat Singh, CO 7 SIKH addressed the battalion before attack. He started with the choked voice that his posting order was already out. "If we do well and win this battle, I will go out as a winner and if we fail in our mission, then I will go as a defeated Commanding Officer." He then warned all officers and men in his fatherly style that the objective has to be captured at all costs. Victory at all costs, in spite of any kind of opposition, victory however hard and gruelling has to be ensured. Without victory in this battle, there is no survival. He made it clear that 7 SIKH was the cynosure of all, in this operation and nothing less than the resounding victory will be acceptable. The reputation of us all, is at stake and specially after Operation Phanne-Shah. This cerebral and inspiring talk had an electrifying effect on all. The officers were ready on all accounts. 2/Lt MS Punia as an Intelligence Officer of the unit had done his job commendably well. The troops had no doubts as to where to go and through what? He laid the white tape as close as 200 yds from the objective and gave clear axis for moving on to the enemy bunkers.

2/Lt Ravel Singh had prepared his Mor position remarkably well. He anticipated each action of the enemy and prepared his plan of moving the Mors to alternative positions accordingly. The unit was lucky to have two fresh company commanders one was Maj Trilochan Singh who was not there with the battalion in Mandi Valley operations, where every man of the unit had faced enemy almost everyday and on every occasion, for a period of over three weeks. The other was Capt Sansar Singh who was out to Rajouri with his 'A' Company.

Catering for all Eventualities

Sensing the temerity of the enemy in holding on to the OP Hill Complex, so deep in our own territory so stubbornly and beating back the attack of 2 GARH RIF, it was felt that the enemy meant mischief and would give toughest fight which required very detailed planning for evicting them. The area had to be cleared of the enemy and there was no alternative except throwing them out. To ensure success everything was coordinated at the Command level. And as it was an operation being fought much after the cease fire declaration, it had to be under the direction and guidance of the Army Commander. Every aspect was catered for and troops earmarked. It was

Lt Col MS Punia (then 2/Lt) conducted an important raid across CFL, performed as Intelligence Officer in Battles of Mandi and of OP Hill

also studied that in case the operation was not successful, the enemy may venture for occupying the area north of Mendhar River astride Rd Mendhar-Punch, immediately after the attack. The enemy even could think of occupying it before the attacks as they did in case of OP Hill Complex, if it came to know about our plan. To cater for such an eventuality a task force of 7 commando platoons of various units ex 93 Infantry Brigade were collected and located in area Balhar and Merol astride the road Mendhar-Punch. They had been given the responsibility of holding the ground firmly and in case required to be launched in any phase of operation, for any task were to be prepared for that too. All the platoons had been under training for over a month under the guidance of Maj (Later Maj Gen) AS Chopra of 3 DOGRA, who had done his commando courses in foreign academies. 7 SIKH Commando Platoon was commanded by the author who was located in area south of Achhard.

Col Sansar Singh, VrC (then Capt), led the attack on OP Hill as 'A' Company Commander, was awarded VrC by Dr S Radhakrishnan, President of India

Phase I of Attack

Phase-I started but about 20-30 minutes late. 2 DOGRA and 5

SIKH LI moved very fast and attacked their respective objectives. While 5 SIKH LI captured its objective after passing through the minefield and enemy Arty DFs, suffering huge casualties, 2 DOGRA after the capture of Twin Pimples could not move for Black Rock due to heavy enemy fire. The following companies going in for Black Rock also joined them at Twin Pimples and it became cluttered up with strength of almost three companies. After having been overrun and completely withdrawn from Twin Pimples the enemy started engaging 2 DOGRA with Arty fire at Twin Pimples which was their registered target and which caused 2 DOGRA to suffer very heavy casualties. One odd medium shell had killed 1 JCO and 13 Jawans of 2 DOGRA. The situation at Twin Pimples had become very difficult as the enemy was firing from the higher feature i.e. Black Rock (See Photo No. 4). On the northern side Lt Col Sant Singh Commanding Officer 5 SIKH LI being with the leading company ensured success at White Rock and made 5 SIKH LI to explore the area upto Twin Trees east of OP Hill Top. Black Rock however was holding on, firmly and caused maximum damage to 2 DOGRA. Testing time for Commander 120 Infantry Brigade had come. He thought that:-

> *"There is tide in the affairs of men, which taken at the flood, leads on the fortune: omitted, all the voyage of their life is bound in the shallows and in miseries, and we must take the current, when it serves or loses our ventures"*

He ordered 7 SIKH to move immediately for their objective. The time of reckoning had come. Companies of 7 SIKH had already been ordered by the Commanding Officer to be ahead of the FUP to avoid being caught by enemy's arty fire, which could be its DF. The troops were at about 20 minutes walking distance from the objective. It paid rich dividends later on, when enemy opened up with arty on all registered DFs in a ring around whole area of OP Hill Complex. 'A' Company was leading followed by 'B' Company, and then 'C' Company. All were waiting very anxiously for the fall of Black Rock, final objective of 2 DOGRA. But it was not to be so and 7 SIKH had to be launched before time.

Leading Company Commander

Capt Sansar Singh was 'A' Company commander. He had spoken to his company at Assembly Area. He himself was a very seasoned soldier, matured in thought and deeds. He always meant business and performed any duty given to him with calmness and total devotion and came out with desired results. He was a man of measured words and was an effective company commander. Battalion was fortunate to have him as a leading company commander in the operation, where the reputation of the battalion was at stake particularly, after the misadventure at Phanne-Shah. He spoke to his men before the operation something like this:-

Capt Sansar Singh, (later Col) who led the battalion attack on OP Hill

> *"I can make out that you people are ready for the attack. I am making it clear to you all that enemy knows that we are coming. The enemy had already beaten back the attack by one of our units and he is determined to hold on. We are*

> the leading company and the success of the Battalion will depend upon the success of our company. The task is not easy. There will be firing all around. Men would die. Some would be wounded. Wounded would have to look after themselves for sometime. I warn you not to take liquor, it will affect your reflex actions and can be a cause of death. I want you to face challenges with complete sense of responsibility and with full knowledge of difficulties. From the Start Line when the Jaikaras are raised, the fastest you go on the objective safer you are. I want to make it very clear and specially to section, and platoon commanders that the company will move like a chess board – enblock. I will be at my place and you will not find me wanting. I have to ensure that everyone is at his place, the section and platoon commanders propel their sub-units on to the objective and if one falls, creates another one as replacement and keeps doing so, and if the time comes, which more often than not will, himself takes the ground and falls or fells."

Response was good, knowing the attributes of a Sikh soldier and specially in attack, where he is so resolute, he felt happy and assured. He knew that,

> "A leader who is a man of courage and is able to command, who knows how to maintain the order in the battle, need never regret, having founded victory on obedience of his men."

Readjustment of Junior Leaders

In his meticulous planning and working out small little details, Lt Col Bhagat Singh had very carefully thought and had given 2/Lt Hardial Singh to 'A' Company as No. 3 platoon commander. 2/Lt

Hardial Singh was physically fit like a "Race Horse" and obedient to the core. He had the swagger and flamboyance of a brash commando. He never cribbed or shirked his duties. In Mandi operations, he moved almost everyday for over three weeks encountering the infiltrators every now and then. Commanding officer had this ace always up his sleeves. 2/Lt Hardial Singh, when asked by the author about his change from 'C' Company to 'A' Company, in a facetious humour quipped. *"Sube asi te spare prick han, zithe marji la den, asi tayar han"* (Sube, I am like a spare prick, they may use for any duty, I am always ready). The other platoon commanders were Nb/Sub Bachan Singh No. 1 platoon commander, Sub Bikkar Singh, No. 2 platoon commander and Bub Bharpur Singh as a senior JCO. Sub Bharpur Singh was an intelligent JCO but had little tendency to be authoritative and talkative. He was more interested in giving suggestions rather than obeying the direct and straight orders/instructions. Nb/Sub Bachan Singh got wounded due to a mine blast while moving to FUP and had to be evacuated from there only. Sub Bikkar Singh was a highly disciplined and a very strict JCO, who was trained, educated and professionally very good and thus was very effective platoon commander. His dealing with jawans was straight and well-meaning and he was a hard task master. His order were seldom disobeyed. He had wry countenances and was a man of few words. *"Real leaders are ordinary people with extra ordinary determination."*

In the mountainous terrain, facing undulations at each step, the move will not be in a text book fashion. The enemy fire will be dictating the next step. The move can be soon individual or group based. However, it is the duty of every commander to ensure that move is not slowed down. It can be a cause of great damage. Here comes the role of a strong company commander to ensure that his sub-unit takes minimum time in the killing ground and moves ahead. If the company commander becomes a casualty, the next person should straightaway take over charge and carries on completing the task. 'A' Company started for the assault line, Sub Bikkar Singh's platoon leading, followed by company HQ, then 2/Lt Hardial Singh's platoon and last Sub Bharpur Singh's platoon, who had taken over as platoon commander as Nb/Sub Bachan Singh had been evacuated due to mine injury. FOO was available in FUP and on his asking, he was told that he should be available during the reorganisation, immediately after the success signal. Same way, MMG section commander was instructed.

Launching of Attack

It was around 0110 hrs on 3 November 1965, the moon had disappeared and the darkness dawned in the area of "Jungle Hill." It was rugged and broken ground. The position of our platoons on the ground was, Sub Bikkar Singh's Platoon on left, 2/Lt Hardial Singh's Platoon on the right, Company HQ in centre and Sub Bharpur Singh's Platoon in the rear. Thinking that the company had covered enough distance and was very close to the enemy, Capt Sansar Singh himself raised the jaikara *"Bole So Nihal Sat-Sri Akal."* The enemy immediately opened up with all available weapons. It was noticed that fire of the enemy came from a distance more than the visualised and probably the jaikara was raised a little early. But it was not the time to question why, but to carry on moving fast, another 150 yards for the objective. The enemy being at a safe distance and little away, got a chance to fire and face the attack with little ease. The enemy started with 2" Mor fire, which was very effective. Our jawans kept on moving shouting jaikaras. The casualties had started taking place and as such the move got a bit slowed down. Capt Sansar Singh asked for the anti-tank grenade to be fired on the objective. It fell short of the objective, but created lot of smoke and dust with a big bang. With this the troops moved another 10-15 yards but again slowed down. Another anti-tank grenade was fired and it did make little difference for the company in moving ahead, but not much. It is a most trying moment for the Company commander, where finally his command, character and personality counts. Capt Sansar Singh started exhorting the men not to go to the ground and instead move faster, otherwise severe damage would be caused. The men were responsive but tense and cautious.

Breaking the Crust

Subedar Bikkar Singh a very brave JCO had moved faster and led his platoon straight on to the enemy LMG which was shuttering on his platoon. This LMG was silenced by L/Nk Achhar Singh and his colleagues in an act of sheer raw courage, but at the cost of three Jawans – a very big loss of brave and trained men in the initial stages only but *'glorious death is his, who for his country falls'*. Company commander got another anti-tank Grenade fired on the objective. This made the men to move and as a result the enemy got unnerved. The intensity of firing in general, from the enemy side diminished a little. With left most LMG being silenced and firing of the enemy getting diminishing, No. 2 platoon of Sub Bikkar Singh took the advantage and moved ahead fast but consciously. The LMG in front of central block of own men was causing maximum hindrance. Capt Sansar Singh fired at it with his sten gun but no effect. Jawans were also firing but somehow it still remained active. 2/Lt Hardial Singh came to Capt Sansar Singh and fired a complete sten gun magazine on this LMG. It worked and this LMG was finally silenced. The Company

HQ and 2/Lt Hardial Singh's Platoon were struggling for a foothold in the enemy defences towards right, which they finally got. They soon captured a right corner bunker. Sub Bikkar Singh in the meantime had reached on top from the left side but his platoon had suffered heavy casualties. His boys had done wonders. Out of six LMGs initially spotted, three were silenced by this platoon and remaining two shifted to some other side.

Table TOP/OP Hill Top

At once stage, there remained no distinction of the platoons, and it was all mixing up due to their moving towards top and the jawans had entered the communication trench. After seeing this development but not before causing considerable casualties, the enemy withdrew from the cliff complex. There was another feature looking like, Table Top, from where an LMG was not permitting the move beyond the Cliff Complex. In fact this Table Top was OP Hill Top. 5 SIKH LI had captured their elongated feature. They occupied the southern tip of Twin Trees and thought that they had captured OP Hill Top (see comments by Col Bhagat Singh on the report, excerpts at Appendix-F). The enemy was very active and was determined not to let the jawans move. Pakistani gunner of 21 Punjab of Pakistan shouted at our jawans

Nk Banta Singh, did as excellent job in eliminating the LMG Bunkers at OP Hill, killed in action, awarded Sena Medal

saying *"come you kafirs, I will not let you touch this place, so long I am alive. It is just impossible for you."* L/NK Saudagar Singh, a very good NCO ran towards this LMG and almost caught him but unfortunately got killed at outside the enemy bunker. Another daredevil NK Banta Singh dashed towards the same enemy, but too got killed just touching the bunker. The enemy kept on holding for some more time. Capt Sansar Singh thought of his plan for execution and felt that:-

"The difficult we do immediately, but the impossible takes littler longer"

Both forward platoons of Sub Bikkar Singh and 2/Lt Hardial Singh were heavily committed. Sub Bikkar Singh's platoon had suffered heavy casualties and was totally mauled, with large number wounded and bleeding profusely. 2/Lt Hardial Singh's platoon was holding on to a very important corner bunker, form where, troop could be launched for Table Top (OP Hill Top) and towards upper side of Black Rock if required. At this stage, it was a pitched battle still being fought at Black Rock by 2 DOGRA, which was to have been cleared in Phase-I only.

Capt Sansar Singh, with a very cool head thought of launching third platoon for the Table Top (OP Hill Top) to eliminate the last LMG, which was still very dangerously active. The platoon commander suggested to the company commander that "we should wait till day light, why to suffer more casualties." Capt Sansar Singh asked Sub Bikkar Singh to move ahead for the said LMG. Sub Bikkar Singh informed that his whole platoon was disorganised having lost nine boys and remaining all seriously wounded. He lamented to say so, but there was no way out.

Role and Place of Reserves

Capt Sansar Singh thought of informing the Commanding Officer, to get 'B' Company pushed forward which was reserve to 'A' Company so that the momentum of attack is maintained. He for some time could not talk to Commanding Officer, as his own operator was not traceable. He ordered the verey light pistol to be fired giving the success signal, so that on this signal, 'B' Company which could not be contacted will move up. That also failed in the rigmarole of Red over Green etc. He finally sent his runner to 'B' Company. There he was told that they will move only on orders of the Commanding Officer. 'B' Company commanded by Maj RK Sharma had come under enemy Arty DF and had suffered five dead and double the number wounded. They could not move as planned. In the meantime, signal operator of Capt Sansar Singh fetched up. Capt Sansar Singh informed the commanding officer that lower rocky area of the main defences has been captured but some enemy were still active on higher ground. 'A' Company had suffered heavy casualties and committed on both edges of the captured objective. Now a little push by the Reserve Company will ensure the complete and clear capturing of the objective, immediately. The Commanding Officer said that he knew about 'B' company and instead he is sending 'C' Company. Capt Sansar then sent the runner to 'C' Company who met Maj Trilochan Singh, Company Commander for guiding his outfit.

Maj Trilochan Singh did not waste any time and visualizing the situation, moved his company fast. Unfortunately, after a few minutes, his JCO Nb/Sub Harnam Singh (Manna) stepped on a mine and lost his foot in the blast. Some jawans gathered around him for first aid. He saw this and asked his senior JCO, to leave one jawan to attend to him and move forward. Maj Trilochan

Singh was suggested that "we could move after first light" which was very irking and disgusting for Maj Trilochan Singh.

Maj Trilochan Singh was one of the senior officers of that time. He was an up and coming officer. He was a hard task master and was known for his strong convictions. He was very effective in his command and whole Battalion knew him well and vice versa. He had been performing as Adjutant for a long time and was very firm in his dealings. He was a man of very stern countenances and a blue-eyed boy of Commanding Officer. He was ruthless in dealings specially with officers and JCOs. He pursued the moves and values of command in a typical OG (Olive Green) way. Socially he was up, professionally very sound and individually a bit egocentric like all careerist. He was a very shrewd officer. When suggested by a JCO to wait for some more time, he looked at him with intense anger and gave a bit of his mind to him for not understanding the sensitivity of the situation. However, he took the company fastest and was soon behind Capt Sansar Singh. He was guided by Capt Sansar Singh to take his company on to the right and climb the Table Top. He was soon in the corner bunker. It was here that the jawans of 'C' Company and raised jaikaras. It was just on the upper side of Black Rock where from 2 DOGRA

Maj Gen Trilochan Singh, (then Major) who pressed the attack for final capture of Battalion's objective in the Battle of OP Hill

were being fired upon by enemy and were held up. The enemy noticing being out-manoeuvered and dominated from top by Sikhs, fled. The pressure on 2 DOGRA was immediately released. 2 DOGRA in response raised jaikaras "*7 SIKH Ki Jai*." They were beholden at heart. They kept on doing so and soon captured the Black Rock. At this stage Capt Sansar Singh, 2/Lt Hardial Singh and Sub Bikkar Singh had also reached the Table Top. It was in fact the OP Hill Top where the enemy had his command post and arty OP.

Elimination of Last Enemy

Now Capt Sansar Singh thought of eliminating the LMG on Table Top. Seeing the jawans rushing towards him, LMG gunner of Pakistan started running towards east, leaving behind his LMG. He was fired at by Sub Bikkar Singh's platoon and having been wounded was captured. That we can say, was the end of battle. The Jungle Hill and OP Hill Top were cleared by 7 SIKH. It was the ground of relative importance in OP Hill Complex. Sub Bikkar Singh's platoon played the most crucial role in the elimination of the enemy and capture of Jungle Hill, but at very heavy cost. It was his platoon, who really beat the hell out of the enemy and made him to run away from Jungle Hill and OP Hill

Col Hardial Singh, SM (then 2/Lt) led platoon attack in OP Hill, was awarded Sena Medal

Top. Commanding Officer was informed who soon was up there. He straight came to Capt Sansar Singh and congratulated him. He made the company commanders to search the whole area well and ensure speedy evacuation of casualties.

Reorganisation at OP Hill Top

Maj Trilochan Singh being a senior and an ebullient commander of troops, after ensuring our own reorganisation at Jungle Hill sounded reveille along with jaikaras. 5 SIKH LI was also raising the jaikaras form the opposite direction as they had come from the northern approach. He ensured there was no clash of own troops. He soon established links with company commander of 5 SIKH LI and helped in reorganisation. Had 'C' Company delayed their move it would have led to more casualties of 2 DOGRA and possible delay and causing more casualties to 'A' Company 7 SIKH, which was already affected badly. Anyway the game was up. We had to pay a very heavy price, 7 SIKH – 18 killed. 5 SIKH LI – 35 killed and 2 DOGRA – 3 Officers and 50 Other Rank killed and proportionately very large number seriously wounded. What a price for folly of the previous Brigade Commander and the unit commanders who permitted the enemy to come so deep into our area and establish a formidable post between two post of ours. Today, there stands a magnificent monument reminding us of the sacrifices of the heroes. They did deserve a monument.

"One owes respect to the living but to the dead one owes truth"

God bless them. They paid in 'cash' for clearing the debt of Mother India.

Crux of the Matter

To lead a company in an attack is the acid test of the company commander. It is, he who has to make sure that the men do not halt and carry on moving. It is important for him to understand the psychology of the ordinary soldiers as well as that of old timers and their reactions to the developing critical situations. Capt Sansar Singh understood his command very well. He put the right man at the right place and conducted his operation like a resolute commander. He maintained his cool throughout and never let the final goal of capturing Jungle Hill, slip out of his mind. He ensured that the momentum was maintained. He sagaciously encouraged, persuaded and led the men where needed. It is a fact that when the BMGs and LMGs are shuttering from front and men are falling, the move does come to a halt. He understood it well and immediately thought of an alternative and acted accordingly. He was clear about the psychology of men moving in face of enemy fire.

He was optimistic throughout and had managed the situation very well. There once came a situation when both the leading platoons were heavily committed. The platoon led by Sub Bikkar Singh, had done superbly well but was decimated badly. Almost whole platoon was incapacitated. 2/Lt Hadial Singh's platoon was occupying a most important captured feature and could not be moved due to most demanding tactical situation. Capt Sansar Singh through the commanding officer sought the move of 'C' Company commanded by another responsible officer in Maj Trilochan Singh who wasted no time and was soon at the required place, which not only facilitated the capture of objective of 'A' company but also provided a "godsend" opportunity to get the pressure on 2 DOGRA quickly released. The whole operation gradually became controllable and both units, captured their respective objectives, but of course not without suffering heavy casualties.

What is the role of a company commander, is the moot point, to be understood with a critical mind. Unit can ill afford to make the company commander to go in for first enemy trench, on the first opportunity. He is meant for a bigger task i.e. for ensuring and capturing of objective. He has to maintain an order in the battle. Company commander of leading company is the life of success in any operation.

It will not be out of place to say that Capt Sansar Singh was lucky to have Sub Bikkar Singh and 2/Lt Hardial Singh with him as his platoon commanders. They both were assets. Both ensured that the job was done at all costs. *"Courage consists not in hazarding without fear but being resolutely minded in a just cause. The brave is not he, who feels no fear, for that were stupid and irrational, but whose noble soul subdues its fear and bravery dares the dangers, nature shirks from."*

Clarification

Area of OP Hill Complex lies between two important Indian posts 636 and 475 and as such there is no big intervening feature in between. The feature is undulating with numerous bumps. In view of the enemy already firmed in, recce parties had not been able to go nearby. It was difficult even for Commander 120 Infantry Brigade to delineate the objectives of the battalions. Everything was planned based on the general knowledge of the area and with the help of the maps. Initially it was occupied by an enemy company but later on its was developed into bigger defended area. Defended localities were prepared and properly connected with each other through the communication trench. On the day of attack there could not be more than two companies plus of enemy, as assessed later. (See Appendix-F)

    The feature of OP Hill Complex, say for the purpose of this study starts from post 475 runs northwards and then takes the turn towards east leading to Twin Trees and Lone Tree area. This features does not straightway join OP Hill Top. There is a depression in between from where originates a nala, which comes down towards south-west leaving Twin Pimples, Black Rock and OP Hill Top to its north-west as the photos attached make it absolutely clear. Ridge line originating from Twin Pimples, leads to Black Rock and joins at OP Hill Top. It means the OP Hill Top dominates the Black Rock and the northern end of White Rock upto which 5 SIKH LI had secured does no dominate Black Rock. The enemy sitting at Black Rock could effectively be dealt with by own troops occupying OP Hill Top. (See Photo 3 & 4)

    OP Hill Top is the ending tip of Jungle still upwards towards KDL 475. It means the Jungle still and OP Hill Top are continuous and hence one elongated feature. This is a small bump on which was sited the command post and the arty OP bunker, of the enemy which was captured by 7 SIKH. Commander 120 Infantry Brigade had written in his after action report that an isolated LMG on Twin Trees continued firing. 5 SIKH LI finally cleared it at 0630 hrs on 3 November 1965. An other enemy LMG which was sited on north- eastern side of Twin Trees, sweeping the approach to Jungle Hill and OP Hill Top, was cleared by 7 SIKH. It shows that Twin Trees at one stage of the battle was occupied by the enemy. 7 SIKH did not attack and cleared Twin Trees area, means it was cleared by 5 SIKH LI, which means 5 SIKH LI after

Photo No. 3: View from Enemy Side

Photo No. 4: View from KDL 636

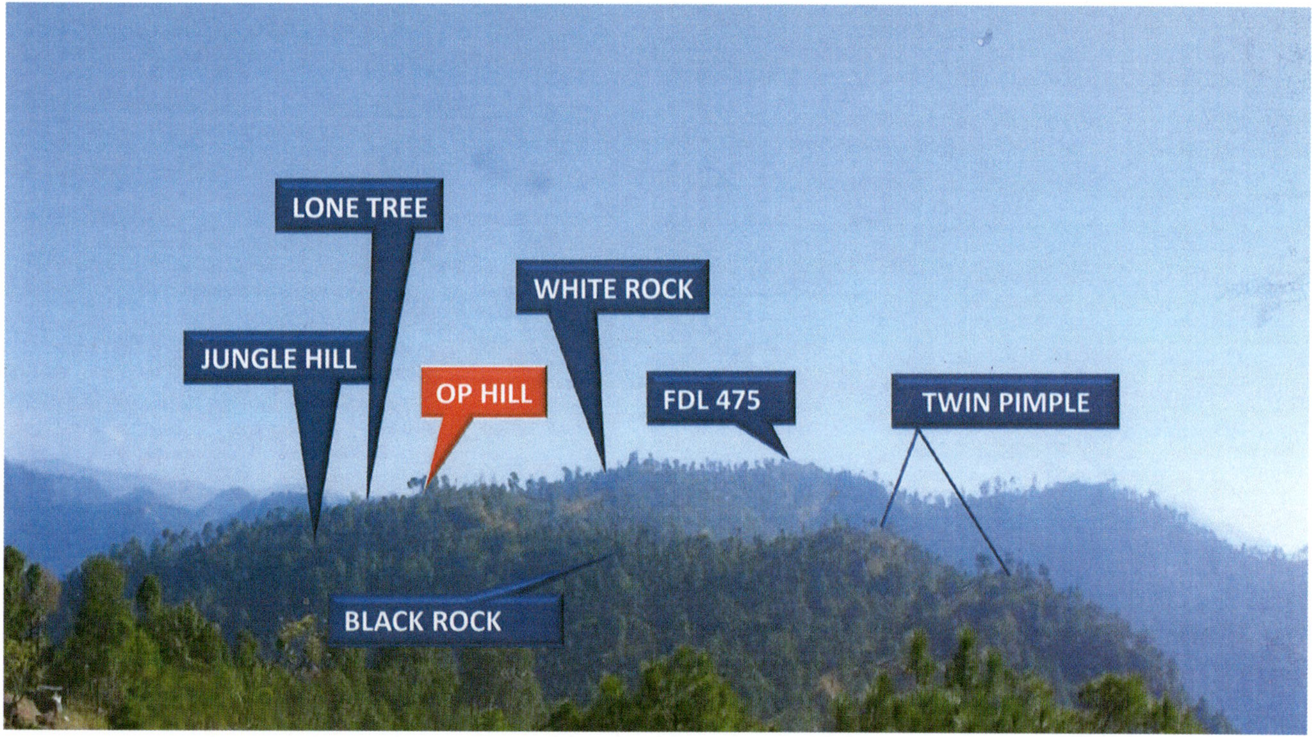

the capture of its own objective went towards Twin Trees and not towards objectives of 7 SIKH. To subscribe to the idea that 5 SIKH LI captured its own objective, captured Twin Trees and also the OP Hill Top, is not correct. OP Hill is the continuation of Jungle Hill and was captured by 7 SIKH and reported correctly. No one had the clear view of the objectives, before the complete OP Hill Complex was captured.

Commanding Officer, 5 SIKH LI was with the leading coy. His own objective was an elongated feature with a gali in between. On reaching the northern tip of the feature through gali visualizing that they had reached OP Hill Top, the message regarding the same could have been given. But it was not to be so as per the understanding of the Commanding Officer, 7 SIKH, explained and proved again as late as in 1982 in a spot study review.

If 5 SIKH LI had captured OP Hill which was higher than and a continuation of Black Rock from western side as said earlier and had sat down there on the head of Black Rock, raising Jaikaras, then how come that enemy kept on sitting at Black Rock till 7 SIKH came much later and the enemy disappeared with the first Jaikara raised by 7 SIKH. It boils down to one thing, that the OP Hill Top is the continuation of Jungle Hill and was captured by 7 SIKH.

Junior Leaders and Ground Realities

Here the aim is to give out the lessons learnt in the context of platoon, company and the battalion in attack. Deliberately the lessons to be learnt at higher level of command have not been discussed in detail but of lower level are enunciated so that the ground realities are realised by the people, who matter. Main points were:

- The morale of the troops was high, preparations made were adequate and the execution was though orderly, but slow at times. Some daredevils, without caring for their personal safety, straightway went on to the enemy, knowing fully well that such an act would cost lives; which paved the way for success.

    "To every man upon this earth,
    Death comes soon or late
    And how can man die better,
    Than facing the fearful odds
    For the ashes of his fathers
    And temples of his gods"

- Every move of own troops to FUP and onwards was a careful thought of Lt Col Bhagat Singh. It really saved the unit from the damage of unconventionally laid mines and enemy's Arty DFs. 'B' Company, 7 SIKH suffered due to arty fire only. Had they moved as did 'A' Company do, away from the likely enemy DF and more closer to the objective they could have saved themselves.

- The enemy conducted an orderly withdrawal after doing colossal damage. It could be very well-coordinated withdrawal as the enemy kept on engaging us till last. They probably covered a longer route for withdrawal over three frequently patrolled positions for the purpose in our area, on the elongated feature south of Sune Gali. The LMG gunner of Pakistan who was caught on Table Top had started running towards east, indicating that they withdrew from that side. Pakis are good in unconventional kind courtesy training of officers at academies in USA.

- Though, defences were there, but there was no enemy at Lone Tree area as was noticed in the reorganisation. The enemy was there at Twin Trees as two LMGs continued firing till last and were captured one each by 7 SIKH and 5 SIKH LI. It means some troops were there, they could have been switched over to Black Rock, as that looked seemingly strengthened being the most obvious approach followed by 2 DOGRA.

- 'A' Company, 7 SIKH captured main defences at Jungle Hill. Three LMGs were clearly spotted and silenced and three others escaped as the enemy had six LMGs in a platoon. .50 BMG could not be captured. There could be a platoon or platoon plus at Jungle Hill, and OP Hill Top, having double the number of LMGs in each section, which could not be judged in the initial stages.

- There should be no illusion about Pakistan's intelligence network in J&K. Ground realities are conducive for cultivating sources in context of Pakistan. As, their intelligence sources are often double-edged, we should have cultivated maximum sources which we did not. We could have got some info at least. Through, the agents and other intelligence sources, observing hectic movements and preparation of our troops for attack and noticing the meaningful arty crunches, the enemy could have known the plan and force level to be used by us and thus planned a coordinated withdrawal of its forces, without leaving much for us to destroy, capture and study.

Critical Appreciation

Leading the troops in attack is not as simple as it looks on the sand model or in exercises. It is the most difficult phenomenon, which needs to be understood in correct prospective. The officers and men perceive the things differently. Age group makes the difference and responsibilities lie the head which wears the crown. These are bare facts and must be understood by officers, who have to face such situations. For critically appreciating a problem, following factors are important:

- Troops do not move from Start Line to the objective in the text book fashion and as they do in exercises. The two situations are totally different having nothing in common – live enemy verses jolly milling around enthusiastically.

- Old people make hundred and one calculations while dealing with actual battle situations and they affect the operation very much. One company's responsible had said, is it the time to move? We will only move after the first light, other one also used similar words, but the company commander being the hard task master and ruthless in dealing with such cases, made him to move fast. Capt Sansar Singh asked the commanding officer to order third company to move so that the task allotted to the battalion is completed successfully. And there was nothing unusual in this. Reserves are created and meant for such occasions only. Reserves are tied to the tail of the leading element and that is their place.

- Different ranks perceive the operations differently. The officers have got the total responsibility on their shoulders and will have to go in for do-or-die missions. There is no way out for them. It is solely their business. For a commander:-

    "The love of glory, the fear of shame, sense of responsibility,

the design for making a fortune, the desire of rendering life easy and agreeable and the humour of pulling down the enemy are often the causes of that valour so celebrated among men"

- People take the advantage of the situation and slip away. The FOO with 'A' Company, and 'A' company commander's signal operator had disappeared, with the firing of the first bullet, only to return later than desired.

- To attend to the wounded is another excuse. Some people take advantage of such occurrences to avoid going in with their sub-units for objective. They should be dealt with a firm hand.

- Everyone is scared of death. It is the sense of duty for a cause which makes one to head for objective. Discipline, Training, Duty and Self Respect are the four vehicles (basic factors) which carry an ordinary Indian soldier into the battle. His psychology is firmly etched on edifice resting on this four-sided structure. They should be trained and educated accordingly.

- With the introduction of new weaponry, there is no possibility of hand to hand fight. There was not a single such case, which exhibited such fighting, in the battle of OP Hill or earlier operations. It was a weapon to weapon all through, though at places, being very close.

- If you think and act patiently, you will overcome every situation.

- Let us carefully observe those good qualities where our enemies excel us, endeavour to excel them by avoiding what is faulty and imitating what is excellent in them. Pakistanis were better in unconventional warfare and left nothing to chance.

- Those who perform individual acts of the highest physical courage are drawn from two categories. Either with quick intelligence and vivid imagination or those without imagination and with minds fixed on the practical business of living, that is, those who live on their nerves and those who have not got any nerve. The first one suddenly sees the crisis, his imagination flashes the opportunity and he acts. The other meets the situation without finding it so very unusual and deals with it, in a matter of fact way. 'A' Company fortunately had both types of persons. In Sub Bikker Singh for first and NK Banta Singh for the second category and they both made the attack a success by breaking the crust of enemy defences.

- Finally it is the platoons and sections which fight battles. Company commander must place emphasis on small unit practical combat instructions, so that battle is conducted with the same precision as close order drill.

All said and done, at the end of the game, the balance sheet was surprising. From both sides, I have to say that it was the game which was played well. The attacker was determined to evict the aggressor and the defender was determined to cause maximum casualties to the attacker and it happened as planned by both.

Multi-directional Attack

7 SIKH was to go in for its objective, Jungle Hill/OP Hill Top in Phase II of the Brigade attack on OP Hill Complex. It was

decided that 7 SIKH will do as reserve to 2 DOGRA for Phase I and capture its own objective in Phase II by following the same axis of advance and passing through the objectives of 2 DOGRA at night. Commanding Officer 7 SIKH Lt Col Bhagat Singh very carefully appreciated that the course suggested would deny him his choice of axis of advance and point of attack. After four days of deliberations and with his convincing reasons, he was given a free choice to select his own axis. As the attack progressed, it was proved by the events that the Brigade attack would have miserably failed and very heavy casualties suffered by the attacking battalions, had his advice not heeded to. It is also mentioned that in those days multi-directional attack was uncommon and this idea of three-pronged attack was given by none other than Lt Col Bhagat Singh, He was not a dashing commando alright but a thinking man he was.

Position of a Commander in Battle

Along with the privileges and authority, the rank and nobility have certain duties and obligations to perform. In addition to all this, there is one unwritten code which says that the leaders must rise above the principles and take unusual steps for the success of the operation, by personally influencing in critical moments. In army during the war, a commander can influence the outcome by being at "hot spot" which directly affects the course of events and the conduct of the juniors, who are automatically drawn to perform. Field Marshal Rommel in his "Summary of the place of the Commander in battle" says that it is always "up front," which can be decisive and this is applicable, equally today to all commanders at all levels.

In the Battalion attack, in mountains the position of the

commanding officer should be, behind his leading company if not with them. He should certainly be ahead of the "reserve" of the leading company, so that he can immediately launch the reserve company if the situation so demands. In war the casualties take place and everybody does not move willingly and automatically as planned. It is a situation, which can only be imagined correctly by those who have gone through such a rut. No commanding officer can have a "physical command" of the scene by being away from the scene. At the time of reckoning, one has to be at 'hot spot' for continuously reading the battle and to have proper control over the situation. Rather than being pushed from behind, through messages, the reserves be pulled up from front by giving physical and verbal orders by commanding officer. Reserves will certainly move to the call of the battalion commander who is ahead of them. The task of leading company is most important and if that is accomplished well, 90 per cent of objective of unit is in hands. For ensuring that, the reserves should be in the pocket of the commanding officer who can launch them on the first available call. They seldom move themselves when men are falling around.

Reorganisation Stage and its Imperatives

At the reorganisation stage too, the commanding officer should reach by being first behind the leading element and at the first opportune moment. It can so happen that commander of leading element is busy in salvaging the situation and giving a semblance of occupation of defences against a immediate counter attack, the other "smarties" will create a scene by moving around, shouting and showing that actually they had done the "basics" of operation, if the commanding officer is not there. And commanding officer can only be there at the right moment, if he has been at the right place all through. Joining when everything has happened and the "simpletons" have been overshadowed by "crafty seniors," the story of the battle would have been changed to at least 50 per cents causing aversions.

7 SIKH in OP Hill

Brigade attack was launched for evicting the enemy from OP Hill Complex. Attack was conducted in two phases, 5 SIKH LI and 2 DOGRA were launched in Phase I on White Rock and Twin Pimples and Black Rock respectively. Jungle Hill was the objective of 7 SIKH which was launched in Phase II of the Brigade attack. Phase, I had gone in, 5 SIKH LI had captured its own objective. The sterling success of 5 SIKH LI was because their commanding officer was with the leading company and controlled the whole situation himself, besides, of course, with the supreme sacrifices made by their brave officers and jawans.

The leading company of 7 SIKH was hugely incapacitated, but major portion of the objective was captured and there was urgent need of immediate launching of reserve company. But the reserve company was nowhere, around. Had the commanding officer been behind or with 'A' Company, he would have "pulled up" 'B' Company and launched them. 'A' Company Commander seeing the criticality of the occasion informed commanding officer who was little behind. He then directed 'C' Company which was behind 'B' Company to move up and assist 'A' Company in completing its task. 'C' Company commander immediately moved his outfit and joined 'A' Company and made up for the delay in capturing the objective by 'A' Company.

Aberrations

In the account of battle fought by 7 SIKH at OP Hill, one finds few aberrations in private versions. Polishing and glorifying individual acts is very common in such writings but reckless altering and adding of "not happened" is bad in view of the lessons for the posterity. It can mar the accounts beyond recognition. Such unscrupulous accreditations prove that history is really a fable, an untrue, imaginary and improbable account. The after action report of Commander 120 Infantry Brigade and comments of the then Commanding Officer, Lt Col Bhagat Singh, 7 SIKH of as late as 1982 do not support such aberrations. How can one justify that when commanding officer and even the brigade commander say that there was no enemy at area, Lone Tree, a pitched battle is being shown to have been fought there. Not only this, couple of officers and JCOs have been shown "wounded." Fortunately no officer from 7 SIKH was wounded in the Battle of OP Hill. Two JCOs had suffered mine blast injuries, no other was wounded. It is rightly said that *historical events occur twice, first as a tragedy and second as farce.*

16

PHENOMENON OF GIBRALTAR AND IT'S CRUMBLING

"Men will never do evil, so completely and cheerfully as when they do it from religious convictions" —Blaise Pascal

Religion as a Weapon

The usage of words like Malta, Gibraltar and names of the Muslim invaders of the yesteryears like Tariq, Khalid and Nusrat etc given to the columns of the infiltrators, had been adopted with a specific aim and purpose as these names have got a history behind them. Pakistan has no other means to incite and unite its people except harping on the slogan of "Islam is in danger" vis-à-vis India. But all what had been done so far and results achieved, certainly did not conform to their wishful thinking. As has been given above one who believes that his is the best religion, does not understand the philosophy of the religion itself, which in actual stance is "the love of God and mankind." All religions are same, the methods of practising are different. Pakistan's philosophy of religion however is to collect the assemblage of people and develop them into a hostile group for seducing the existence of others. The Pakistanis express such sensibilities in all walks of life with regard to India. For them their own religion has taken the place of reasonableness.

Malta

Malta is a small island in the Mediterranean Sea roughly between Tunisia and Sicily. In the distant past, it was raided and occupied by the Arab Muslim crusaders in their exploring missions by throwing away the original settlers from there. They by occupying Malta had established and controlled the maritime communication in the Mediterranean Sea. It was then a grand success, where from Pakistanis try to draw and manage inspiration, generally for their folks and specially for their Muslim Army.

Gibraltar

On the southern coast of Spain there is a sheer, lime-stone rock which rises about 1394 feet high from a promontory i.e. a high ground projecting into the sea, also called 'headland' overlooking the entrance to the Mediterranean Sea. It basically serves as an observatory and a check post for controlling maritime traffic. It is where, around this entrance the present Gibraltar town is situated. Since the ancient Greak settled there, this entrance has seen many invasions. In 1711, the Moors (Islamic crusaders) arrived from North Africa and this headland was captured by them and as such there is a curious expression connected with the naming of it as Gibraltar. It is named after Muslim General, Jabar-ul-Tariq (generally called Gen Tariq), who had captured this rock and then through this entrance conquered Spain and who on landing on the Spanish soil had all his ships destroyed to make any retreat by any element of his force impossible, just to ensure that this important entry point remains in their hands.

This peninsula remained under the Moors almost continuously till 1462 when the Spanish people drove them out. It is valued as a strategic naval and air base and communication centre for monitoring naval traffic in Mediterranean Sea and hence lies its utmost importance.

What is in a Name

It is because of this stupendous success of the legendry Muslim crusaders of the yesteryears that Pakistan tries to derive religious incitement for its troops by correlating with those names. As the Arabs had captured Malta, and Gibraltar was captured by General Jabar-ul-Tariq, Pakistan planned to capture Jammu and Kashmir using the same names and analogy as an inspirational dose for its troops. Even in 1947-48 operations the amalgam of raiders consisting of Afridis, Mahsuds and regular army was commanded by one Maj Gen Akbar Khan who was also given a pseudo name of 'Gen Tariq' of Gibraltar fame. Even 'Operation Topac' launched by Gen Zia-ul-Haq in July 1988 was named after Topac Amru, a Prince who fought an unconventional war against Spanish rule in 18 century – Uruguay. In all its wars and actions Pakistan has always tried to flaunt its self-created Islamic superiority, arrogance and haughtiness. Of late the atomic bomb fabricated by Pakistan is called the Islamic Bomb, as if, by becoming Islamic the bomb which has been made to frighten and annihilate India has acquired some extra ordinary prowess and dimensions.

Pakistan hatred towards India

> "Pakistan is like Israel. Take out Judaism from Israel, It will collapse like a house of cards. Take Islam out of Pakistan and make it a secular state, it will collapse."   —Gen Zia-ul-Haq

Before starting Pakistan Army had wanted war of 1965 to be taken by her people as a holy war on "infidel" India. As mentioned earlier, the words Malta and Gibraltar were expected to arouse the religious zeal and fanaticism of the raiders. But most of the raiders did not even know the languages of Punchhis, Kargil people or Kashmiris whom they wanted to incite and instigate against India when they came all the way for the purpose. Having failed to seize J&K in 1947-48, they planned again in 1965 based on these false notions. Their commanders thought that their troops would also draw inspiration from the exploits of previous Muslim warriors who invaded India in the past. They were of the opinion that if Mahmood of Ghazni could plunder India seventeen times, if Shahabuddin Ghori could lay the foundation of the Islamic state here by invading ten times, if Babur could establish Mughal Empire in India in his fifth attempt and if Ahmad Shah Abdali could overrun this country eight times, Pakistan could also realise its aim of conquering India by invading this country again and again. To rally their ranks in view of above given philosophy they coined a new slogan for poisoning its people against India "Hans ke liya hai Pakistan, Lar ke lenge Hindustan" (By asserting joyfully we got Pakistan and by force of arms we will conquer Hindustan). Ever since the creation of Pakistan, its people are being fed on hatred against India, which is reinforcing the opium of Islamic appeal, and that in their view helped to keep that country together. But for how long? Scientific advancement, philosophy of reasoning and modernisation will take its toll one day – either play or perish.

Obsession Kashmir

Pakistan has got an undying desire to capture of erstwhile Kashmir which includes the Valley and Punch. It is its life long agenda and it has been daydreaming about it from day one. It serves two purposes for Pakistan. One, unless there is some problematic issue, there is no requirement of army and a strong army is the answer to keep that country together. Secondly, Kashmir is main source of water for its rivers and this issue has to be kept alive, for getting it permanently recognised by India at International level without which their survival itself will be in jeopardy. We can safely assume that water is even more important than Kashmir. Why Punch, because their Mangla Dam is based to quite an extent on Punch river and its tributaries, which are with India and blockade can be resorted to in hour of need and that can be a cause of great concern for them. Even for safety of Mangla Dam, the securing and enlarging of this area is important.

Also, as the origin of that country is hate based, its aim is to do maximum damage to India by any means because they feel their existence is related to it. Kashmir Valley being Muslim dominated is attracting Pakistan as they are of the opinion that it should have been their part. Deep-rooted obsession for Kashmir thus mires their rational thinking and forces them to go in for Kashmir time and again. As a result of all this, they once again thought of annexing Kashmir by force in August 1965 and launched an operation, initially known as Malta, which was later on changed to Gibraltar conducted by a force known as Gibraltar Force, of about 15,000 troops. This force was trained as guerrilla force which started entering the Indian territory of Punch Sector and other places in July 1965 and completed administrative dumping etc by end July 1965. The first report of their ingress in our area of responsibility was reported from Gali post in Punch Sector on 5 August 1965 and they fired first bullet on Gali picquet on 7 August 1965.

Enlarging Hold on Punch Basin

Besides their misplaced notion of the valley to revolt against Indian authorities and then establishing the Regional Council and declare independence in the valley, Pakistan had planned to cut off Punch bulge by advancing from Mandi Valley from north and Mendhar Valley from the south and joining in general area Kalai Bridge, once the scheme enunciated earlier comes to fruition. Punch as given earlier, has got its own importance for Pakistan. Punch River basin is the second biggest catchment area for filling the Mangla Dam, which Pakistan has developed near Mirpur in POK. Pakistan had planned to capture Punch, so that the danger to the dam can be minimised which is so very important for its agricultural and economic survival. In fact Pakistan has always given priority to this area comprising of Mandi, Surankot and Punch etc. for that obvious reason. They also believed that Muslim population in Punch area will be easily instigated as was done in 1947-48. Also capturing of this area would provide much needed depth to Hiji Pir bulge.

The Northern Pincer

Well-trained guerrilla columns were organised, planned and launched accordingly. It was also with this aim that an area, which later came to be known as OP Hill Complex in Mendhar Sub-sector, between two of our own posts, was occupied on 5 August by their regular troops, whereas irregulars kept on operating in guerrilla fashion in general area Mendhar and around. This southern column of Gibraltar was known as Nusrat Force. They started blocking the move of men and vehicles of 120 Infantry Brigade in Mendhar and Balnoi areas mainly by Arty and Mor fire. Own infantry columns and posts were also subjected to intense firing of all kinds. Same way Sallahudin Force launched, a sub-column known as Mann Force from Kopra (POK) for moving and capturing the heights dominating Gali, Sauji, Khet, Mandi and Kalai Bridge. But here 7 SIKH did not permit them to stick and Mandi, though once captured by enemy was wrested after two days in a fierce and fast action by 7 SIKH. The plan of Pakistanis was audacious. This was to be solidified by a conventional attack on Punch from north or north-west. The area around Balnoi and Mendhar was the responsibility of 120 Infantry Brigade. There the enemy, had established strongly at OP Hill Complex, which ultimately had to be cleared by one brigade group comprising of 7 SIKH, 5 SIKH LI and 2 DOGRA under command 120 Infantry Brigade on 2/3 November 1965.

Mann column, a sub-column of Sallahudin Force which came with full fury was blunted by 7 SIKH, responsible for the entire area starting from Kalai Bridge to Gali (602), the main axis of advance of infiltrators. The unit had fortunately been active in this area since its arrival in August, 1963 and was totally acclimatised and familiarised and was well-versed with the activities of the enemy, attitude of the civilian population and the normal enemy intelligence set up around. This helped it in great deal to blunt the move of Pakistanis. 7 SIKH did not permit the enemy to get a foothold in Mandi or Kalai Bridge area as was unfortunately done at OP Hill Complex in the area of 120 Infantry Brigade which remained under their occupation till 2/3 November 1965. The enemy was successful in crossing the CFL and reached its pre-decided "Bases" making use of weather conditions and the terrain. But once out they were checked by aggressive patrolling and laying of ambushes by 7 SIKH in entire Mandi Valley. The enemy did not dare to come out at night and move freely in general area. He was blunted everywhere, besides being totally unsuccessful in instigating the civil population.

Planning by the Enemy

Basically the aim of the enemy was to wrest Punch area alongwith the Valley of Kashmir. For doing that they had dispatched, various columns all around in Jammu and Kashmir. Depending upon the success of these columns, Pakistanis had planned a conventional attack on Punch from Gulpur/Pritam post side in coordination with an infiltration thrust via Mandi or Pir Mangot Ghazi on the Krishna Ghati ridge west of Khanater Gali. (See Sketch 15) This was visualised by CO 7 SIKH that any breakthrough by the enemy forces and joining of strong mobile columns at Kalai Bridge and around would entail the conventional attack on Punch immediately. Western Army Commander Lt Gen Harbakhsh Singh was more than clear on that issue and had ordered the move of HQ 52 Mountain Brigade with 8 Grenadiers which reached Sekhlu in Mandi Sub-sector on 11 August 1965, giving a much needed relief to the heavily engaged chain of posts along the Mandi, Sauji and Gali axis manned by 7 SIKH. Enemy had gone into jungles in small groups, which is always possible in such an area but they could not dislodge the battalion from that area. The credit to save the Punch bulge from Mandi side by blocking the enemy who was desperately trying for a link up at Kalai-Khanetar or Pir Mangot Ghazi goes to 7 SIKH. In Mandi Valley, the Gibraltars, were not permitted to consolidate and pursue any course towards fulfilling their aim. Once the situation was restored HQ 52 Mountain Brigade left immediately after and the whole situation was controlled by 7 SIKH alone. Though Gali Piquet was totally undefendable, isolated and sited in a bowl against all teachings, but still the unit gave a sterling and noteworthy account of itself by holding it for eight days against the well determined enemy. Had 7 SIKH buckled under the pressure of the enemy, the Punch bulge would have faced a very serious threat.

7 SIKH – The Saviour of Punch

It is a hard fact that:-

- A Sikh jawan is psychologically not worried about a Pakistani and reacts to his every move very boldly and tackles him with success. Even in very difficult situation, he comes out successful when led properly. This is his firm conviction that Pakis cannot beat him.

- The Commanding Officer, Lt Col Bhagat Singh had the advantage of serving in this area twice before and he knew the whole area backward. Fortunately the troops also had been operating in this active area for the last two years and were feeling confident all the time to face the enemy anywhere and anytime. It was never thought by any element of the battalion that Pakistanis could dislodge them from this area and establish and consolidate themselves.

- The establishing of the Battalion Tac HQ at Sauji gave a clear signal to the infiltrators that this unit is not going to allow them to move around freely. Sauji with battalion HQ became a nerve centre and was a big psychological boost for the CRPF and own unit personnel deployed on various posts like Kath Panjal, Kinari and Khet etc.

- The unit was made to look after a very large areas. Maintenance also was unit's responsibility. Thus the unit could not spare troops for creating reserves for launching proper mobile columns.

- There was no arty support available for the troops deployed in far flung areas in Mandi Valley. The unit had to manage everything without arty fire. This was the area, about which the corps commander was though most worried but still no additional troops or the arty support could be made available. As per them this was most threatened sector of 25 Infantry Division, but somehow dealing with the enemy was left to 7 SIKH.

- When the troops fell back from Gali, Sher Post was established on Molsar Ridge on the track junction, south east of Khet. This stopped the moves of the raiders in this area from north along the ridge and from Loran. Though the unit suffered few casualties but the enemy move was altogether blunted. The enemy did not use that approach for coming from Loran to Mandi Valley, anymore.

- The unit did suffer casualties at all the places like Mandi, Molsar, Sauji and Gali but befitting reply was given whenever contact was established and chased the enemy out, wherever reported from. Security demands sacrifices.

- The civilian population was largely non-supportive of Pakistanis except some odd person, but that happens every where. That was the main reason that the enemy could not find any foothold because the unit used to get info about their presence immediately from the civilians and through other reliable sources.

- District/civil administration was given all possible help and that kept on functioning which created confidence in civil population. Re-capture of Mandi gave lot of confidence for sustaining the morale of the civil officers.

- The main aim of the enemy was to make the public revolt against the Indian Government and Civil administration and hence the plan was made first to establish in the area and then the conventional attack could have come at later stage for capturing Punch.

- Lt Col Bhagat Singh, Commanding Officer 7 SIKH though very cautious had always ensured that the whole area was patrolled and screened and the enemy was tracked after, religiously. Patrolling was planned and executed vigorously. There were certain heights which were occupied and dominated by the enemy for a short while but soon these heights were also cleared and the enemy could hold no ground in Mandi Valley. Once the area of track junction, just north of Mandi town was occupied by own troops enemy could not do much against the posts or column of 7 SIKH. Psychologically, the troops were neither surprised nor scared of Pakistanis as such activities had been taking place even before the actual hostilities and Operation Gibraltar.

Conclusion

Pakistanis were hoping that the Muslim population would revolt against the Indian Government and they would be welcomed but it was not to be so. Their move was first reported by the civilians only on 3/4 August 1965 and Brig Zora Singh was up at Gali Piquet on 5 August and Lt Col Bhagat Singh had established his HQ at Sauji on 6 August. The Gibraltars could have never imagined that they will be stopped at Gali only and they will be thrown out from Mandi so soon. They were made to deliver by indoctrination on religious basis stating that there was a total persecution of Muslims in India but they forgot to note that *"He that toucheth pitch shall be defied there with."* Gibraltars had big dream and they had made plans which could have looked workable but the strength and the will of Indian troops, which was going to confront them was miscalculated and proved to be miscomfiture in the long run. They planned meticulously but ignored the fact that their strength was only false sense of religion and not logic and reason.

17

YOUNG COMMANDERS AND LEADERS

"War is just when it is necessary, arms are permissible, when there is no hope except in arms" —Machiavelli

Nature of the Man

Man has been fighting since his evolution. Fighting becomes necessary for one's survival. Nobody can avoid it for long. To safe guard his own interest is part of man's primary thinking process. Man finds a reason for fighting and gets involved into it. Not only man alone, all living beings fight for supremacy and controlling the surroundings. War is never good and peace is never bad, but it is out of the control of human beings, who all are ambitious. All the talk of the history is nothing else but fighting and killing, primarily coaxed by politics. All the great civilisations in their early stages established themselves, based on their successes in the wars. Eminent scholars in the long distant past of the Indian history advocated war as an essential element of maintaining the society and its values. War is mentioned in our scriptures as an inescapable requirement for living peacefully. There are not many countries which could equal India, in advancement of war

Author (Left) with Lt Ravel Singh, Lt SK Singh and Lt MS Punia after the war

for preserving peace in the bygone centuries. Vedas, Puranas and other such scriptures have all glorified war. Ramayana and Mahabharata are among the noted ones. All the heroes of Ramayana and Mahabharata have been excellent warriors. Even if we take these as fictions, very rightly they depict the then prevailing thinking on war machinery and role of leaders and commanders.

Kautalya's Arthashastra is a masterpiece on warfare besides being a guide on business of State affairs. It is part of great Indian mythology. Going to the battle, in Indian context even today is taken as a sacred duty for a young man specially of countryside. Before the advancement of Buddhism, preparing for war was an essential act of the State. During the emperor Ashoka's time, it got a severe jolt and warfare came to be considered as an evil. Since then the Indian philosophy changed and assertion, aggressiveness and martial advancement on warfare unfortunately took the back seat.

War is thus a necessary evil and it cannot be avoided. It is ordained by human nature that a stronger will try to subjugate the weaker and for surviving himself, the so-called weaker will arm himself for maintaining his sovereignty and freedom. It is better, he thinks, that we should die fighting rather than being outraged and dishonoured. It is worth dying then to serve in slavery. *"When all peaceful means fail it is righteous to take up sword"* – Guru Gobind Singh.

Foreign Invasions

Our country in the past couple of centuries, has gone through a bad patch of historical ground where the outsiders came and destroyed, looted and denigrated its people and raped its surroundings. Muslim invaders came, established their rule in India and made the people to convert to Islam and later, the Christianity too, exploited the country to the worst limit. India has been subjected to a foreign onslaught for long time. Mercenaries came, plundered and left with the spoils of war, with little or no resistance from us. We were a divided lot and could not unite in face of external aggression. Later the colonial powers ruled us ruthlessly with impunity. During the foreigners rule the country was deliberately and manipulatively divided on the basis of religion, region, cast, creed and colour and the outsiders made full use of it. During this period though the armies were there, but they were only with the individual different States. Indian Army, as a Central Force was not existing. The country could not assert itself as one entity and the result was, the country remained under a foreign yoke for a very long time. The British after defeating one state used to make it join them and help fighting against the others and thus subjugated them all, one by one.

The birth of a "Khalsa" is the result of continuous atrocities of Muslim rulers on the population of the country, culminating into conversion of the masses. There was no way out except picking up the arms against the mighty Mughals. Guru Gobind Singh, seeing the outcome and pattern of continuously bringing war at it doorsteps, raised the army of Khalsas, so that the country and its population were saved. That gave a new twist to the whole system and for the first time after a long spell of history, the idea of nationalism sprang up during Maharaja Ranjit Singh's rule. But British again broke that Sikh Army, however fortunately, the identity of the nation had come into being for recognition which helped reorganisation of its Army and the State, though a bit later.

The above given details are enough to understand that the war is necessary and even a must for preserving the interest of the State. So to be prepared for war is a duty of the power that be in the country and the primary role of all commanders and leaders of men at all levels for developing and innovating new methods of warfare. Developing the war machinery and educating the men to the level of a jawan in essentials of warfare is therefore very necessarily important.

Command as an Element of Power

Command is an element of power of authority or control to give orders or instructions, invested in a person by law, based on his professional skill, competence and merit and whose orders are to be obeyed ungrudgingly and willingly in toto, taking them as one's duty for his prescribed role and the commander uses his authority, influence and esteem or all for fulfilling it. In simple words 'Command is Enforced.'

There are various types of commanders who come up depending upon their native qualities, interest, training and situation. That is why every commander varies his style of command and as such, no two commanders are of the same type. One excels because of his specific quality, the other does it due to his own peculiar characteristics. Army is a set-up by itself, which is the combination of human beings and material equipment, brought together in a systematic and effective coordination to accomplish a desired task. Man forms the main cog of that machine. Any weakness in this part will have a direct bearing on the whole organisation. Man is a thinking machine and is versatile and start oscillating with a slight wrong push to its sensitivity by unwarranted and uncalculated nibbing. The regular and constant study of this aspect by commanders is thus very important, before the doubts are cast and damage is done. The problems have become more acute and vexed with educated and well informed persons joining the force, which entails placing of considerable emphasis on splendid and good relations and unwavering commitments of the power that be. For venturing for total success, the aspect of maintaining the 'Man' part of army machine can never therefore be lost the sight of. It requires perpetual repairing and greasing of this "thinking" machine by its commanders.

Role of Officers

The officers are the life of an army unit. The officer is a commander who must be a capable person. The commander who gives an order should be an example in himself for performing that and the order must be practicable and within the capabilities of the men. The officer cadre therefore becomes the most important part of the whole organisation. The officers are to be kept fully fit in all respects. They are to be trained and educated properly so that they can lead the men. A weak officer will not be able to earn goodwill, lead the troops in battle and achieve desired results. The officers are to be made fully responsible and clear cut orders are given to them for the job to be done. A person who is expert in taking timely and appropriate action, weaponry, tactical deployment of troops, ways of blunting the move of enemy, who is not a boy but a matured, brave and trained person in soldiering and is able bodied and who is intent on performing his duty, and is always loyal to his superiors, such a person from whatever caste or parentage, will make a good commander for military duties.

Every officer commissioned in the army cannot reach the highest point as promotion is unfortunately in a pyramid shape and only one will be on top. The officers who do not get the opportunity or do not make to the higher rank start losing interest. Such officers are required to be managed effectively by government through policies and by senior commanders on the spot. Give them fair deal, ensure their entitlements and give them job and deal with them firmly. They are to be told that they are being paid for a job and that job has to be done by them and done well. For dealing with such elements, who have developed a little sense of arrogance and lethargy, a commander of high repute, as boss, is the only answer. "Don't trouble troubles unless troubles trouble you" should never be practised by senior commanders. The problem can be solved only by a man who is fair, impartial, firm, competent, honest and well-meaning. Ninety nine per cent officers, who are in need of the monthly emoluments will have no cause to be disinterested in front of right and firm commander.

Ambitious Commanders

Ambitions are natural with human beings. Though an ambition in itself is a vice, yet it often is the parent of virtues. It is the germ from which all growth of nobleness proceeds. But it is also to be understood that ambition is like love, impatient of both delay and rivals. It is not a weakness unless it be disproportioned to the capacities. To have more ambitions than the ability is to be unsatisfied and unhappy. It is the ambitions which make men liars and cheats, who hide the truth in their hearts and like jugglers, show another thing, to cut all friendships and camaraderie to the measure of their interest and put on a good face, when there is no corresponding goodwill. In our context commanders at certain levels are over ambitious. As a result, their self interest causes many hardships to the subordinates. It has to be checked in the right earnest. A wise man will know his own capabilities and work accordingly and achieves deservedly. It is a point worth pondering that commanders keep on changing enjoying field and peace and hard and soft tenures but the man remains the same and does face the hardship as a new and ambitious commander puts the unit to spin. In case of the same tempo is not maintained the commanders attitude becomes punitive rather than sympathetic. But it is also to be kept in mind by all that success in war depends on a particular standard to be achieved. Proper balance therefore between fairness and commitment is to be maintained. However, the ruthlessness does play a role at the crucial movement, let us face facts. A weak commander will not be able to take the men into battle. A commander with impeccable integrity, high professional caliber, total commitment to service, broadminded and a tough task master who is feared and yet respected by his subordinates, only can take the men in battle, make them to fight and achieve success.

Men Joining Armed Forces

Men coming to the army, now a days in a free country like ours are better educated and more democratic in their approach towards various issues in military life. They are apt to clarify and reason out, the ifs, buts and whys and hows of the things. Mere seniority for officers or JCOs will not solve the problems. Officer should be well read, competent in his profession and capable to answer all points or queries raised by the subordinates. He is supposed to know the life style of the men to be in better position to deal with them effectively. As he belongs to the same stock, as that of men has got the added advantage. If a man is given fair deal, he will find no reason for not to have interest in his job and faith in commanders, which is so crucial in battle. He should be given his due everywhere. Giving him his total entitlements and asking him to perform should be the aim and it is the best 'mantar'. Scrupulous observance of rules for promotion, honours and awards and punishment too, should be adhered to, for keeping the man in his element. Unfair dealing is bound to have abated his spirit, where a justified decision will create a positive and assuring climate. A good order will never be disobeyed, even in most difficult circumstances.

The weak civil administration and corruption in civil life cause troubles to the families of men and that will have direct effect on the efficiency of men and their devotion to duty. The officers will be required to help them out. Though too much of familiarities will breed contempt but at the same time informal visit to the men in leisure time and at times meeting them individually with regards to their problems will solve lot of them and help officers in consolidating their command. Appreciation of the work done, avoiding over supervision but being firm in dealing, will keep the men on right track. There is no short cut other than maintaining a highest degree of discipline – obeying orders and get your orders obeyed.

To be precise, we can say that "to bully or bluster, pamper or please, spying or sneak or giving punishment or fatigue in not command, to give a just and fair deal is command."

Leadership as an Obligation

Leadership is nobility or rank which has got its own obligation. Everything hinges on leader. He has to give his best at every occasion. Beside duty, it is his obligation to do and do it right way and for the interest of all. For success everyone in his place is to be honoured but for every failure, he has to be responsible and that is what his position conveys to him. In order to understand the qualities of a military leader, we have got some definitions of great military commanders of our times, which are immensely useful.

> "Leadership is the will to dominate, together with the character which inspires confidence" —FM Montgomery

> "It is a projection of personality. It is that combination of persuasion, compulsion and example that makes other people do what you want them to do." —FM Slim

> "Leadership is the knack of getting somebody to do something you want done because he wants to do it" —General Eisanhower

Kautalaya the great ancient Indian military thinker has described the qualities of Military leader in even more acute details like:

"Possessed of sharp intellect, strong memory and keen mind, energetic, powerful, trained in all kinds of arts, free from vices, capable of paying in the same coin by way of awarding punishments or awards, possessed by dignity, capable of taking remedial measures against dangers, possessed of foresight, ready to avail himself of opportunities, when afforded in respect of place, time and manly efforts, clear enough to discern the causes necessitating the cessation of treaty or war with an enemy or to lie in wait keeping treaties, obligations and pledges or to avail himself of his enemy's weak points."

From the above definitions, it becomes clear that various leaders would like to do the things differently in their own way, depending upon their own dominating qualities. Leaders have to lead by their action to command and control and order the men to move and perform and not by himself becoming the first casualty when not warranted. For a situation, where a commander becomes a casualty an other capable man groomed to take over is made available, to pick up pieces and carry on regardless.

Military Leadership – A Complex Art

Leaders are required in all fields of activities. Wherever there are men, some one has to lead them. It is an important requirement but for military career and profession, especially, it is crucial and is of paramount importance. It is that element of unpredictability in the field of war, which makes military leadership such a complex art. Warfare is an art and not a science in its practical sense and as such no formula for victory can be prescribed. The training in peacetime can help tying up details and drills, but can never stimulate the real battlefield conditions and develop crucial responses, which is the need of the hour to deal with the fast changing situation in war. *Man in peacetime training and in war are two different personages and the reactions to actions are totally different*. Psychology of the two in two different situations will be altogether different. All leaders can be good commanders, but all commanders are not necessarily be the good leaders as already said that *command is enforcement of orders whereas leadership is obligation for leading*. War is the best training ground and the leadership is an art which is actually learnt in war. Though it is generally taken now a days that leaders are not born but made, but the basic Native Qualities are still essential. We see various actions, embodying the same situations that various commanders of same age, same background, same education and same training behave very differently. It means the aspect of being born as commander cannot altogether be ruled out. But this all besides, hard and advanced study on warfare will find out and make them as such and that is why so much time is spent in military academies all over the world, for the training of future military leaders. In this connection, for understanding whether leader are born or are made, the words of Admiral Sherman of USA are very apt.

> *"We can take average good men and by providing hard training, develop in them the essential initiative, confidence and magnetism, which are necessary in leadership. I believe that these qualities are present in the average man to a degree that he can be made a good leader if his native (innate/inborn) qualities are properly developed; whether or*

not he possesses that extra initiative, magnetism and moral courage, which make the difference between the man and above average man."

Traits of Military Leadership

The aim of the military leadership is to create required faith and confidence about himself, in his men so that they may go in, whenever ordered or they may follow him, in any situation against the enemy. The style of each commander is different which depends upon his own mental approach to it, thereby dictating whether he leads from a position of authority or influence. In war, the influence affects the outcome, but authority is also very important without which, the difficult situation are seldom overcome. Let us face facts and understand that everyone is scared of death and does not go on to the enemy so easily. It is the authority, discipline and training coupled with personal influence, of leader which makes it a success. In short, if an influential leader is placed in a position of command, he can lead with great flexibility and use both of his power i.e. authority when necessary and influence when appropriate. In other words the status and esteem, both are necessary for coercion and persuasion in an hour of need. Anyway, whatever style and power leader uses, he has to have certain inherent qualities which make him an effective leader. These are enumerated in the succeeding paras:-

- **Organising Ability**: A successful leader is a good organiser. He has to organise training and coordinate various aspects of management to make the organisation fit for participating in an action. He has to discard the non-essentials and makes sound plans. He organises his unit/

sub-units and provides them guidance and supervision where required. He has to ensure that every unit or sub-unit performs its given task. To make everyone do his duty at its required place is the crux of ability for organizing.

- **Willpower**: A good leader has to have a willpower to do a job. In face of enemy, it is the willpower of commander which counts. Both, enemy as well as self are affected, incapacitated, worn out and disorganised, but the winner is he who, coolheadedly and with strong will power sticks to his ground for an extra minute. He who seizes the right moment is the winner.

- **Professional Skill & Knowledge**: A leader is required to be a voracious reader. He must know his job well and keep improving in view of the latest development in organisation, methods of warfare, and the new technological advancements. It will give him added confidence to command and lead the men in war.

- **Initiative & Determination**: When the time of reckoning comes, it is the commander on the scene, who has to take decision according to the situation. He has to take initiative and no one else except his common-sense will help him at that crucial moment. He has to be determined to act assertively and survive to defeat the enemy.

- **Integrity & Character**: a leader has to have integrity which will straightway endear him to his subordinates. A man of character will withstand any assault on his prowess. There is a great hope for men, in the character of the leaders. It is diamond only that scratches every other stones. Where the talents are best nurtured in solitude, the character is best formed in stormy billows of the world and truthfulness becomes the cornerstone of character.

- **Dedication & Commitment**: Leader, who is dedicated to his profession, can be an example before his men. He has a commitment to the profession and if he is ready to sacrifice his life, when duty demands, no one dare ignore his orders, however difficult the situation may be. Fact is that there is no command without leadership and effective leadership is required for wining a war. It is necessity and necessity makes even a timid, brave.

Leadership of 7 SIKH

7 SIKH was raised in 1963 at Meerut by Lt Col Bhagat Singh, as a new unit. The troops for new 7 SIKH came from almost all old units. Some senior officers were also posted from other units such as Maj Sukhmal Sen from 2 SIKH, Capt Jagdev Singh from 18 SIKH and Lt Trilochan Singh from 5 SIKH etc. 2/Lt Surjit Singh, 2/Lt Santosh Kumar and 2/Lt Sansar Singh were posted directly as regular officers from IMA. Quite a large number of officers from Emergency Courses came and joined the unit. The unit organised its training and after the needful was done, it was moved to Punch Sector in Jammu and Kashmir in August 1963. Maj KG Belliappa took over as the Second in Command, Capt Jagdev Singh became company commander and Lt Trilochan Singh took over as an Adjutant. The author joined the unit on 17 September 1964 at Punch.

Conventional Training

Training for a new raising is very-very important. Without proper training, the unit cannot be in a shape to go and take part in active operations, which will be very risky. Training is light and lack of training is darkness. If a peasant does not know how to plough, he cannot grow crops. Same way untrained man can achieve nothing. A properly trained man is worth ten in battle. Training therefore for the job is a marvellous thing. At Meerut, the elementary training was carried out, field firing was done, night training and long marches were resorted to but the collective training for taking the battalion for attack, infiltration and assembling across enemy lines, and battalion in defence with the exercises finishing at Brigade, Division and Corps level etc could not carried out. The fact is that the unit had finished its assembling process, and could not carry out rigorous training, which is the bread and butter of profession. It was primarily due to the immediate move of the unit to field area, a national imperative.

It would not make any sense to have a military outfit if it is not properly trained in practical military aspects for knowing basics of operations. The old formula, firmly etched in the primal reaches of army's memory, from the days of the thousand years ago when army first came into being is SKILL + WILL = KILL and this simple and fundamental formula still holds good. Agreed, some people are born brave but they are a very few. Most become brave through hard training and force of strict discipline. The unit however did carry out required training at Punch before occupying posts but that hard training as mentioned above demanded larger wherewithal which was not there. Urgency necessitated it to occupy defences on the CFL against Pakistanis.

Practical Training on Posts

Punch was operationally an active area. The unit was deployed in two sub-sectors, Mandi Sub-sector and Betar Sub-sector and occupied posts along the CFL. There used to be regular firing and encounters between Pakistani and Indian troops. Except arty, all type of firing including MMG and 3" Mors used to be a routine affair. The young officers used to go for ambushes and patrolling during night and almost entire area of responsibility was effectively dominated by the battalion. Then came the Kutchh operation, which is discussed separately whence nothing much, save, the regular exchange of fire took place in this area, though the activities got intensified. The requirements of the operations were well understood and learned. The whole battalion, by virtue of its stay and getting regularly engaged in activities for two years on FDLs got practically trained and became competent to deal with the enemy confidently. 2/Lt Ravel Singh, Lt Sansar Singh, 2/Lt Hardial Sing, 2/Lt SS Sandhu, 2/Lt MS Punia, Capt Santosh Kumar, Capt GP Bhandari and 2/Lt SS Ahlawat were the officers who were most of the time on the posts and carried out independent missions across the CFL.

Officer's Training Cadres

Regular orientation cadres were organised for newly commissioned officers as they all had done only about six months of training in IMA/OTA and did require regular training to be fit for fighting and leading troops in an operational area. All young officers were compulsorily made to attend these cadres first at the battalion level and then at the Formation level. Another point which I would like to make here is that commanding officer had to give the responsibilities to certain selected JCOs to do as senior JCOs of the companies who could also fill the gap as officiating company commander, if the permanent incumbent was away and no other officer was available. This practice was picked up immediately after the Independence and during the organizing of the army for 1947-48 operations, when there was acute shortage of officers in the army. It however, had plus and minus points. For controlling the men and disciplining them, there could be need of the JCO, and that is okay but operationally a JCO cannot take the place and role of an officer due to his training in leadership, age, education and capabilities. The unit became popular with the civilians, due to human approach of the commanding officer and battle worthiness of Sikh soldiers in dealing with the enemy.

The civilian population in Punch area, though dominantly Muslims there were Hindus and Sikhs also, who were very helpful. Muslims were sandwiched between India and Pakistan and those who had divided loyalties in some cases, had to lead a difficult life. As the part of this area like Kotli, Muzzafrabad etc were under Pakistan's occupation, their families were divided and had relations on both sides of CFL. As such, in some cases their loyalties were suspected. But by and large the Muslim population was not pro-Pakistan. Pakistan could neither understand the Kashmiris, nor Kashmiriat. These Muslims were different from the Muslims of Pakistani Punjab. Historically also, Kashmiri Muslim is from a different stock and culturally, he is not having much in common with others like Punjabi Muslims, Pathans and Baluchis. Even Sindhis, Pathans and Baluchis of Pakistan considered themselves different from Pakistani Punjabis. In such a situation, during 1965 we were better placed to deal with the civilians for cooperation and positivity due to commonality of agriculture as profession, language to a large extent and culture and traditions.

Commanding Officer and His Team

The aim of inclusion of this chapter in the battle account of 7 SIKH is to compare the performance of the unit operations against the parameters of command and leadership traits mentioned herein. As mentioned the SIKH regiment has been doing the yeoman's service for the consolidation of the united India by being at the front in all the operations fought. In fact a Sikh solider has got hereditary love for his weapon and serves his honour and has never been out of any military adventure. 7 SIKH an outfit command by a dedicated, methodical and God-fearing officer did well in the 1965 operations. It is a different thing that commanding officer may have not come to the expectations of some, at some places, who could not judge the difficulties, commitments of the unit and enormity of the tasks given to the battalion. Lt Col Bhagat Singh was a respected personality who was equally feared by those who could not come to the required standard of a soldier. He like everyone else, could have one or two weakness but he was clear, prompt and able. He at times looked to be influenced by the views of few in whom he had more faith and who basically could be cause of his difficulties in some of the actions fought by the battalion. Certain people were seen enjoying greater liberty beyond their sphere and used it for professionally seducing the others and serving their own cause well. Lt Col Bhagat Singh was a man of his own ideas and conveyed the same fearlessly and forcefully to Brigade Commander 93 Infantry Brigade. He was more than emphatic about Gali Post to be readjusted and get more resources for Operation Phanne-Shah (details of both these Operations are given in the respective chapters). He was not one of those who could enjoy life in golf, cards or sip drinks. He was concerned about the battalion and that endeared him to the men. He was a voracious reader and maintained an excellent collection of military history books in officer's mess including Kautalya's Arthshastra, Maccivelli's The Prince and Sun –Tzu's Art of Warfare etc. He made the officers to read every book available with the unit. I remember having been ordered to go to English Book Depot Delhi and Dehradun and get number of books from there. Being a man of strong convictions he could not carry along certain senior officers in the unit and thus could not use them properly. That made him to wholly depend upon a few officers and JCOs.

Young Leaders and an Active Area

Punch Sector was an active area even before the outbreak of hostilities. The unit was fortunate to have large number of junior officers, who were loyal, hard working and very matured, while dealing with men. They were groomed well, made to go for various operations very often and were committed to the cause. Maj Trilochan Singh (later Maj Gen) remained as a strong adjutant for a very long time, who finally commanded 'C' company very successfully in OP Hill and contributed to the success of the operation. Maj Santosh Kumar was with the battalion through out and in operation Phanne-Shah, he was with the forward most element. He commanded 'D' company in OP Hill. A person with a very jovial disposition, had been the life of functions and festivities before and after the war. In Late Capt Surjit Singh and Late 2/Lt SS Sandhu, the unit lost two very good officers at a time when they both were required most, Capt Sansar Singh, VrC (later Col), who is our hero of the OP Hill, where he commanded 'A' Company, is a man with cool and very matured habits. He proved, as commander in the battle where he ensured that his command was intact after having suffered lot of casualties and propelled them on to enemy, by being at the centre of his command. 2/Lt Ravel Singh, a very bold, young, energetic and forthright officer, who was popular with the men. He was Mor Platoon Commander in all operations fought by the battalion. He did his job marvellously and needed no supervision. In all operations with diligence and thoughtful assertion, he gave the most intimate support to troops with his mors. In the Battle of Mandi, he ensured that with his Mor fire, Mandi town was totally cleared of enemy before the troops passed through for the capture of feature dominating the town. 2/Lt Hardial Singh was one of the officers, who was available for all operations. A bold, young, and physically fit person, he was the architect of chasing the infiltrators from Mandi Valley, engaging them boldly at Molsar Ridge, leading the troops in Phanne-Shah and securing an important foothold on the Jungle Hill, which facilitated the capture of the respective objectives by 7 SIKH and 2 DOGRA, in Battle of OP Hill. Capt SK Singh was the MMG platoon commander, who remained very busy during operations. Leading maintenance column to Mandi Valley, through the bullets of infiltrators and reinforcing and evacuation of the casualties from Sauji and Molsar ridge, goes to his credit. 2/Lt MS Punia a very sober, matured and a well read officer who took part in all active operations. He carried out successful raid across the CFL before the battle in later half of 1964, which earned appreciation of senior commanders. He did as intelligence officer in Battles of Mandi and OP Hill. It was due to a great determination and courage on his part for having laid the tape as close as 200 yards from the objective in the Battle of OP Hill, which helped the troops, a great deal in maintaining the axis of attack. He has been an asset to the battalion and the commanding officer besides being a lively and affable colleague.

Sense of Commitment

2/Lt Dewinder Singh commanded the troops at Gali Picquet. Inspite of all odds against him, the officer stayed put at Gali and gave a most thrilling account of himself by delaying the enemy by fighting for eight days. He himself killed two enemy men with his personal weapon and was an example of cool courage and boldness. Seeing him, the man fought like tigers and gave an account of conspicuous bravery. He delivered with efficiency and alacrity and measured himself to the expectations of all. Everybody talked about his actions at Gali post in glowing terms.

Yours truly, 2/Lt SS Ahlawat (later Lt Col) was as an officer who was present in all actions fought by the battalion in 1965 operations. I was the leading platoon commander of 'B' Company in the capture of Mandi, where Pathan enemy soldiers of the so-called dreaded SSG of Pakistan were killed in face to face encounter. It was because of this incident that we came to know the involvement of the Pakistani Para Commando Force. Led a raid on a Pakistani post first at Kabar Ki Dheri and later on a Pakistani post at Ring Contour, north-west of Punch before the Battle of Phanne-Shah. In the Battle of OP Hill, formed the part of force of hard trained commandos who were placed astride track leading to Punch via Achhahard, north of Mendhar River for launching anywhere anytime for any task, if situation so demanded. 2/Lt RS Cheema, Capt GP Bhandari, 2/Lt AJS Ram and others who were with the battalian played no less a role. 2/Lt RS Cheema took part in Operation Phanne-Shah and Battle of OP Hill as a platoon commander. Capt GP Bhandari was commanding Adm Company and was really hardpressed for doing the needful for troops. 2/Lt AJS Ram was the MTO and did a good job in the battle of OP Hill for transporting men and material.

They Made Things to happen

In the end, I would like to say that true commander has some specific traits like wisdom, humility respect, integrity, dignity and courage and the young commanders of 7 SIKH gloriously displayed these traits in 1965 War with Pakistan in Punch Sector. They with their wisdom humbled the enemy, with their humility they were endeared by men, with their respect they selected the right man for right moment, with their integrity they solidified their command, with their dignity they kept the whole lot unified and with their courage they raised the moral of troops at various occasions. I do not want to bemoan the fact, though the unit faced the untoward situations at times, but never because of these enthusiastic young leaders. They were those who made the things happen and not those who watched the things happen or those who wondered what had happened. They all were the men of action. Their role was to command and commit themselves to the tasks allotted, decision-making was always with the commanding officer.

18
JUNIOR LEADERSHIP

"One man with courage makes a majority"
—Andrew Jackson

Junior Leaders

Junior leadership, in real sense of the word means the leaders at the lower rungs of the ladder. It includes NCOs and JCOs. Some senior officers try to include the junior or young officers also in this but officers is a different class by itself. An officer is specially trained as a leader. His selection in a protracted way taking almost five days and then his training for over a period of almost four years mainly deals with inculcating of leadership qualities required in the battlefield. They in turn have to train, guide and lead their own sub-units in battle. It is a well researched technique, where everyone is made to accept duties and take responsibilities for performing the assigned tasks.

Creation of JCO Rank

A JCO is a promotee from the lower ranks and over a period of time reaches to this rank. Basically he is not trained, in the real sense of the term, as a leader, in our context for leading troops.

This rank was created by the British as a link rank which still exists but only in Indian and Pakistan armies. No other country of the world is having such a rank in its army. At one stage the British were willing to grant the independence to India but with one rider that it will be self governing territory of British Commonwealth. It will have an autonomous character, with its own Government machinery including the military. They were articulating that as the contemplated Viceroy's Government in India will be tutelage of British Government in England, its army will have the Viceroy's Commissioned Officers who after sometimes, with the advent of education will get better stuff and with training at academies in England and India, they as officers will be able to shoulder the responsibilities of commanding the Indian troops in peace and war. It simply means that Indian Government will be independent with its complete wherewithal but a protege under Government in Britain. It was this reason that this rank of JCO was propped up and created. Of course the genesis of the theory lay in the link criteria, required between British Officers and Indian troops for understanding the problems of culture, traditions and language. This ideas was however rejected, outrightly by the Indian leaders fighting for complete Independence i.e. "Puran Sawaraj."

JCOs and Mercenary Army

British used to make the JCOs to lead the men in battle but under their direct supervision. The casualty rate of the JCO rank in those days used to be much higher than the British officers. It means that the JCOs were, those promoted persons who were capable of leading the men into battle and could understand the tactical requirements. They had very intimate relationship with men and knew their capabilities better than officers. If they are properly trained and made responsible for leading them into battle and face the consequences thereafter, they can produce better results. The British made them responsible and at the same time awarded them for gallantry very liberally. But that army was a mercenary army of a foreign power and the soldiers were paid for fighting for them. The context was different. The things are totally different in free India. It is not a police state under a dictator but a welfare state where humanism plays a big role. The British were never worried about the casualties of the Indian soldiers, whereas, in our context, avoiding the loss a trained man, means something. The aspect of warfare has undergone a substantial change. The concept of hand to hand fighting is no more relevant in view of the technological advancement of weaponry. The concept of fighting itself has experienced a sea change.

Factors Affecting Performance of JCOs

There was and still there is a very large number of JCOs in an infantry battalion. Even during days of British, the number of the JCOs in a unit used to be quite large. The requirement was that they must lead the troops into battle as platoon commanders and occasionally as officiating company commanders. In thirties the Indian officers Commissioned from IMA and some from British academy had started coming in units. In free India, however army carried this along and used JCOs extensively in 1947-48 Indo-Pak War. Their performance in the Indo-Pak War of 1965 however was really not very complemental. That was the reason that every action had to be led by a young officer. Some young, good and educated JCOs, of course led the troops and made a good work of the enemy. Why did the JCOs, in overall view, not perform well as required, was due to following reasons:

- **Education**: The JCOs were mostly uneducated or educated upto primary level and to understand the new tactical requirements, education is very important. Tactical concepts cannot be cleared to an uneducated person though once he is made to understand as to what he is supposed to do, he can produce results. But that is the role of a jawan and not that of a JCO. A JCO in our context as a platoon commander is required to lead his sub-unit and we should make him to do that. There is tremendous pressure on the national exchequer towards the payment of the dues of JCO class as a whole and their services should be utilised to the maximum, which was neither done during 1965 operation nor even now to be precise.

- **Age**: Age is a very important factor. A man at the age, roughly around 40 years and above cannot lead the troops. There is certain age to perform in war, after which strength forsakes and debility increases. That is why most of the senior JCOs managed to sulk down to the level of an administrative JCO. Very few and that too, the young and bold individuals only did produce results and contributed to the success of the operations.

- The stark reality is that once he becomes a JCO, he loses interest and tries to play from outside. He realises that he has nothing more to gain and plays safe.

- **No Provision of Training of JCOs as Leaders**: There was hardly any training carried out for the JCOs to be the leaders. To lead men in the battle, one is required to have proper tactical knowledge and one should have capabilities of a leader which can be inculcated. Everyone cannot be the leader of troops in war. For that, special training is required which was not organised for JCOs at that time. It is not available even now. But some JCOs being educated and otherwise as intelligent persons used to do well. 7 SIKH was having few good JCOs who could contribute in the operations but majority of them were slow in uptake and were not willing for leading the men in do or die missions.

Making Best Use of JCOs

However, notwithstanding the above, as far as the training on weapon, understanding the terrain, ground configuration and individually facing the enemy, goes JCOs were well-trained. Only important point to be understood here is that they were not capable as leaders and in most of the cases they were not even willing to lead the troops in battle and take risks. This has been very vividly brought out by various battalion commanders. But still the JCOs rank forms the major portion of the leaders at junior level. Some points which merit attention for making best use of JCOs are:-

- They have got general experience of the service life and have enough experience for the conduct of operations. As far as 7 SIKH was concerned the JCOs had the complete knowledge of the area and helped the officers in their tasks for going in for any operation. General contribution of the JCOs specially the young ones was good. They had the rationale and professional approach and knew their men well. The commanding officer wanted them to perform and he used to stress upon them for performance. He had quite a faith in JCOs more than young officers in certain cases.

- There was, then, no system of training of JCOs like officers do in OTA/IMA. The JCO should be young and should be trained in an academy minimum for a year to year and half without which they will not be able to lead the troops in battle. The deficiency in office rank can be, somehow temporarily made up by putting young and good JCO in responsible jobs. Officers are heavily burdened in an infantry battalion, whereas JCOs being such a large in number, relatively are not that hard pressed. Selected havildars, who are likely to be made JCO should be trained in the established academies. Even the direct recruitment of young as JCOs like in BSF, CRPF and other Central Police Organisations as sub-inspectors, will be better than the present system. We cannot afford to tire out young officers for the sake of JCOs.

NCOs and their Contribution

A Sikh NCO is brave, courageous and willing to perform his duty very well provided he is led by a very competent leader. He is like a wild horse and a weak commander will not be able to handle him. He is sensible, intelligent and responsible but needs strong handling. NCOs of 7 SIKH played the most important role in all operations. They led their sections very well and were not found wanting, where guided by the capable officers. They were very successful and proved their worth in Mandi, Gali and OP Hill operations in an exemplary manner. Their understanding of the ground realities is excellent as they are primarily from farming communities who are out in fields day and night. He is thoroughly rooted to the soil and is a member of hardy family of farmers. The fact is that his career including punishment and awards are entirely in the hands of commanding officer, whereas after his becoming a JCOs the criteria changes and power and authority to deal with him get diluted, rather transmitted to higher ranking officers. It makes a difference.

Performing Team

Battles are won by and large by the intrepidity of men of the ranks from a jawan to captain, because they are always quick to act and are bold. Fear is contagious but courage is no less so. The courage of any one man reflects in some degree the courage of all those, who are within his vision and view. To the man who is in terror and bordering on panic, no influence can be more steadying than that of seeing some other near him who is retaining self control and boldly doing his duty. The role played by 2/Lt Dewinder Singh and Nk Shangara Singh at Gali fits in here very aptly.

Food for Thought

Lt Gen Harbakhsh Singh of SIKH Regiment was an outstanding field commander, the Indian Army had produced who was popularly known as, War General, because he fought all the wars as commander and came out with sterling successes. He was an astute authority on warfare in the Indian context and his comments are taken as "Golden Rules." He after having seen the performance and contribution of the JCOs in the army during 1965 War had this to say. *"I have recommended the elimination of the rank of the JCO in Indianised units for whatever arm, as this is a legacy from the days of British, which has become an anachronism – (outdated)."* He explained that there was an anomaly that exists in our Army since British days – that is the JCO formerly known as Viceroy's Commissioned Officer (VCO).

VCO was created by the British to provide a link between the British officers and the Indian other ranks because of the different cultures, customs and languages. He is senior than a warrant officer and junior to a commissioned officer. It is a typical colonial legacy. When they introduced Indianisation in the army in early thirties, the British themselves abolished this rank and replaced the VCOs with young Indian Commissioned Officers trained in the IMA Dehradun. This measure unfortunately had to be shelved during the Second World War, as the output of the officers from the newly established IMA could not meet the requirement of rapidly expanding Indian Army.

Beating back a Deadly Raid

Regular dominance with single minded devotion and steely resilience will surely stave off aggressive activities of the enemy. Old lot of JCOs of the pre-independence days had little different opinion about the duties, because the British used to give them specific duties and wanted definite results. In that system, the JCOs used to be made responsible and were never spared for non-performance. That produced number of good JCOs, who at places, changed the course of events. There were couple of JCOs of this brand with us also, and that was the reason that the commanding officer, who was also of the same vintage had quite a faith in some of them.

Shahpur was a small village at the base of the spur, leading towards Doda to the north-east and close to the CFL. The track to Shahpur passed through another village named Guthrian, which was connected to Punch with a jeepable road (See Sketch 17). We had two important posts at Doda on to the right and Post 405 on the left as we face the enemy. At Shahpur and Guthrian, we had

Sketch 17: Beating Back a Raid

platoon each. There was a vast grazing ground with Dhoks in front of Shahpur and Guthrian, on the other side of CFL. There was a very influential man who was very active and used to get info about own movements through the civilians living on our side of the CFL. A raid was planned to capture or kill him. 2/Lt MS Punia was detailed for the raid. The raiding party left at about 2000 hrs and straight reached the spot. The spy was caught in a very fast and daring action. He was brought along and party reached back at Shahpur at 0300 hrs. Lt Col Bhagat Singh was already there with 2/Lt Hardial Singh. After debriefing of the raiding party, the spy was taken to Brigade HQ and handed over to them for further action. No firing took place and it was an excellently conducted mission with complete surprise.

Our posts at Shahpur and Guthrian were warned to be careful as we expected retaliation. As the things would have happened, the enemy planned a raid on our post at Guthrian. Guthrian, as given in the sketch is situated at the lower level at the nala-track junction. It was meant to check the movements of enemy, smugglers and way-wanders, besides securing the route of maintenance and troop movement along with the supply columns to Shahpur. It was held by a platoon and Sub Sant Singh was the post commander. In the last week of July of 1965, Pakistan had planned Operation Gibraltar and its troops had been issued with all the new weapons procured from USA and other friendly countries as given earlier. Besides others, 83 mm rocket launcher and .50 BMG were especially effective and deadly weapons.

One night the enemy planned a raid at Guthrian. It was before the starting of Operation Gibraltar. The enemy raiding party armed with BMG and RL came to area Bump, fixed their weapons and started firing at Guthrian post. Sub Sant Singh, a very alert JCO immediately got up, being dressed only in under wear (desi kachha) ran to 2" Mor pit and himself started firing towards Bump. He fired over 20 about HE bombs. Fortunately and of course with his lifelong experience, he hit the target with a deadly precision. By this time the whole platoon had occupied trenches and engaged the enemy. The enemy made a very hasty retreat towards the grazing grounds leaving behind the complete lot of RL ammunition. Sub Sant Singh then himself took the patrol and reached Bump and made search of the area. He could find no enemy dead or injured but found large quality of live rockets, left by the enemy in haste. The commanding officer reached there and was presented with live ammunition of 83 mm RL. Two boys had suffered minor injuries with the fire of RL, but no other damage was done to the post due to acute sense of urgency on the part of Sub Sant Singh and his men. It was one of the rare actions, where a well-planned raid by the enemy was beaten back by an equally vigilant and brave team of Sub Sant Singh. Samples of the captured ammunition were sent to various HQs. Quick action by the platoon and specially part played by Sub Sant Singh was duly appreciated by all.

19

HONOURS AND AWARDS

"Soldiers generally win the battles, Generals generally get credit for them" —Napoleon Bonaparte

Man and Machine

War machinery is a complex mixture of human minds and machines, interwoven in such a fashion that any weakness, in any part can be a cause of concern. Man behind the machine has got his importance and the machine alone without the man will be useless. But it is also a fact that man alone without the machine will not be able to do much, against an enemy equipped with better machine. Gone are the days, when battle revolved around the strong and physically mighty. People used to be killed in hand to hand fight on the battlefield and the force which could muster more skilled and strength to kill or avoiding getting more casualties, used to be the winners. Realistically taking it, the old adage of calling hand to hand fight is no more relevant and such mention in relation to the modern battle is all farce and a concoction. Using the same logic, it could be called "weapon to weapon fight." Any of the two, who has got the better weapons and uses them effectively wins the day. But out of the two cogs i.e. man and machine, the thinking machine (man) has got its own importance as compared to the working machine (gun). The man therefore has to be maintained like machine, if not better. The broken parts of the machines are required to be repaired, replaced, greased and reused. Same way, the physical, mental, emotional, spiritual and moral maintenance of the man behind the machine has to be resorted to, for getting the required results of him. Only a mentally tough, physically stout and morally high person can deliver in battle. There is no place for half heartedness in war. The result will be a chaos.

Rights of Leaders and Men

Senior commanders are simply the men who plan the battle but do not actually go and kill or get killed. They are for bigger roles of organising, managing and ordering the men and to ensure that the men go into the battle and perform. As we come down in the hierarchy, the junior leaders are closer to the fighting men and machine and are in fact the part of that team. Their role, therefore becomes little different than the leaders up the chain. Duties and responsibilities are not the same for all in one operation. The role of the junior leaders is therefore important rather critical. Everything revolves around men. But at the same time, alongwith the roles of the men and within the ambit of duties of leading, the roles of the senior leaders also requires critical examination. After the battle, the contribution of men should definitely be given due place in post battle considerations. If we do not do that, the men will lose interest and will not take responsibilities. Therefore, at places in the battle, the men unless led by a willing desperado, will not move onto the enemy. For making the man move, he has to know first that his interest in the way of looking after his family, respect, reputation, contribution including awards and honours is safe in the hands of his commanders. He is obeying willingly and lays down his life, if duty so demands. By nature, Indian jawan in general and a Sikh jawan in particular will not let down a commander who means business and looks after him. Today men and officers belong to the same stock. In a family in Punjab, Haryana, UP and Rajasthan and to be more precise in all the states, occasionally one finds men, JCOs and officers all three from the same family. In certain cases couple of brothers are there in different ranks in the same unit or regiment. It therefor will be difficult to ignore someone's legitimate right which will straightway reflect in administering the unit.

Maintaining Merit a Must

It requires proper study and scrutiny of the problems of command and other allied issues. It was okay, when the foreigners were commanding but now scenario is totally different. We were slaves then but today as a free nation, we are our own masters. We cannot afford to treat our men on any other criteria than the merit. In those days there used to be two classes, the foreigners as commanders and Indians as subordinates. The roles and aims were different but today situation is totally changed. The aim is one and the same – to serve India to the best of our capabilities. Good officers will have to remember the credo of IMA – "always and every time." The feeling of (*Hamen Kya Milega*) what will we get, will creep in if the jawan is not given his due. In most of the battalions, it is thought and done scrupulously on merit but not in all. In a battalion attack, if the unit loses its couple of brave hearts in capturing the objective and unit getting nothing for them and the brigade commander is getting gallantry award say, Mahavir

Chakra, the same cannot be justified on any account. Men and junior leaders know, who is the pillar and who has to be given his earnings. I am afraid in certain cases it is not happening. After the reorganisation stage say in attack, they and their contribution go into the background and the manipulators come onto the centre stage for taking the whole of the cake. The man who has laid down his life following orders, most faithfully, must also be treated most faithfully. The trend of ignoring them will not pay. Let us be clear that where there are serious rewards, there will be valiant men. The Indian Army is a fort of concrete and its bedrock is hardy man of rusty, dusty and remote village. If the bedrock is decayed, the fort will crumble. *Hey – the man responsible, please note, it will be well-nigh impossible to raise that fort again.* It has taken centuries to build up to this level of standard.

Honours and Awards

There are various types of awards which are bestowed upon officers and men, having taken part in a battle. These are gallantry and non-gallantry awards. The units get the Citations and Battle and Theatre Honours as these things are very important for heralding new josh (spirit) in the units and celebrating them becomes methods of having set the traditions which propel the new generation to imbibe them and follow them in battle. But after most of the battles, one finds more often than not, that the awards are not given to all the ones who really deserved. Certain gallantry awards given to the higher officers who were not directly involved in the battle, do raise hackles. There are thus lot of factors which should be kept in mind before forwarding names for awards. These are:-

- Judicious selection of names for awards, duly recommended

by the immediate superiors up in the chain.

- Gallants must not be left out at any cost. Their roles must be researched rather than ignored.

- Ratio of awards for senior officers, junior leaders and men must be seen are per the direct contribution in the battle.

- Company commanders, platoon commanders and in certain cases battalion commanders do contribute directly and should not be ignored at any cost.

- The recommendations should be as per the general opinion and knowledge of the leaders and men on the spot and around.

- Cases must be got recommended by all the leaders up the chain of command for genuineness and without any prejudice.

- Outstanding performance must be awarded irrespective of overall losses or gains in case of the unit or sub-unit or individuals.

- Personnel views, likings, dislikings and rivalries ought to be checked. That is most disturbing aspect of the issue.

- Loss in one action should not overshadow the successes in the other actions. Our is a democratic and open society and this should be understood properly and followed judiciously in selecting and recommending the cases.

- Sufficient time should be given for getting correct info about the operation and the role of individuals to be correctly ascertained for awarding them.

- What we should not ignore is that in almost all the battles, dead and the wounded, while leading or being led, come chiefly from the best and the bravest. We must do justice to them. To my mind it is greatest of the human values.

7 SIKH in Battles of Mandi and Gali

7 SIKH took part in capturing the Mandi town and the heights dominating it. It was a good action, which ensured that the Gibraltar Force of Pakistan dreaming of cutting off the Punch salient was checkmated. More important than that, was the importance of the town of Mandi which mattered a lot with the propaganda and publicity connected with it. It gave a very big relief to the higher HQs. It helped in giving an idea that this area will not be easily won over by Pakistanis and as such the operation in general area Haji Pir could be launched without any fear, which was undertaken and succeeded. Mandi valley was the biggest worry of the corps commander, 15 Corps, by the way.

The swift and dashing effort by the column of 7 SIKH should have been recognised as such lapses affect the morale and psychology of men. Though it was our own area and Mandi was wrested from the infiltrators, but the way it was captured immediately in a swift and daring action, needed recognition. The reason for ignoring it probably was that Gali post (602) held by a platoon of 7 SIKH with the element of CRPF & 7 MADRAS under overall command 7 SIKH, was abandoned two days after. It was sited on a nala track junction in a bowl and was not tactically sited. It had to fall unless resited/relocated. It was not permitted to withdraw or change its position. The garrison suffered heavy casualties, 12 killed and very large number seriously wounded. This abandonment having not been appreciated by higher ups not only affected the gallant acts of our jawans at Gali but it affected the victory gained two days earlier at Mandi also. Gali was fought under 93 Infantry Brigade and 7 SIKH was part of this Formation. But only for Mandi action the task force commended by Maj KG Belliappa second in command was put under 52 Mountain Brigade which after clearance of Mandi and establishing order moved away, and thus the action of Mandi and the contributions of the jawans was totally forgotten. 7 SIKH played a very crucial role at both the places. But its action at Gali was not appreciated by Commander 93 Infantry Brigade and the most daring acts of some boys alongwith 2/Lt Devinder Singh were simply not recognised. 2/Lt Dewinder Singh himself killed two enemy men, Sub Jagir Singh of 'C' company 7 SIKH proved to be a pillar for the morale of troops at Gali. L/NK Amarjeet Singh killed two enemy men and restored the order at the command post. The roles of Sep Ram Singh and NK Shangara Singh, were a very rare acts of bravery and sacrifice, who challenged and killed all the enemy men coming near them but at the same time lost their own lives in the gruesome battle which ensued. All these actions should not have gone unnoticed. In an operation like this, elsewhere the unit could have got MVC and PVC for Sep Ram Singh and NK Shangara Singh respectively, if I am permitted to say so.

Whatever could be the reason, the efforts of the men should have not gone waste. To ignore the contribution of the gallant and brave men will definitely send wrong signals for men in uniform and particularly lower ranks who are ultimately the ones who crack the crust and face bullets and settle score with the enemy. Both these actions of Mandi and Gali should have been recognised and names recommended for awards. A special Shabash was given to the Task Force by Brig RD Hira Commander 52 Mountain Brigade after the capture of Mandi who unfortunately was moved away after this action and the unit got robbed off the recognition of Mandi action. Such actions are important not only as a welfare measure, but an inalienable right on men if taken in correct spirit. We gleefully notice even now, the British keep inquiring about their old companions of those times of World War II and sending money and enhancing their entitlements. It is a very great gesture and lively tradition, we must not let it be forgotten.

7 SIKH in OP Hill

7 SIKH was loaned to 120 Infantry Brigade for the battle of OP Hill Complex. The unit was ordered to capture the most important part of the objective – The Jungle Hill/OP Hill Top. The battalion did a commendable job involving all from Lt Col Bhagat Singh down to a junior most sepoy and captured the objective. Not only their own objective, but also it helped 2 DOGRA to capture their objective of Black Rock which was gratefully acknowledged by them by raising Jaikaras like "7 SIKH Ki Jai" for minutes together. Everyone up the ladder was appreciative of this, but the awards given to 7 SIKH were certainly not commensurations with the efforts, importance of objective, contribution and sacrifices made by the unit personnel. Officiating Commanding Officer 2 DOGRA, though a fine officer sitting behind throughout got Sena Medal, Commanding Officer 5 SIKH LI got Mahavir Chakra but Commanding Officer 7 SIKH was not even considered, for any award for reasons best known to the higher commanders. The Army Commander Lt Gen Harbakhsh Singh of Western Command fame, who was the main architect of this operation praised this operation in these words. "This was the biggest and the cleanest infantry battle fought in the mountains at night." It was one of the

most efficiently conducted battle of 1965 War of free India and the efforts of all units were praiseworthy. 7 SIKH was no less and got numerous laudatory messages.

Lt Gen Harbakhsh Singh asked all commanders, after the Battle of OP Hill, to send citations for awards. But the corps commander promptly spoke in between and asked for forwarding all the names "through me," whereby the deliberate cuts were applied to the list forwarded and 7 SIKH, was made to make amendments and the net result was disappointing. After the war, the author happened to be with Lt Col Bhagat Singh at Jammu. During the discussion on actions fought by 7 SIKH and commensurably winning of awards, he lamentably commented something like this:-

"Sube, this is part of the game and as a soldier, you people should learn to take such things as they come" After a pause he added *"The consciousness of having attempted faithfully to discharge our duties and the approbation of our country should be sufficient recompense for our services and sacrifices."*

Operational Analysis and Relations Among Senior Officers

Personnel relations between the commanders whatever be the reasons, do affect and in fact have always been affecting the outcome of any action by any Unit or Formation. The man on the spot gives out his own viewpoint but that is not liked or taken well by the higher commanders. This has been a human weakness. There are hundred and one criteria, which can affect the thinking of a commander. Holding on to Gali (602) for example, was the result of different thinking of Commanding Officer 7 SIKH and

Commander 93 Infantry Brigade. In the bargain the jawans who fought the heroic battle and displayed indominating courage and determination could get nothing. Along with that even the boys who killed the commandoes of Pakistanis elite force SSG (19 Baluch) who were part of guerrilla force at Mandi a day earlier also got washed off. The only recipients of award probably was Brig RD Hira Commander 52 Infantry Brigade under whose leadership Mandi town was wrested from Pakistanis by the task force and who moved away to another theatre immediately afterwords.

Planning of the operation Phanne-Shah, where a total strength of 270 all including Mor platoon, MMG platoon and Medical platoon etc. was made to capture and hold three posts just opposite highly sensitive and formidable post of Pakistanis i.e. Pritam with almost negligible arty support, 7 SIKH suffered badly due devastating enemy arty fire. It infact affected the winning of awards even of OP Hill, a battle fought a month and half later. The unit which got the Ground of Tactical Importance with comparatively less casualties and then facilitated the capture of the objective of sister battalion got one VrC and two Sena Medals alongiwth two Mentioned in Dispatches. How could it be justified? Personal liking and disliking should be forgotten for the sake of sacrifices made for the country and the interest of the fallen heroes should be uppermost in our minds. It can be demoralizing to see the supreme sacrifices made by Late Sep Achhar Singh, L/NK Sadaugar Singh and NK Banta Singh, in a most daring charge on the enemy machine guns and silencing them, facilitating the capture of the objective of the national fame, not being duly awarded. Concern for such heroes should never be forgotten among our diagrams and personal equations.

Welfare of Troops and our Own Commanders

To my mind, it is a fact that the Government of India is very meticulous and accepts whatever names are recommended for awards. It is our own organisation which does not know how to play or they do not want to play. We must change our mindset on such issues and should recommend all the genuine cases. It will go a long way in improving and motivating our troops in performance of their duties. If we do not give their dues to the deserving and oblige undeserving then, the battle accounts will have to be changed and rehashed to accommodate undeserving and thus the history will be taken left-handedly. Unit battle accounts will be changed beyond recognition and thus will be spurious.

Out of Context - But

Though out of context, but certainly rare combination of greatness in human values and love for justice really seducing the enemy in their own way, affected me quite a bit to cite the example here. This is case of the large-hearted commanders like Lt Gen KK Singh Corps Commander 1 Corps, Lt Col VP Airy and Maj Hoshiar Singh both of 3 Grenadiers who in 1971 Operations went even to the extent of writing and recording the gallant act of a fallen Pakistani Commanding Officer who had launched a counter attack on a company post of 3 Grenadiers commanded by Maj Hoshiar Singh, who in this action got PVC. Not only one, this Corps got three PVCs, the other two were Flt Lt Nirmaljit Singh Sekhon and Lt Arun Khetarpal.

Lt Col Mohd Akram Raza of Pakistan Army was commanding 35 Frontier Force Regiment. He led the battalion attack in a most daring fashion on Maj Hoshiar Singh's company but was killed by an equally brave and determined Maj Hoshiar Singh and his gallant men. When Brigadier Sher Baaz Khan of the Pakistani Army came to collect the bodies of their soldiers after the ceasefire, feeling that death levels everything, he was given a sort of citation, when so requested, about the role of Lt Col Mohd Akram Raza, by Col VP Airy himself, with permission and info of the corps commander (See Appendix-G). On this recommendation the well deserving but the fallen enemy battalion commander got the highest gallantry award of Pakistan – Nishan-e-Haider, through the hands of commander of Indian troops having acute sense of duty and integrity. What a great feat and quality of leadership of that Formation of Indian Army. What a consideration for human sacrifices.

Incidentally 3 Grenadiers, later happened to go to Somalia on UN Mission. Maj Yusuf Jamal an officer of 35 Frontier Force Regiment (Pak Army), in one of those rare occasions, visited the 3 Battalion during their Battle Honour Day celebration as he was posted there as UN observer. Despite being the son of our adversary, Lt Col Mohd Akram Raza who got killed while attacking 3 Grenadiers in Battle of Jarpal, the officer proudly accepted the invitation of the Commanding Officer and stayed in the unit for two days. The then Commanding Officer presented Maj Yusuf Jamal a portrait of Lt Col VP Airy later (Lt Gen), accoutrements and a memento of the unit for 35 Frontier Force Regiment of Pakistan. Maj Usuf Jamal attended the Regimental functions, the Mandir function, homage to Martyrs and the Special Sainik Sammelan. He addressed the Battalion and said 3 Grenadiers was considered a revered unit at home (in Pakistan). He also assured the unit that portrait of Lt Gen VP Airy would occupy a place of pride of 35 FFR. On returning back from leave (from Pakistan) Maj Yusuf Jamal presented two oil paintings on behalf of 35 FFR, a portrait of Lt Col Mohd Akram Raza of Battle of Jarpal and a landscape of Lahore. The episode conveys lot of meanings to lot of commanders.

The issues of denial of well-deserving awards are very sensitive and if no attention is paid can be a cause of difficulties one day. No one has got the right to scuttle the entitlements of those who give their everything for country's honour. The great Kautailya in Arthashastra is told to have said to King Chandra Gupta Maurya with regards to the entitlements of soldiers, in these words *"the day soldier has to demand his dues will be a sad day for Magadha, for them, on that day, you will have lost all the moral sanctions to be the King."* Indian commanders in the battlefield can ill afford to forget that all books of statecraft warn against neglecting the interest and entitlements of the soldiers. We can risk this aspect only at our own peril.

Some Home truths

- There has been no battle in which there has been no decorations. Some people call them baubles and it is these baubles that make one to lead the men in war.

- War is not an affair of a chance. A great deal of knowledge of all issues, study and meditation is necessary to conduct it well.

- All a soldier desires to drive him forward is recognition and appreciation of his work. For a Sikh soldier, the love for honour and dread of shame plays even the greater part.

- A sense of vocation should be a greatest virtue of the military man. It is the fittest profession for a Sikh, where he is always in his best. Punishment and fear are necessary for keeping him in order in peace time but in field and war, he is more influenced by hope and rewards. And I think he is very right in thinking so.

20
LAST FEW YARDS

"The Army is a school, where obedience is taught, discipline enforced, where bravery becomes a habit and morals too often are neglected, where chivalry is exalted and the religion is undervalued, where virtue is rather understood in the classic sense of fortitude and courage than in the modern sense of moral excellence." —Ladel

Planning as a Phenomenon

The success in war decides the future action of a nation, which it fights for preservation of its national values. For fighting a war, major issues are worked out by government in consultation with the higher HQs of Services. At the formation and unit level, required arrangements are made by the commander/commanding officer and his staff. Units are then organised and arty and mor fire support etc is made available to them. Defences are prepared and the minefields and wire obstacles are laid around. In attack the requirement at the battalion and company level are met and troops are launched into battle to settle scores with the enemy. The above exercise is done in the typical staff way. But, how to go from the Start Line to enemy trench and how to surmount the difficulties encountered, the study with meticulous care is to be devised and adopted only by the respective company commanders. The crossing of start line and going in for the enemy bunker in attack and in dealing with the enemy coming on to your trench in defence, is a peculiar phenomenon, on which no one issues any instructions. It is the baby of the commanders at the levels of section, platoon and company and they are to play with it. Human machine working under peace time conditions, and during exercises etc knows full-well that nothing will happen as there is no live enemy. It will work totally in a different fashion, when the BMGs and LMGs are raining bullets upon one. The casualties are taking place, command structure is affected and the move is slowed down. The men run for cover, behind which they step on unconventional mines adding more to the casualties. The company commander at such a movement has a onerous task at hands and he and his men have to fight for ascendancy.

Unfortunately this aspect is neglected in the training of the units and the things are taken for granted as to what happens beyond the start line. It is a real tragedy. The reason is that seniors are not involved and hence no one is bothered about. The heart of the matter therefore is that the company commander himself has to ensure, for including this aspect in training of his sub-unit. How will a men behave when the firing is coming onto them, is to be made clear to the respective commanders and other junior leaders.

Training Schedule at Each Level of Command

In all battles fought by 7 SIKH in Mandi, Gali, Phanne-Shah and OP Hill in 1965 Indo-Pak War, the company and platoon commanders had to face such situations and could only manage, because almost all commanders had the experience of dealing with the live enemy for over two years, before the war started because the area was already active. They had learnt in the field, on the spot. The ground taught them, combat experience taught them and enemy taught them and that is the datum line. For dealing with such phenomenon, there are certain prerequisites which should be ensured before going in for fighting a formidable enemy:-

- Adequate Arty and Mor support with extra ammunition.
- Mutual support provided by weapons as well as sub-units.
- Reserves and their earliest arrival.
- Double checking and carrying of all items and requirements by the men before, during and immediately after battle.

Bitter truths:

"Experience is the child of thought and the thought is the child of action. We cannot learn men from books"
—Benjamin Disraeli

Everyone is a unique individual with crocked arts and dark alleys. It requires special efforts to study such characteristics. There are certain other well-tested and established but bitter truths which should be kept in mind for taking corrective measures, while going in for serious adventures. They do have the effect on the outcome and therefore are important to understand and register. These are:-

- The person who has less worldly liabilities, does serve the cause better. *"He that have a wife and children, hath given hostages to the fortune for they are impediments to great enterprises"*

- To take the old persons in battle is likely to be impeding. They make different calculations which affect men too. Troops including leaders should be young.

- Exercises exclusively at the company level encompassing real and practical aspects be conducted. Situation is to be created on the actual scene of the battle, like men falling one after the other due to enemy fire etc. No company commander of the Indian Army does it, made to do or encouraged to do. That is why almost 75% attacks fail in the first attempt or achieve nothing much or suffer very heavy casualties.

- Reliable means of communication at the level of section commanders should be provided, which at present is just non-existent. Section commander loses command and his contact with his seniors and thus goes out of scene. He is and should always be recognised as the main cog of the fighting machine, history is the testimony to this fact.

- Certitude of actual happening should be understood and practised. Mere lip service will not do.

- Right choice of man for a particular moment and job is the key to success.

Personality of Company Commander

Any commander leading the men in battle has to be a man of impeccable character. His order must be obeyed to the hilt and be taken as that of one, next only to God. There are numerous qualities of an officer or leader of troops, which help him in command of his troops in battle but few given below have the added effects:-

- **Ability**: It involves responsibility and power to its last particle, is duty.

- **Clear Hands**: A man of probity and honesty and dedicated to the cause of troops will find the command smooth. He should have a very clean image. It will help him at every step in a multiplied way.

- **Dispatch**: It means promptness. Battle is not a simple affair, even seconds matters. He studies situations and passes clear and firm orders. Delays have dangerous ends. A man of very fast reflexes is the need.

- **Patience**: It is genius in battle which speaks of a matured mind – hold on, hold fast and hold out.

- **Impartiality**: In the promotions and punishments one has to be very-very fair. This is the weakest element of the personality of most of the officers. There are a few rather very negligible number of officers who could stay wholly impartial. There are varied factors to influence the human element in an officer. I feel for a human to be impartial is a Herculean task. Even devils require to have given their dues, and we should not ignore that.

Characteristics of Junior Leaders

In the battle, it is the junior leaders, whose role is important to make any operation success. He has to be trained and made to feel that he is the real leader. He should be permitted to raise his team in the way he thinks right and effective. A junior leader must understand the background and nature of each individual. An individual is what his home, religion, his society and the moral codes and ideas of his society, have made him. The army cannot unmake him. No line can be drawn as to what should be characteristics of junior leader but the important ones are:

- Conscientiousness in the care of his men.
- Resolute justice in all walks of life, be it a promotion, allotting duties or punishment.
- Military bearing – of an excellent soldier which include exhibition, development of military culture and maturity.
- Nourishing the spirits of his men and lives in a novel way.
- Courage, creative intelligence and top class physical fitness, fit for all occasions.
- Innate respect for the dignity of the position and the work of other men under him.

Layout of the Ground

"Our business like any other is to be learned by consistent practice and experience and our experience is to be had in war and not only in reviews"

In certain cases, it has been noticed that some individuals are of the opinion and do say so, that it is company commander's personal business in taking the company into battle. Some of them like certain lower level leaders do subscribe to such a canard. It is to be understood by one and all that they have been drafted, recruited and trained for a specific job, which requires priority over everything else. The instructions on charter of duties are clear and simple – 100% obedience, at all 24 hours. Based on this edifice, the army is raised and organised for fighting a successful battle.

A rifle company is the basic sub-unit of an infantry battalion, which invariably goes to war as one. When in field formation on the ground, it looks like a "compact block," where the place for everyone is marked, like players on the football, hockey or basketball ground. The moment one member is disturbed the space is to be covered by the other, who is nearby and ensured by the respective section and platoon commander. The mantra is that sub-unit as such has to carry on with its functions. Reserves and replacements for the task will have to be pushed in or created there only. In the battlefield, the troops are arranged to face the enemy. If one falls, the other comes in. It is to be a automatic process in a good sub-unit, but what happens, when faced with odds? It will only be realised and surmounted by the company commander himself – no one else. The buck stops there. He knows for a fact that human equations and group responses will radically change under fire from the enemy. Therefore, he should prepare his command for that task very carefully, deliberately, consistently and continually.

Making best use of Everyone

The discipline is the backbone of the army. It is more strict in the infantry because of nature of their duties, entailing in face to face dealing with the live enemy. Only disciplined people do contribute towards the success and there is no denial. However, it has been seen that some who are otherwise awkward, arrogant, indisciplined, rogues, ruffians, ignored for promotion and certain players etc., also do play an important role in the battle, at times. As they all are overbearing by nature and have tendency to boss around, are capable of taking a leading role. They must be made full use of. I have seen this happening, while attacking a feature in Mandi where a superseded NCO, came forward recoiling angrily, shouting at everyone to move up and himself taking lead and throwing grenades at the enemy. These men who had been consistently bad actors in peacetime, marked by the faults of laziness, unruliness and disorderliness, become lions at the battlefield, with all the virtues of aggressiveness, warm obedience and thoughtfully planned action. When the battle is over, they invariably relapse again. They could fight like hell but they could not be good on permanent basis. Of course, disciplined ones only as said earlier play the major and crucial role in battle in the long run.

Moving from Start Line to Enemy and His Reaction

"On the battlefield the real enemy is the fear and not the bayonet and the bullet"

The actual battle, say in attack starts at the stage of moving from start line towards enemy. It is a historical fact that about 25% attacks go as planned and achieve desired results. The reason is the understanding or otherwise of the implications of the process of 'perform' or 'perish' at that particular moment.

Just before such a crucial moment, the company commander, the Man Friday of the battle, being on a silent mode invariably, thinks and talks to himself something like this.

"I have been given the task and I have accepted it. I have put up the Compact Block of my men on the ground. I am firmly held at my place and will have to prod my men, because I am the commander of the situation and have given orders to my men accordingly. My orders are to be obeyed, is my duty to ensure. My men know me well to have confidence that when, at times, I have to remain behind, it is good for the company.

I am the chief manager of the show and not to save myself from enemy bullets."

The troops are lined up, battle cry is raised and the troops start moving fast towards the enemy. The enemy is alerted. He opens up with all weapons, at his disposal. What happens at this moment is the most important, crucial and a deciding factor. Any light reading of the situation can lead to a disaster. The commanders, who have gone through such experience will never forget it. But the war does not take place every now and then. Many officers reach the top of their career with no such experience and they are the people, who will base their plans only on the outcome of exercises and sand model discussions. The performance and reaction of men, in exercises, will be totally different from those in the battle. What happens in the battle and which does not happen in peace time exercises is summarised below:-

- Some men will fall and others will be seriously wounded. Others by their side will also be affected and run for cover and as such move is hindered.
- On either sides of them too, the same thing would be happening with the other sub-units and the momentum will be checked by the enemy.
- Command particularly at section level will be affected and the enemy gets the time to engage easily and deliberately with enhanced courage.
- Not getting respite from the enemy fire, own casualties will increase.
- Some men will face supremely testing experience of their life almost as a total stranger to the situation and develop fear.

- The perfect order on the ground will be disturbed. The company commander gets anxious and at times perplexed as he knows slowing down is courting death.

- Highly anxious moments are there for company commander who has got the responsibility solely and heavily, planted on his shoulders.

- Any leader at any level can become a casualty. If the company commander is killed, there could be a finish of operation, unless a forceful person so authorised and fully trained takes over and does the required pushing from behind, immediately.

- Wounded will create a most disturbing scene, crying for the lives. It is natural but should be looked after a few minutes later.

Remedy

"Warfare is an art and not a science and no set formula for victory can be prescribed"

To overcome the difficulties faced by men in last few yards, certain steps are required to be taken which will help in keeping the pace of going good and raising the morale of troops. These are:

- Individuals, should not be left alone. Immediate commanders or comrades should be nearby, it will enhance his courage. Man is a gregarious animal. He will perform better with a companion. Being unarmed but in the company of companion, will feel better than being armed, but without a colleague, (one is one, two together are eleven) holds very correct. Man will always do better when others are around.

- Commander should keep speaking giving "Shabash" and raising morale. He will be required to ensure pushing the men on to the objective. Speaking but calculatedly will give lot of strength in the cold atmosphere of battle.

- Encourage accurate and intensive fire at enemy positions. Fire and mobility are interrelated and firing on the enemy position is the only answer for making own men move. Slowing down the fire, is dangerous and impeding. Only fire-beats-fire.

- Use all methods at your command for counseling, warning and even threatening for making all to move. "Fastest you go on the enemy, better it is" should be impressed upon time and again. It is an eternal truth.

- Move of the 'compact block' is very important. The semblance of that even in the worst of times must be maintained, otherwise junior leaders will lose the command and all gains, earned so far will be squandered.

- Going down to the ground should never be permitted, once the troops go to the ground, it will be difficult to make them move. They will never get up. Experience is the witness.

- Move is to be coordinated, somehow, at all possible levels. Individual alone will not move for long.

- The bunker of the enemy should be spotted and fired at intensely and violently unless his "white of the eye is gone" alongwith the "thuk-thuk of his weapon."

- Pass whatever positive info you have got, to all. The is the biggest morale booster, but the need to know principle be followed.

- Each company commander must be informed of:-

  - Latest info about the progress of move or success of sister battalions/ companies.

  - The company HQ should also serve as a distribution points for info to lower and sister sub-units.

  - When in doubt pass it along. It's good.

  - Maintain inertia – keep moving at all costs. Be ruthless rather than getting sentimental on seeing the casualties.

  - Move has to be there at any cost. There is no alternative. Once halted, even if there has been no damage, the troops never move as strongly or as willingly again. After three or four such delays men will become morally spent and psychologically hesitant and rested.

- On insistence of strong commanders, the troops will move but haltingly and gropingly, again becoming a biggest and easy target. Such tendency is to be checked and curbed.

- Commander will have to come forward and ensure that everyone leaves the cover and moves ahead. At no stage, at any cost they should be treated as castaways. Commanding voice will help such element to join and move forward.

- In extreme emergencies, when the stakes are high due to failures of juniors to act and the need is imperative, such acts warrant the leaders to himself lead, boldly. For a soldier, there is no alternative except doing that.

- To get the men moving again as a group, at most sensitive a moment an officer must expose himself to the point of killing or being killed, if situation so demands.

What happens at the Unit Level after the Battle

It is such an unfortunate phenomenon in almost all armies of the world, that the individuals who were so badly involved in dealing with the enemy till now are no more asked of anything after the success signal. Reviews and discussions take place but the company and platoon commanders are just not invited. Senior officers discuss among themselves about that. After the war, the first thing should be done, is the detailed debriefing and progress report from all commanders upto section level, by commanding officer. If we do not listen to the men, who fought on the ground, how will we know about the truth of their roles and difficulties they faced. The important points in this regard therefore are:-

- Discussion first at company level, then at battalion level and after that at higher HQ should be held for getting into the nitty and gritty of the operations. More openness is the the key for strengthening of the organisation.

- Awards given must be judicious. The cases must have the written recommendations of the company and platoon commanders. How can a division or brigade commander get highest gallantry award, when his man who broke the crust and was killed in doing his duty so assiduously be neglected. Sheer lack of discussion at the lower level and warding off their views by self-seekers is the only reason for disappointment and disgruntleness at lower levels.

- Incapable heads, must roll after the battle, if their respective roles were not as per the expectations. Such issues are generally ignored and covered, after success, under the weight of happiness which is so very unfortunate.

- Promote the people who got victory by placing their lives on hand and facing the ordeal. It will help bringing openness in the system and make the men to come forward willingly.

- Even devil deserves the due and he must be given. We generally ignore them.

- Gospel truth is that those who deserve monuments are not there to see them. We owe the truth nothing but truth, to them as has been said earlier.

What should be done in Peace Time

We prepare for the war in peace time. Without proper knowledge of what could happen say in attack, no training worth the name can be given to troops. Unfortunately the training is limited to the presentations to be given to the senior officers. Exercises are not conducted for the training of troops but to find out the suitability of a Formation Commander and also for tying up administrative details and mastering movement drills. New concepts must be developed and given a chance. What actually happens in fighting and how should we go about it, is totally out of the view and preview of the present day peace mission commanders. Fire and move of old IMA days is totally forgotten. What happens to the man, when his colleagues are falling and he is left alone, is given no thought. Psychology of the man facing bullets is not given even the cursory feel. The result is that troops are launched just like that in the battle, who suffer heavy casualties. Some strong-willed men will come forward and lay down their lives one after the other, in succession. To avoid such loss of men, the correct and well-thought of training on the lines given below will help to a great extent:-

- Exercise should be organised and conducted in such a way that pertinent points about causing of casualties, falling down of men, taking cover, not getting up and moving forward, pushing by commanders, being alone and in frightened state of mind, respective commanders taking over the control and then leading themselves etc are incorporated and practised hard.

- Only bold and talented individuals be promoted to the NCO rank. There is a difference between a nice guy and a bold man.

- Maximum info based on the need to know basis should be made available to all. It helps a great deal.

- Moving fastest, without holding in between, is the best way to avoid casualties and overpower enemy, but it is not that simple. Intensive training on all crucial and practical points at company level is the answer. It has to be meditatively drilled both mentally and physically.

- Occurrence of casualties, in case of slowing down, be explained and practised in right earnest.

- Realism on the scene of last 15-20 yards be explained to all concerned and such situation be created and practised galore during exercises.

- After the exercises, lower level discussions by the company commander with his subordinates must be held and views ascertained which is an inescapable requirement. Unfortunately this is just taken for granted and normally unit suffers very heavy casualties, if in war which should be avoided by taking practical steps.

- Super inducement of changes in teaching new ideas is a must. Elasticity of mind is very much desirable. Rigid mental attitude of the commanders will be harmful for one and all. It will destroy the energy of young enthusiasts. The difference between rigid and firm including pragmatic must be clearly enunciated.

21

WHAT MAKES A MAN FIGHT

"When thou has profited so much that you respectest thyself, thou mayest let go thy tutor" —Seneca

General

After my retirement from the Army, I have been working as a Principal in some of the very reputed schools of Rohtak which is an educational centre in Haryana. The area is considered as nursery for recruitment in the armed forces both in the rank of officers and men. Almost all schools, have been preparing the students for the entry into the NDA, IMA and other academies and institutions for the armed forces, with reasonably good success.

A few questions which are generally asked of the instructors with defence background by the students are "What makes a soldier to follow the maxim of do or die? Does not he get the feeling of fear? What make a body of men to obey an order, which at times, gives the clear message of death? These are very relevant questions which will be often asked, by the students who are preparing for that career. Within the precincts of these questions, lie the meaning of army, its welfare measures, war, discipline, training, command structure, obedience, qualities of soldiers, elements of cohesive working and et al. For clearing the fog on such questions, we should as such understand the meaning and effects of some of these terms more deeply with attendant implications. The deep insight into these issues will explain to us as to what makes a man fight.

Army and its Ethos

Army is a very old profession which had been raised to protect one's society and subjugate others who oppose its freedom, philosophy and challenge its survival, since time immemorial, meaning thereby, involving fighting against them. Man has always been fighting for one reason or the other, be that a woman, pasture, territory dominance, loot, exploitation or subjugation, without which, such ventures are not normally undertaken. For coming to terms with such requirements, the army has developed its own ethos of working, which are beautifully enshrined in the following adage:-

> *"Theirs is not a reason why*
> *Theirs is but to do or die.*

In other words the strength of the army lies in its strict discipline and undeviating obedience to its superior officers. Discipline is the bedrock and soul of the army life. It makes small number formidable, procures success to the weak and esteem to all in the organisation. Ethos of the army, are very strong and develop over a period of time. It does not permit the lot to leave the line of structured obedience. *"To have respect for ourselves guides our morals and to have deference for others, governs our manners"* – Sterne

War and its Causes

Before going into the core of this very important issue, let us be clear about, as to what is war and what does this involve. The life of the countries is like that of men. The later have the right of killing in self-defence, same way former can make wars for its own survival and preservation. Nevertheless, wars today have got numerous reasons also but the ones given below are rather the main:-

- Either actual or threatening wrong by one country to the other
- Suspicion by one country that another intends to do it wrong.
- The bitterness of feelings dependent upon substantial question of difference. It is sort of permanent hatred.

The basic reason of these three causes of war is actual injustice. Right causes are the strong motivation for carrying out duties by army men. Right the cause, right will be the effect. Reasons for war, in a democratic country, like ours must be conveyed in a forceful manner to troops. It will have effect on their performance.

Soldiering and State

Soldiering is a profession, where the man becomes a part of the machine in such a way that he is propelled automatically to play his part and there is no escape from that. Such an army becomes the important arm of the State and the State uses it as and when required. For safeguarding the State, the use of the soldiers is a must. It may be correct that in many cases ignorance, poverty and vanity could have forced some people to join soldiering but once they are within the four walls they have to learn how to save the interest of the country and if needed, at the cost of their own lives. Soldiering therefore can be termed as a pious profession irrespective of the outcome of the war. Soldiers, in fighting the war will do their duties in the best possible manner, if following are ensured:-

- Political will of the country to fight for its interest.
- Support of the masses due to a genuine cause.
- Preparedness of the armed forces to deal with the adversary.

The wars will take place and continue till all the anomalies are removed, which are, in reality beyond human endeavours due to varied perceptions of problems by various countries. Therefore, it is important that well-trained and highly motivated army is maintained by the country. In an educated society, soldiers are not as dumb as they used to be. For giving his best in war, he has to be satisfied with the cause and also for preparations of war.

System of working in Army

The army works on three important pillars of order, authority and seniority. The meaningful training with the above-mentioned points in mind, makes a junior to treat his senior as demi God. Whatever a senior says and it is finally understood and accepted by juniors has to be carried out. There are no two ways about it. The man has to develop an animal within himself, which forces him to work the way he does. He in all activities in armed forces has to measure himself in terms of enemy's capabilities and strength vis-a-vis his training and discipline. Successive stages of command ensure that orders rather than getting diluted get accentuating effect for firmness. Everyone is made to obey his superiors and that is the ethos of the armed forces. Therefore, a senior commander has to be a man of extraordinary capabilities, so that no body dares to challenge his orders. A good leader works like a good root, out of which branches off the courage of the soldier and that springs out further. And to be finally prepared for war is one of the most effectual ways of preserving peace but it can be done only by capable commander, who is selected one. The right of command, is no longer an advantage transmitted by nature like inheritance. It is the fruit of labour and price of courage. For soldiering, the up-stepping order of precedence is very very important. For all in the chain, therefore, the reputation is uppermost in the mind of everyone and same makes him proud and working to the best of his capabilities. It helps in our understanding as to why a soldier fights, and what makes him to do so.

On the Job Training

The author passed out from IMA Dehradun in 1964 and was commissioned in 7 SIKH. The unit was located at Punch in J&K, where I joined them. It was an active area, where exchange of fire with the enemy, used to be a routine affair. Similarly going out for pursuits was not uncommon. The life on the posts was totally operation oriented. In such a situation one learns those aspects of military life, which one could not have learnt in IMA where there is no live enemy. Here one learns his tasks the hard way. This profession demands a high degree of obedience, courage, physical fitness and promptitude. In case of difficulty, the troops look towards an officer. The officers, therefore, are required to have a high standard of training and possess an effective personality. The troops will take the officers seriously only when they see them, as a perfect human being with very high personal standard in all respects and with a learning attitude. A sensible leader will realise that nothing short of required standards will work with the command of troops. In an operation the troops look towards an officer, for everything, be that an order, reaction or action. It means that one learns when he gets a chance and that way keeps learning through out life. In other words whole life is a learning process.

Officers and Men

Officers and men, join together to make an outfit a bedrock of discipline, worthy of warding off the enemy's manoeuvers and moves and achieve success. They both are part of the same machine having their respective roles to play, which require clear understanding.

Officers

The lot of officers makes the unit as all orders emanate from them. They before becoming officers are subjected to a very thorough and systematic scrutiny for selection and then a rigorous training for years at the academies. Once fully trained and passed out as Commissioned Officers are supposed to be cream of the society, strength of the army and jewels and property of nation. For them the fighting against the enemy means:-

- To uphold their own reputation and self respect among the juniors, equals and seniors.

- To uphold the honour of the position and rank, one holds and its obligations and be proud of one's behaviour and dignity.

- To uphold the honour of the society, caste or community, they belong to.

- To uphold the safety, honour and welfare of the Indian army and the country.

- To uphold the pride, "izzat" and traditions of the Indian army and the regiment, he is commissioned into.

There are different types of officers, coming from totally different backgrounds with their special community traits and reactionary attitude. It initially makes difference for their settling down in a unit, his grooming by seniors and guiding him in the profession. All officers are not lucky enough to be placed in a favourable atmosphere, but that is what, which happens in a country like ours with diverse customs, traditions, culture and ways of life. One has to learn, how to get adjusted wherever placed. One cannot blame the circumstances but should do his best. He has to circumvent all hurdles himself and come up as an able person to be obeyed to the hilt in his unit/sub-unit. Everything cannot come his way without concerted efforts. Difficulties have to be faced and surmounted to the best of one's capabilities. I am reminded of an incident. A young officer just posted in the unit, wrote about his well-being etc. to his friends. One of his friends wrote back asking him *"Dil Lag gaya Ki Nahi"* as to how was he feeling and should be settled by now. He replied him *"Dil to lag gaya lekin pair nahin lage"* as he was feeling alright but cannot say 'settled' because he was pushed around hell of a lot as the "Man Friday" – the adjutant in the unit wanted to establish his authority on the youngsters. Officers make the unit and see that the men go to the battle unhesitatingly obeying their orders and that is what is required. He is a class apart and has to maintain that throughout. He leads by example and his location is always at the head of the pack. He has got the sanction for the command which has to be enforced.

> *"It is essential that the authority of officers in military service be preserved. That is the reason, they have set rules for the methods of communication between ordinary jawans and higher officers. If there are too much rubbing of elbows, it will soon affect the structure"*

For getting on the right track, the officer should ensure that his orders are not taken lightly. The officers are the backbone. If officers are able and capable, an ordinary soldier will not at all be thinking of ignoring their orders. That will make him to go straight into the battle and perform as ordered. The officer should take stand and abide by his convictions. He cannot afford to burn the candle at both the ends, he has to be a man of the men. For the faith reposed by fellow countrymen, he has to ensure service before self, a price one ought to be proud to pay. *"He cannot be hybrid product between both a careerist and a man who takes stand."* The officer has to maintain a very high standard of his conduct, competence and character to make the men realise and see that they obey him to the point of giving their last ounce.

Training of Junior Officers

Another side of the study is also worth mentioning. That is the treatment of juniors by seniors. An officer will normally not have any problems from the men but the attitude of certain seniors can be a cause of spoiling the lives of certain youngsters due to various reasons bordering narrow-mindedness, parochialism, caste, creed and what not. Here comes the role of commanding officer, who must rein in such elements. They try to win the favour of the commanding officer by using very clever manoeuvring and have rollicking time. An officer was posted back in his unit, located in a peace station after the staff tenure. Knowing the attitude of a very senior officer, who had a say and sway in the unit, the officer decided to report a day earlier so that he can get settled for a day after which he would definitely to shuttled around. As expected he was given the royal treatment, in the first hour of his landing in the unit, without being asked for a cup of tea or lunch and was made to carry his stuff on the firing range joining the troops carrying out practice. Such tendency must be observed, checked and uprooted by commanding officer. We all have seen the careers of many outstanding officers being permanently ruined by the machination of self-seekers. Such noddings will have a direct bearing on the theory of what makes a man fight.

Men

There are various types of troops, one has to serve with. They have got their specific qualities and characteristics, which play very important role. An officer has to understand the traits of the troops which help him to settle himself and command them effectively. Unless one knows the unit well, he will not be able to lead them. Same way the troops understand the officer, as per the quality of talent, boldness and courage to face the difficulties and react accordingly. An order of an accomplished leader will not be disobeyed. They will take you seriously when you prove to them that you mean business. This is what, will make them to fight and lay down their lives at the time of need. For an ordinary soldier, the meaning of fighting an enemy is the same, as to an officer, but for him, his caste, comrades, immediate seniors and to some extent unit and regiment also play a role. A demand of duty to men as compared to sense of performance of duty, to officers, makes the difference. Personal honour and discipline matter quite a lot in case of men. For them the fighting means:-

- Welfare of the country.
- The community and its respect.
- Comradeship and esprit-de-corps.
- Pride in his profession and personal honour.
- The pride in the unit and the regiment.

Age and Performance

Age plays very critical role. The psychology of soldier too, does change with the advancement of age. It is the young who actually delivers. It is almost an accepted fact that those who won gallantry awards being young, except the exceptions, have not been able to deliver that well in the senior ranks. And higher one goes more susceptible in thought and action he becomes. Most of PVCs, Ashoka Chakras, Sword of Honours, Gold Medalists awarded so, while young specially among officers, in our context have not been able to make to the reasonably higher ranks in their career. The officer or a man alone, will not be of any consequences and will not be able to do anything. Cohesiveness based on single chord of order, authority and seniority passing through the organisation becomes a key to success. It has to be understood that a soldier will fight as he should do if the criteria of order, command, discipline and obedience are adhered to, firmly and decisively beyond any uncertainty. And that makes a man to fight as he does.

Special Characteristics of Sikh Soldier

The SIKH Regiment is one of the oldest regiments of the Indian Army. Its first five units were raised in the later half of the nineteenth century and formed into two Sikh brigades. The units were raised from the remnants of Maharaja Ranjit Singh's army, after the Anglo-Sikh Wars from 1845-1849. Soldiering for a Sikh is therefore inherent in his birth and furthered to be widely tipped, the hard way. The significant point to note is that a Sikh was not made into a first class solider by foreigners. He was already a highly trained and disciplined solider, when drafted by them after the SIKH wars. He had the experience of fighting a long and sustained war and the credit of making him as good, as he is today goes to his ancestry and history. He is the product of his village, where the atmosphere is different from cities. The cities in all walks of life are different. There is a special virtue in those country houses, in gardens and orchards, in fields, in streams and groves, in rustic recreation and plain manners that neither cities nor metropolitans enjoy. He in such an atmosphere develops certain typical values and characteristics, which make him different from urbanites. He can be best understood by his likes. The battle records of all the Sikh units in 1st World War, 2nd World War and 1947-48 War with Pakistan, 1962 Indo-Chinese conflict and all other operations speak volumes, for a Sikh solider's quality and contribution as a warrior. He has characteristics which make him to stand apart from others. These are:-

- Hardihood of his character.
- Dominating courage to survive under most difficult situation and menacing crisis.
- Honour for his words – fidelity to oath.
- Never say die attitude – product of strong culture and traditions.
- Spirit of adaptation.

Conclusion

It is not one factor, but a combination of various factors mentioned in the forgoing paras that inspire a soldier to manage fear, withstand the stress and strain and give his best in war and peace. Once a soldier adapts himself to these requirements of the profession, it is taken that he will stand and fight like a man against all odds, making it clear as to what compels him to fight and will lay down his life, if situation so demands. In a good unit, there is no alternative but doing the things right way, as one is bound by various criteria. Where an officer can never afford to lose his equanimity and come out to be a man of high moral rectitude, the men must also be trained the hard way and disciplined to the core to fulfill their duties at all costs and to make him as to why does he fight.

"When we build, let us think that we build for ever"

Field Marshal Helmuth Graf has described as to why does a man fight. He says that war is an integral part of God's ordering of the universe. In war, man's noblest virtues come into play. Courage and renunciation, fidelity to duty and a readiness for sacrifice that does not stop short of offering up life itself. Without the war the world would become swamped in materialism. It is already given that "war is like love it always finds a way." If a person happens to be in circumstances where fighting is a norm, he is automatically drawn into its ethos and that conveys as to why does a man fight.

22.
LESSONS LEARNT

"History repeats itself mainly because men do not study it and those who do, forget its lessons" —Lord Birdwood

General

As has been already brought out and given in relevant chapters, this in an account of a unit, which played a pivotal role in saving the Punch bulge from the Pakistani's clutches in 1965 operations. 7 SIKH single-handedly fought against designs of Gibraltar Force of the Pakistan in Punch sector in J&K and blunted their advance and fought valiantly in its area of responsibility in Mandi Valley. The enemy's plans of linking the Mendhar Valley with Mandi Valley and then cutting off the Punch bulge along with creating chaos in the Kashmir Valley, was brought to a naught by this excellent outfit, officered mainly by young but highly dedicated lot. In performing its duties steadfastly, the unit had to undergo untold hardships, amounting to isolation, suffering casualties and going without rations and ammunition at times. The unit was involved from first week of August to the end of first week of November 1965 in intense operations and learnt lot of lessons, important ones of which are given herewith in succeeding paras:

Familiarisation and Knowledge of Area

An infantry battalion is the unit which faces the real brunt of the enemy fire in almost all operations of war. It therefore becomes incumbent on it to understand the importance of various factors like weather, terrain and population and everything pertaining to their area of responsibility for proper conduct of battle. It is very rightly said that time spent on patrolling in various places and recce is never wasted. The unit must familiarise itself with the whole area very well and as quickly as possible. The unit which dominates the area by offensive action like patrolling, laying of ambushes and conducting raids on the enemy positions, will achieve desired results during the war. Such a unit will not be surprised, overawed and buckled down under the pressure of enemy activities. 7 SIKH operating in Mandi Valley, knew the area well and had got detailed knowledge of its history, geography and sociology. It was the reason that the unit was successful in blunting the thrust of Pakistan's Guerrilla force. At Gali post (602) which was located in a bowl and was surrounded from all sides by high features, where from enemy kept on engaging it, gave stubborn resistance to the enemy and when the post had to be abandoned after eight days, conducted a planned withdrawal.

Creating of Reserves

The unit should have minimum one company strength as reserve which can be launched without any loss of time as per the demand of the situation. The unit did not have the adequate reserves and had to manage from within. Had one company strength been available, it could have occupied the Molsar heights and dominated it adequately and that could have checked the offensive of the enemy, in the initial stages only. When it got the troops, who fell back from the Gali Post, it did smart itself and checked the moves on the Molsar Ridge particularly toward Mandi town, which was so very important.

Bold, Audacious Offensives

Brig RD Hira Commander 52 Mountain Brigade, immediately on arrival on 11 August 1965 in general area Sekhlu-Mandi, ordered the task force of 7 SIKH to be launched for clearing the Eastern Ridge dominating Mandi town at the earliest. He got the Mandi town bombed by arty fire and 3" Mors of 7 SIKH at the first instance as it was held by the enemy for the last three days i.e. since 9 August 1965 and then launched attacks from two opposite directions on Eastern Ridge. It paid rich dividends. Enemy was uprooted and Mandi town was secured. Gut feeling must be given a chance. Transitory chances should be grasped immediately. The enemy lost their administrative base, were put off balance and that action helped salvage the situation, putting brake on the propaganda being unleashed by Pakistanis. It was a good psychological, tactical and above all a physical defeat of their purpose.

Provision of Supporting Fire

Arty fire is a great morale booster. A good infantry battalion will be able to deal with the enemy infantry but without arty support, it feels helpless when on the other side, the enemy is getting the required support. In case of 7 SIKH in Mandi Sub-sector, there was no arty support available. Same was the case at Phanne-Shah. 7 SIKH was made to withdraw from the feature only due to the lack of arty support. It is worth remembering that the whole corps arty of Pakistan was firing on that feature Lahori

Shah. There was not a single casualty caused by small arms. It was all due to enemy debilitating arty fire, that the unit was forced out.

Commanding Officer, the Best Judge

The unit should be permitted to be commanded by its commanding officer. Any stipulation and not permitting him to act as per the study of the situation may not result in desired success. In case of Mandi, the brigade commander and corps commander were more worried about the operations to be conducted by the battalion. Lt Col Bhagat Singh was not given a free hand in dealing with the situation at Gali and Sauji. Phanne-Shah operation was the brainchild of senior commanders, who did not realise as to how a unit will hold three features just opposite a most important post of Pakistanis in the whole of Punch sector without adequate party support. It was totally ill conceived plan and did not work as expected. The operation should have been launched in two phases and with maximum arty support. Same day moving from Punch, crossing of Betar Nala, moving on to the objective, fighting and occupying the features with the meagre strength of two companies plus, was asking the battalion for too much. I wish commanding officer could put his foot down. Factually, it should have been tackled, by a brigade size force. It was far from an achievable task.

Offensive Defence

Moving of the troops from Gali to an alternative location was not allowed. The commanding officer had suggested but it was not agreed. Offensive moves could put the enemy off balance and should not have been ignored. Even from Sauji we could have moved the troops for offensive operation which was not done because it was perpetually being fed to the battalion that the enemy was likely to make a thrust through Mandi Valley and hence no troops in excess should leave the posts. It was passive approach and should have been avoided. Small offensive operations at unit level also were avoided by the unit.

Appreciation and Awards

Even if the enemy had made momentary success at one odd place, which normally happens in war, the best efforts made by sub-units and individuals at other places should have been recognised. There was no plausible reason for ignoring the contribution of the fallen heroes of Gali, who faced the enemy for consecutive eight days, occupying a most disadvantageous location and not yielding to their pressure. It does affect the morale of the troops besides sending wrong signals of ignoring the good job done. 2/Lt Dewinder Singh and his boys did excellent job at Gali against all odds. It was a most difficult situation, a young commander could face.

Ruthlessness

The commanding officer should be absolutely forthright and ruthless both in peace and war as far as dealing with the officers and JCOs goes. There should be no manipulative advisors around and they should be told what to do, in clear and simple terms. Officers should have been dealt with more firmly particularly in operation Phanne-Shah and even in OP Hill. The result was the loss of face for this fine unit in Phanne-Shah. Officers failed in their duties and could not move and occupy the objectives, where they were supposed to go, fight if needed and hold. It was young

2/Lt Hardial Singh who rushed to his objective at Ring Contour in operation Phanne-Shah otherwise, we could have not even gone there at all, the way the things were progressing at the crossing site at Betar Nala. In OP Hill, reserve company was nowhere around, when leading company was facing difficult situation. The defaulters should have been dealt with properly.

Young Officers

The unit was lucky to have very good young officers in 2/Lt MS Punia, 2/Lt SK Singh, 2/Lt Hardial Singh, 2/Lt Ravel Singh, 2/Lt SS Sandhu, 2/Lt Dewinder Singh, 2/Lt RS Cheema with Capt Santosh Kumar, Capt Surjit Singh and Capt Sansar Singh, who were all matured and very capable officers and had come up to the expectations of the commanding officer. The commanding officer however who belonged to Second World War generation had quite a faith in JCOs, could not see and feel that they could not grasp the tactical situations as clearly as officers. During the operation it was felt and proved that the young officers and good NCOs were the backbone of the battalion. However, he had his own reasons, the unit being new and most of the officers not being that experienced.

JCOs

The performance of the JCOs except a few like Sub Bikkar Singh in Mandi and OP Hill, Sub Surjit Singh in Mandi and Sub Jagir Singh 'C' Company in Gali and OP Hill and Sub Sant Singh 'C' Company at Sher Post and earlier operations at Guthrian was not very complimentary. Young ones of them must be made to go on independent operations and given training accordingly. It was noticed that they were under-utilised for active operations. A

JCO has got better knowledge about the man and surroundings. He on this aspect is better placed than an officer. However, role of higher age group JCOs and their contribution in almost all operations was found wanting as a result, the officers were very hard pressed.

Training of Troops

It was felt that the companies should be trained and organised in most cohesive manner like a commando company and should be capable of moving independently at least for five to seven days. It was a bad show while going for Phanne-Shah at crossing site on Betar Nala. It was a total mix up and chaos.

Time

Time taken by a patrol, platoon, company and battalion should be worked out judiciously. When our own fighting patrol took seven and half hrs to reach and do its job at Ring Contour on night 17/18 August 1965, the time to be taken by the battalion, a larger wherewithal for advance to crossing site and capturing objectives was not carefully calculated. The whole issue should have been gone into more deeply and realistically. I could see at the beginning that it could be very doubtful to accomplish the task, as we had been on this feature two days earlier. Infact the whole operation should have been conducted in two phases, first crossing the nala and establishing firm base and second launching of the operation with proper strength, not less than two units in any case, with proper arty support. Even putting the platoon which had been there two days ago, at the head of advance column, could have saved some time.

Jawan

A Sikh jawan is an excellent soldier but should be led by a well-meaning strong commander. He will invariably provide you with success, if guided and led well. However exceptions could be everywhere and that is not to be counted. His understanding of the ground and the general grasp of the things happening around is very clear. In our operations in Punch Sector, I am yet to find an instance, where our jawans caved in under the pressure of Pakistanis.

Physical Courage & Fitness

It is physical fitness and courage which beat all dangers. Once we are in operation, physical fitness counts a lot. Our jawans are physically very fit and that standard of fitness should be maintained. It was felt that certain senior JCOs and older officers were not fit to command the troops in battle. The first virtue on an infantry soldier is endurance of fatigue, the courage is the second one.

Digging Tools

It was seen that seniors normally do not carry the digging/trenching tools which is so very important. In Operation Phanne-Shah when the enemy corps arty started pounding, it was observed that all were running to get picks and shovels from here and there. The main culprits were the the officers and JCOs. Everyone should carry the digging tools and it should be impressed upon all. Numerous precarious situations in various battles have been saved by deeply digging down and sticking to the ground firmly, resolutely and coolly.

Organisation of Enemy

Razakars from Pakistan, during 1965 were the people who were residing near the posts. They were trained, fed and paid by the Pakistan army. The aim was to make use of them on posts and for subversive/intelligence tasks. Our troops must be properly educated on such issues. These things should not be taken casually. The enemy Razakar will say that he is a civilian but his word should not be taken as correct. Two Razakars were captured at Lahori Shah and brought by the fighting patrol on 17/18 August 1965. They were kept at Brigade HQ and when 7 SIKH moved for Phanne-Shah, they were surprisingly given to the unit as guides. How strange it was? They both disappeared on our reaching at crossing site at Betar Nala and gave total info to Pakistani Posts at Pritam and Langur and as a result the enemy gave a dressing down with accurate arty fire. They were required to be taken seriously. Casual handling of such cases can be a cause of great damage.

Conduct of Withdrawal/Fallback

Withdrawal is a most difficult operation. It has to be thought of very carefully and conducted with a bold face. 2/Lt Dewinder Singh, though out-maoneuvered and out-numbered at Gali conducted his abandoning of Gali post in a most efficient manner, not leaving a single wounded behind. The dead however could not be disposed off. But in Phanne-Shah, it was just opposite. Everybody was on his own. The command and control had gone for a six, firstly because the whole strength got mixed and secondly because enemy arty was really playing havoc and this was the situation when enemy was not physically pressing or following. The enemy itself was worried about the probable attack at night by this battalion on Pritam. Had this operation been planned properly, it would given a big name and fame to the battalion as enemy was demoralised and stunned after losing Haji Pir bulge. It was most ill-planned operation at the Corps level and with the same sense of casualness, the unit followed the course and result was there, for us all to see. The enemy's withdrawal at OP Hill on the other hand was complete and perfect, leaving nothing behind. Own troops suffered over one hundred killed and double of that as wounded, whereas, whole Brigade got only six PsW, two dead and four wounded soldiers of Pakistan.

Attending the Wounded

Wounded and injured would be there in a war. In an attack, the casualties will be due to arty fire, mines, machine guns and direct fire from other small arms. It was noticed in Mandi in 'A' Company advance on Eastern Ridge on 11 August 1965 and OP Hill on 2/3 November 1965, that men surrounded the wounded casualties which occurred due to mines, machine gun or arty fire. While on their way to FUP, a shell landed on 'B' Company causing couple of casualties. Company got involved in salvaging the situation and never moved from there for the task. In their place, 'C' Company was launched for pressing the attack. Company should keep moving and if need be one odd man can be left with the casualty. There is no requirement of whole lot of men to stand by and waste valuable time. It is to be ensured by all officers and JCOs that the momentum is maintained. When the enemy is firing and the move to objective is started, then it will be suicidal to waste even a minute on or ahead of Start Line.

Enemy's Information

Any info about the enemy at any stage should be passed to the required level of command without delay. It is incumbent upon the officers and JCOs to understand the designs of the enemy in respect of weapons, new concepts and organisation. From our own experience at Mandi and Gali, we had come to know that enemy was having new fire power in the form of 81 mm Mors. 83 mm RL and BMGs. Increased number of light machine guns in a rifle company of Pakistan which was noticed only in the OP Hill but was never passed by any other agency. The set up of enemy organisation became clear in Mandi Sub-sector quite late, that, it were not probably infantry battalion launching the attacks but amalgam of regulars and guerrillas in different dresses.

Move of the Reserves

It was felt in OP Hill that 'A' Company had been grossly involved in fighting and had suffered heavy casualties. Two platoon commanders, Sub Bikkar Singh on to the left and 2/Lt Hardial Singh onto the right had secured the two important edges of the Jungle Hill and hence it was really not possible for 'A' Company to launch another attack on Table Top (OP Hill Top) a higher and second step on Jungle Hill for clearing the remaining enemy element. 'B' Company was reserve to 'A' Company and it was not following as it should have been. They were bogged down due to some casualties caused by enemy arty fire. It was 'C' Company which was up behind 'A' Company in minutes and helped clearing Table Top and in reorganisation on Jungle Hill besides saving the situation for 2 DOGRA and linking with 5 SIKHLI coming from opposite direction.

Signal Operators and Others

It was noticed that at the very crucial movements, the signal operator of 'A' company commander was found missing. He bolted with the first Jaikara at the Start Line, to be traced, much later. It was felt that there should be two of them in case of any eventuality, the second can take over the duties and two together will seldom disappear. Same way Arty OP and Medical persons alongwith the Engineer's representatives be present at the first opportunity and at the required time. In OP Hill all these points were noted with concern. In the crucial movement of the battle, these specialised persons should be available at the first call and it is the unit with whom they are attached, who should ensure that.

Disposal of Dead Bodies

Proper disposal of dead bodies in a dignified way, goes a long way to maintain the morale of the troops. Seeing the dead bodies, being ignored in a undesired manner hits the very soul and command of the unit. At Gali, to bring down the dead bodies or carry out a respectable disposal was not possible. However, they were placed properly in the trenches and all the wounded were very courageously brought alongwith, after abandoning the post. At OP Hill, of course, it was a planned cremation. In Phanne-Shah the bodies were just left, which should not have been done, but situations for both the places were different.

Administrative Functioning

The battle at the battalion level can only be fought, where every single individual is made accountable for his actions and duties. There is no place for casualness. Operations deal with the lives of men and the careless handling can be a cause of loss of men, which could prove to be very costly. To lose a trained men in battle and more-so an officer or for that matter any other leader can prove disastrous. In Phanne-Shah Capt Surjit Singh, who was doing as Adjutant of the battalion, accompanied the battalion in attack. He was not required to be there, and the same cannot be justified. He was killed with the first firing by the enemy and we lost a capable and good officer for nothing. It is not the fault of unit alone. The general atmosphere of easiness due to anticipated declaration of ceasefire prevailed at all levels including Brigade, Division and Corps HQs.

Position of the Commander

In an attack in mountains, the move from Assembly Area to FUP will be in little dispersed single file. The companies will move one after the other. In such a situation, the commanding officer can ill-afford to be away i.e. with the third or fourth company in the order of move. He should be at the place, from where he is in a position to influence the battle. He should either be with the leading company or just behind or maximum, he can be behind the reserve of the leading company.

In the battle of OP Hill, commanding officer 5 SIKH LI was with the leading Company. He directly influenced the battle, Not only 5 SIKH LI captured their own objective of `White Rock' they exploited the area upto Twin Trees and claimed even the capture of OP Hill Top. Commanding officer 7 SIKH was little behind. 'A' company commander having read the situation asked the commanding officer to launch 'B' company so that the battalion objective was captured immediately. But he being away could neither pull up 'B'. company, nor push them up from behind and result was 'B' company did not move to, where required. It was third company i.e. 'C' company, which moved up and joined 'A' company. It is also because of this act that various versions of Battle of OP Hill, with regards to 7 SIKH accounts are found. The After Action Report of 120 Infantry Brigade and that of Commanding Officer, 7 SIKH noted that there was no enemy at Lone Tree whereas a fierce battle has been described in other accounts.

Lt Col Bhagat Singh and Recording of Historical Facts

There was another reason for different versions. Commanding Officer Lt Col Bhagat Singh, moved out on permanent posting within days after the battle. Had he stayed for some more time, say about a month or so, he could have put all the records straight. He was honest, hardworking and a man of letters and could not have permitted different versions of the operational records and other anomalies mentioned in the earlier chapters.

Taskent Declaration – Bargaining Table

The war ended and then came the time for playing the roles by government on the negotiating table keeping in view the national interests and sacrifices made by our gallant officers and men.

The president of US, Mr JF Kennedy was assassinated and Vice President Lyndon Johnson had taken over as President of America. His chemistry with Field Marshal Ayub Khan was different and as a result, Ayub Khan got tilted towards Russia. Russians did not miss the chance to take Pakistan into their camp, soon got engaged with him and offered themselves as the facilitators between India and Pakistan, with regards to 1965 Indo-Pak War for solving the tangle.

Shri Lal Bahadur Shastri, Prime Minister of India and Field Marshal Ayub Khan President of Pakistan reached Tashent. The discussion on Kashmir and 1965 Indo-Pak War ensued. When Lal

Bahadur Shastri was dogged in his determination not to vacate Haji Pir Pass and Uri-Punch Bulge taken with so heavy sacrifices, the talks got stalled. The Soviet Premier Alexei Kosygin offered to prevail upon the then Vice Chief of Army Staff Lt Gen PP Kumarmanglam who was also present and he applied clever logic in clinching the issue. He asked Lt Gen Kumarmanglam, whether in the fresh outbreak of hostilities, it would be difficult for Indian troops to recapture these features.

"Not at all," replied Lt Gen Kumarmanglam. "Then why haggle about them," declared the Soviet Leader. The hard-earned area, with blood, bones and sweat of so many human lives was lost in one sentence.

We in Army keep cursing the civilian officials and bureaucrats for ignoring us and not looking into our problems, but at times we also contribute for creating difficult situation for ourselves. Had Gen Kumarmanglam played the game, Lal Bahadur Shastri was playing, we would have not vacated the Haji Pir Pass and the heights, Point 13620, Saddle and Black Rock in Kargil Sector and that could have changed the course of history of India and Pakistan in respect and J&K, then and there only.

23

DEALING WITH PAKISTAN

"The passionate are, like men standing on their heads. They see all the things the wrong way." —Plato

Genesis

The Hindus, Sikhs and other Non-muslim communities had been treated very harshly under various Muslim regimes in India. They were crushed, tortured and forcibly converted to Islam at occasions. At the time of attainment of Independence and selection of democracy as way of governance, the things were destined for a great change. Muslims and their main leaders like Mohd Ali Jinnah became apprehensive of their living together with the other Indians, saying that they will not have any say in a predominantly Hindu India.

Britain and United States played a dirty role in the whole sordid drama of partition, where former was the main actor, who added fuel to the fire. They never let the Muslims feel that they were safe in a free India. Thus Pakistan was created based on fear and hatred for Hindus and India and that mentality still persists and keeps multiplying with advent of every new year.

Nehru and Army

The political leaders in India have no military background. Their knowledge of military matters is very sketchy and raw, at best. This could be easily attributed to the fact that Jawahar Lal Nehru, the first Prime Minister of India himself was against the idea of militarism. It is a fact that when Gen Sir Robert Lockhart, the first Commander-in-Chief of the Indian Army, presented a paper, outlining the plan for the growth of the Indian Army, in the light of an assessment of threats it faced, Nehru retorted, "We do not need defence plan and the growth of the Indian Army. Our policy is non-violence. We foresee no military threat. Scrap the army, the police are good enough to face the security threat and to meet our needs." It was, these theories developed by Indian leaders that were, the cause of their lack of knowledge and interest in armed forces, which are always and the only tools for preserving peace and ensure safety. Nehru, though was a great man with superb intellectual thinking but he had his weaknesses also. He did not rely on Sardar Patel for his views on defence. He ignored the views of Army Generals also, as mentioned earlier.

As result of all these imponderables of history, Pakistan got emboldened and raised a reasonably strong army, which she uses against India as and when gets a chance. For Pakistan, with the historical background in view vis-à-vis India, doing right is not their concern, using any means for annexation of Jammu and Kashmir is the aim. She had already tasted blood in 1947-48 and got a large portion of the state of J&K and almost 35% of it is still under her occupation. Its policy towards India will never change. Pakistan will never reconcile to our gestures. The whole thing has to be judged in view of its hatred for India. We in India feel that how unfortunate we were that our country was partitioned, otherwise we could have achieved wonders by now, as undivided India could have stolen a lead in world affairs and advanced growth by couple of decades, whereas Pakistan thinks and says "thank God we got separated and saved ourselves." Two divergent views and as such there does not seem to be any possibility for reconciliation on their part in a normal course of historical happenings.

Pakistan and its Army

Pakistan Army is very important part of its establishment and is not in favour of any reconciliation with India. It has got its own interests. This is the power centre which dictates the foreign policy of Pakistan. For being able to do that their "thinking" type officers of higher command structure are given lessons for in-depth study of strategy encompassing Central Asia, West Asia and South Asia. For such lot of officers who are certainly not monoliths and are quite different from the "fighting" type of officers, intensive educating is done on the important strategic issues. For different neighbours, they have different assumptions of "operating codes." The current versions of theirs, with regards to world in general and India in particular seem to be:-

- Full fledged war with India is to be avoided and no yielding to Indian pressure on important issues.

- Keep supporting Kashmiri separatists, but ensure that it does not lead to serious confrontation with India, however, the attrition to bleed India should continue.

- Maintain good relations with all Muslim States, both for broadening the economic base and required military support. We should show no tilting towards any one State for avoiding sectarian conflicts within our own country.

- Nuclear programme must be maintained and expanded, but without risking Pakistan's relationship with the United States of America and other anti-proliferation States.

- The relationship of being totally dependent on USA be avoided, but should be close enough so that the Indian influence in balanced.

- Whatever is possible should be done to maintain and enrich our relationship with China, which is our most important ally.

These are the permanent features of Pakistan's strategic policy towards India, US and other countries. There will be no change in its thinking in the near future and that is what we should never ignore any aspect of this strategy with regards to our country.

Measures to Deal with Pakistan

The two concepts, of India having a desire to improve relations and of Pakistan professing hatred, are totally contradictory. Therefore India requires altogether a different mindset to understand, react and finally deal with Pakistan. In such a situation the following measures and ways only, will hold water and as such these be made permanent features of our foreign affairs policy towards Pakistan, to get at something worthwhile :-

- You can take a horse to water but can't make it to drink. For them India is allegedly a biggest threat, bigger than anything else and they are suitably arming themselves. In such a situation, to deal with them with kid glove will be suicidal. They do not believe us, nor they ever will, then why not to deal with them on the same plane. Pay them in the same coin always and every time, diplomatically, militarily and commercially. Once an enemy is always an enemy, simple as that. An old saying still holds good.

- *"Never argue with a fool. First he will bring you down to his level and then beat you with his experience."* We must educate ourselves.

- High Commission to Pakistan should be recalled, immediately after a major willful dastardly act. Contacts can be reactivated, whenever needed, through other channels.

- Cultural and sports contacts need to be restricted to internationally committed by us.

- Not a drop of water of Satluj, Beas and Ravi rivers, exclusively meant for India, should be permitted to flow to Pakistan. Water is their biggest worry even bigger than Kashmir and infact Kashmir is also more for water, because it is the main source of their rivers which originate from here.

- Aspirations of Pastuns and Afghans, on Durand Line should be sensitised by us, whole-heartedly, by a covert action; with the crystal clarity of mind, with out missing a chance.

- We should forget the shared history. They hate to talk about it. It needs realisation on our part. They are praying for the old generation of pre-partition days to fade away so that, old link between people of both countries is washed off quickly and permanently.

- Carnage like at Mumbai and other places should neither be forgotten nor forgiven. The message should be clear.

- For China's role towards Pakistan, there should be no illusions. It was China who blocked the move to declare – Jamaat-ud-Dawa as an international terrorist organisation. China is against India on all accounts, vis-à-vis Pakistan.

- Cancel 1960 Water Treaty with Pakistan if the things don't improve. Consequences will dictate new theory. It should be abrogated because Pakistan has not lived upto the unwritten assurances given to the then Prime Minister JL Nehru, who had cleared the treaty because the then Pakistani ruler Gen Ayub Khan had assured him, that if, they could sort out the river water dispute amicably, the Kashmir issue will not come in the way of good neighbourly relations between the countries. For the friendly ties with Pakistan, Nehru had conceded more that 60 per cent of overall quota of water of all rivers to Pakistan.

- To be able to deal with the present situation created by Pakistan and China, robust economic growth, corruption free and clean administration and strong military is the only answer.

- Pakistan is not a country who will understand logical arguments. She has illusions about Jammu and Kashmir and the time has come, when she should be told in forceful words to keep her hands off, Kashmir. Conciliatory approach sends a wrong message to them. Our Kashmir policy must be most vocal and clearly unambiguous.

- There are other Muslim countries in the world, who are liberally contributing to the world peace. Pakistan almost a failed state, has got nothing of its own and lost the independent power of rational thinking and behaviour. From its birth, it has got congenital defect embedded in its working. It has developed its own character, which is a permanent part of its personality, and is anti-India. *"Should one tell you that a mountain has changed its place, you are at liberty to doubt it, but if anyone tells you that a man has changed his character, don't believe it"* – Mahomet (Mohammed)

- Pakistan will never change, what she has been preaching against India, as its survival is based on such a diseased aspect of philosophy. They will always preach like:-

    - Islam is in danger.

    - Hindu is a Kafir (enemy of Islam).

    - India is number one enemy.

    - Kashmir must be conquered, being a Muslim majority area and also a source of water for them from Chenab, Jhelum and Indus, which can be blocked by India to a large extent at any time, if situation so demands.

- Unfortunately No 1 Power of the world, USA does not try to understand the real intentions of Pakistan. But one day the American policy on Kashmir is destined to flounder, as it is based on seriously flawed premises. The Americans refuse to acknowledge that Pakistan's support for terrorism is not the work only of the element of ISI but constitute the considered opinion of the entire Pakistan Army Establishment. It is not only the fear of India, but the fear of Pashtun Nationalism and revival of Afghanistan territorial claims over the Durand Line that drives the Pakistani Military efforts to convert Afghanistan into a medieval, isolated and extremist client state which should be shunned by the international community. Only such a country may allow Pakistan to provide fuel to the idea of strategic depth, which Pakistan is pursuing with all its might vis-a-vis India. Pakistan seeks to subsume the Pashtun Nationalism at all costs. Afghanistan has not reconciled to the division of Afghan Nationalism by Durand Line, forced on them. It is also pertinent to note that Afghanistan was the last country to recognise Pakistan in 1947 and Badshah Khan was buried at Jalalabad in Afghanistan as per his last wishes and express desire of being a Pashtun.

- There are many politicians and bureaucrats in Pakistan and hundred percent military persons in Pakistan Defence Establishment who in their heart of hearts seek revenge for the 1971 disaster. This we should be able to guard against. Almost all of them without a single exception through propaganda or belief remain convinced that "India will destroy Pakistan." It is not for nothing that they have unleased a war of terrorism throughout India. Even their orchestrated propaganda, that the the Muslim population's place in the Indian society is that of second class citizens is enmeshed with that conviction. This propaganda is adversely affecting the gullible Indian Muslim population at places. We have to do everything to restore the confidence of Muslims. It will be unwise to ignore this issue. It is really not only shocking but also disturbing. We must take house clearing measures, so that such propaganda is reduced to a farce in the eyes of

Muslim population. In fact it is bias, suspicion and mistrust of Pakistanis towards India which is affecting the lives of certain percentage of Muslim population in India and as such Pakistan is awash in various incidents in Kashmir and rest of the country.

Conclusion

Pakistan is hypnotically obsessed with India, persistently engaged in thinking about its moves and checkmating it and we should always brace ourselves for any adventure by them. "Bleeding India with a thousand cuts" which is an avowed state policy of Pakistan should be clearly taken as a permanent challenge with no deviation whatsoever. Of what use the decisive victory in battle will be if we are bled to death as a result of their war of attrition. It has to be replied with befitting measures.

Trust Deficit. Pakistan is fed on the above agenda for the last so many years. The hate campaign unleased against India, in that country will only be stopped with robust economic growth and military prowess of India. To change their mindset, otherwise is very difficult. Hate India, bleed India, defeat India and conquer India policy of Pakistan can be thwarted by firmly telling Pakistan to butt out, otherwise they will never stop spewing venom against India. Distrust of Indian intentions is embedded in their DNA (Deoxyribose Nucleic Acid) and is really becoming difficult for them to surmount that. There is no trust of its Army in its Government itself, how can they have trust in us. So long as the Army rules the roost in Pakistan, there is no question of any reconciliation with us. It can be struck deep into our DNA also that "They can never be trusted." India is the prime target, because of unending hostility of Pakistan over Kashmir and the unseizing activities of jihadi organisations. India should be prepared to face prospects of unending jihadi attacks not only in Kashmir but also in the other parts of the country. Eternal vigilance is the price of liberty, India has to pay.

Definite Defence Policies. Country should have a definite defence policy. At present there is no defence policy, and a large force is being maintained as a usable commodity rather than a deterrent force. Pakistan will never stop the process of sharpening its teeth to cut India. India cannot blame anyone, if it is too late and caught on the wrong foot. The history of failure in war of attrition can be summed up in two words, (Too Late) enunciated by Gen Douglas MacArthur "Too late in comprehending the deadly purpose of a potential enemy, too late in realising the mortal danger, too late in preparedness, too late in uniting all possible forces for resistance, too late in standing with own's friends." We must watch out, before it is too late. Pakistan will always keep debilitating pressure on India and resort to war whenever in a position to do that.

24

THE LAST WORD

"It is the deeds rather than thoughts which count in war"
—Aristotle

Free Exchange of Views

How an infantry battalion deployed on separate independent axis will perform, in a sudden war, forced on the country by the enemy, has been brought out here systematically. The battle progresses and the situations keep changing. To adjust according to the operational requirements and the dictates of the senior commanders is though, an essential criteria of functioning of the army, the difficulties faced by juniors within the range of their duties also must be gone into carefully and clearly. Only the wearer knows where the shoe pinches and he is the person, who has to say, in no uncertain terms as to what his problems are. The people with weak & submissive responses are pushed around, as per the whims and fancies of certain senior officers on the perceived enemy moves. The person who performs has to see the possibility, probability, workability and achievability of the task given and must get it clarified in unambiguous words. To see that the problems are addressed squarely is also his job and concern. Levelheadedness has got its own awards. Your views on operational planning must be hazarded boldly, frankly but respectfully. Nothing clarifies knowledge like free exchange of views.

The Command

During the operations, the deliberate discussion of fleeting opportunity may not be possible but whenever a chance occurs, the matter should be discussed and deliberated wilfully. The commanders who are given a chance to perform, will study the situation more deeply than the others. Their minds start working immediately as to how the task will be performed, the moment they are assigned the task. The old adage "Plan deliberately and execute violently" always holds good. Wherever serious matters have been discussed, cursorily among the top two-three self seekers only, results have always been below expectations. And when the whole game is discussed and views of all upto lowest level are taken, it will pave the way for success and make a very difficult for any one to shirk responsibilities.

Good relations with the superior HQ is a prerequisite. Higher HQs cannot be taken lightly who can always create hurdles if they are not positively inclined towards you and your problems. Professionally everyone is qualified and equally trained, it is the personal disposition and equation which make all the differences. Certain persons carry certain things in their minds till last and their conceptions and perceptions are required to be cleared at the earliest opportunity. One cannot afford to be at loggerheads with seniors. It can only be at the cost of his own command.

The command of an Infantry Battalion is direct, which is independent, intimate and personal and authority of commanding officer is absolute. Views of the infantry Battalion commander are required to be given due weightage. He studies the ground realities, terrain, weather, strength and time and space and is the best judge to take recourse to a course. He is required to be listened to. Whenever he is ignored and the issues are forced upon him, the results have been significantly different than the expected ones.

Junior Leaders

Fate of an operation of any magnitude is decided at the level of platoon and company. Their defended localities, which are held by the junior leaders whose capabilities are normally not duly appreciated, are the leaders who matter most. They are not managers but the leaders who influence the outcome of the battle by giving personal example, whereas a manger manages the resources at his disposal. The contribution of each requires clear spelling out, by defining art of war and art of leadership.

The operational task and duties given to JCOs must be clearly discerned, based on their inherent qualities, capabilities and qualifications. JCOs and specially those who are taken as experienced, did not play any specifically useful role rather they were seen as hindrance being suggestive at number of places. The mental appreciation of the situation, the will to lead the men in battle on the part of a JCO cannot be equated with that of an officer because of his poor sense of appreciation of situation, higher age group and other implied calculations. Astonishingly, on one hand they were placed as juniors but at the same time they were made responsible for the performance of the companies, which did create little difficult situations at times for young officers. Their will to perform or not, did make difference in couple of situations, the unit had faced.

Essential Safeguards

There are certain basic issues essential for smooth functioning of the unit which the senior and middle rung commanders should always keep in mind:-

- The sycophants and manipulators is a dangerous community in army and their designs should be visualised and addressed firmly. These are the people who do greatest damage. If the man at the helms of affairs judges everyone based on former's actual capabilities to perform, nothing will go wrong in the unit. One has to be ruthless to deal with this element, who creates serious lags and biases for their personal gains, whenever they get a chance.

- All officers be involved for arriving at decisions. The man who is going to play with his life under the cloak of his duties, does deserve a right to know all possible info he needs. He should not be rubbished and taken as castaway, branded so by the intermediaries. Doer applies his mind more acutely than other thinkers or even planners.

- General working conditions are to be created in the unit. The things should not be left to certain selected ones. It creates unpleasant situations where the officers are not heard, and as a result they start looking the other way. Cohesiveness will be the first casualty. It could be ensured in the pre-war period only, so that it stays effective in war.

- It should be ensured that the principles of seniority cum-merit and equality of law are maintained and applied at all levels, at all costs. Any deviation for giving preferential treatment to selected ones will pay you negatively in the long run.

Summing up

In the end, I would like to say that I have tried to be exact, sincere and impartial in writing this account. In fact the various additions and deletions, manipulations and modifications and distortions and anomalies were the factors which made me to take the pen and write down the battle account at this age and after almost 47 years of its occurrence. To my mind it is free from passion, unbiased by interest, fear, resentment or affection and is faithful to the truth. My aim has been to bring out the facts, so that both sides of the coin can be studied, known and relevant lessons learnt. To include the flops and bad patches is very important, though unpleasant at places.

I am sanguine that the readers will find it worth reading and knowing as what and how the things happen in battle and how the same can be presented with all the veneer and aura, later on.

Appendix – A

Col Bhagat Singh, Retd

7/7 HP HB Complex
Shoghi, Shimla
May 26, 2005

My dear Shashi,

It is for quite some time now that I have been thinking of writing to you but for some reason or the other the thoughts could not materialise earlier.

Soon after attending Bn's Raising Day function at Pathankot early this year, some old officers of 7 SIKH shared with me their hurt sentiments over certain aberrations in presentation of OP Hill Battle and coupling it with the PETHAHEER fought by old 7 SIKH in 1948. The points raised by them may be briefly summarised as follows:

(a) Mixing up operational achievements of present 7 SIKH and old 7 SIKH as if both were one and the same entity.

(b) Distortion of OP Hill Battle as fought by 7 SIKH.

(c) Suffixing a hypothetic name of CHOINAR to the name of 7 SIKH when it had no relevancy to the OP Hill Battle objectives.

While expressing their hurt sentiments, the said officers sought my guidance in the matter in my capacity as the eldest members of the 7 SIKH fraternity, to have the records set right. I had, therefore decided, though reluctantly, to write this letter to you as you being the present captain of the team, are best placed to remove the ambiguities. I would therefore like to deal with the three alleged points in detail.

7 SIKH as an Entity

It may interest you to know that the old 7 SIKH never ceased to exist. It was simply re-designated as 5 SIKH. As is well-known to all of us, 5 SIKH inherited the history, traditions, silver, trophies, funds & other properties of old 7 SIKH. Incidentally, the battle of PETHAHEER fought by old 7 SIKH was never recognised as Battle Honour. On the contrary, the present 7 SIKH has the rare distinction of fighting a major battle & earning Battle Honour besides gallantry awards within three years of its life. We should all be rightly proud of its battle performance. A battalion with such a distinguished records does not need to borrow somebody else's battle achievements for flying their flag high.

Distortion of Battle Account

My experience has shown that there is a tendency among every sub-unit commander to exaggerate his own role in the battle & understate that of the others. But, the version of the Commanding Officer, whose assessment is based on impartial observation is ought to be correct being based on sound reasons. To avoid any further controversy, I had placed on records an exhaustive account of 7 SIKH's role in OP Hill Battle. This version was given out during Review of the Battle at Mendhar on 5 Nov. 65 in the presence of Army, Corps, Div & Bde commanders, besides of course the commanding offrs 5 SIKH LI & 2 DOGRA. It was further authenticated by me during `Battlefield Study' held by 120 Inf Bde at the scene of battle in early 1982 where most of the leaders who participated in actual battle were present.

Phenomenon of CHOINAR

I was surprised to read this word when I first saw it suffixed to the name of 7 SIKH, particularly when viewed in the context of OP Hill Battle, because, I could not understand its relevance to the said battle. This word never figured anywhere in either the Bn or Bde Op Orders. I lately learnt through certain officers that it was derived from the name of a stream which was not even remotely connected with our objective.

So much so, even the then Comdr 93 Inf Bde (the fmn to which 7 SIKH belonged) is believed to have taken serious objection to the 7 SIKH using CHOINAR as suffix. Since nobody cared to consult me on the matter, I preferred to avoid interfering in the matter. But, the fact remains that we have to pause & ponder over the wisdom of using a suffix to Bn's name which has no relevancy to the operation fought by the Bn.

I am writing this personal letter to you with the earnest hope that you would view its contents from correct perspective. Although I am a retired person but I still claim live long membership of the team that you captain. It is in this context that I strongly feel that we must ensure that the concern of 7 SIKH's sanctity in all respects remains at the centre of our collective endeavour and commitment. Being in a position, as you are, I am sure that you would take corrective measures to remove the alleged aberrations, if and where these have occurred.

At the end, I would like to seek your forgiveness if you find that I have exceeded by limits anywhere in the text of this letter.

With kind regards & Fatehs.

Yours Sincerely

Col Shashi Shekhar Prasad, YSM
7th Bn The Sikh Regt.
C/O 56 APO

SD/...............
(Col Bhagat Singh)

Appendix – B

PROCLAMATION OF WAR OF LIBERATION

The Revolutionary Council of Kashmir Proclaims:

Brave Kashmiris,

ARISE, for now is the time.

We have suffered long enough under the oppressive and treacherous rule of imposters and enemy agents.

Long enough have we allowed the traitors, to further the enemy designs.

Remember that a Hindu despot who ruled over us, in utter disregard of the wishes of the people, sold us to India in 1947. This was the second sale of our land through a fraudulent and ignoble deed which brought the might of the cursed Indian Army into our beautiful and peaceful land.

Betrayed though we were, we fought the enemy on every inch of our sacred soil. And we should have won but for the intervention of the United Nations who obtained an undertaking from India that we will exercise our inalienable right of self determination under a free and fair plebiscite.

The United Nations was duped and so was the whole world. India dishonoured her international pledge shamelessly and with utter contempt for world opinion.

She played for time to occupy our land. Since then every day that has passed has been a day of misery and every night a night of crime. You know what acts of cruelty, sacrilege and barbarity the enemy has been perpetrating under the shadow of guns and bayonets.

For years our great leaders Sheikh Mohammad Abdullah and Mirza Afzal Beg have been languishing in Indian prisons but their determination to throw off the yoke of Indian Imperialism remains unflagging.

We have seen our children butchered but every drop of their blood has illumined the path of our struggle.

Our women were dishonoured but in their agony they sanctified the course of our freedom.

Our brave fighters lost their lives but their dying calls stirred the hearts of their compatriots.

The will of our people remains unbroken; their united might unshaken.

The enemy is on the run. We will not rest content till we have chased him out of our land.

The time has come for us to deliver the final blow and hereby we take a solemn pledge to take up arms once again and continue the fight till:-

(a) The usurper are expelled out of our land;

(b) Our leaders now in jail are freed; and

(c) The will of the people is allowed to determine the future of our land.

The Revolutionary Council which consists of patriots of unimpeachable integrity and men of unswerving faith, has set up today the National Government of the People of Jammu and Kashmir which decries as here under :-

From Today:-

(a) All alleged treaties and agreements between the imperialist Government of India and Kashmir stand annulled and are no longer binding on us,

(b) The National Government of Jammu and Kashmir formed by the Revolutionary Council of Kashmir is the sole lawful authority in our land.

(c) Only the National Government will be legally competent to receive taxes and public dues from the people of the state;

(d) Any Kashmiri national who willfully cooperates with the Indian Government or their puppet administration in Occupied Kashmir will be treated as traitor and dealt with as such;

(e) Every national of the state of Jammu and Kashmir who may be employed either by the Imperialist Indian Government or its puppet administration, in civil or military capacity, shall support the freedom movement of the Revolutionary Council in every possible way ;

(f) The National Government will issue orders and decrees on the Kashmir National Radio representing the 'Voice of Kashmir;'

(g) Any national of Kashmir who impedes the freedom movement or disobeys any order or decree of the National Government will be dealt with as a traitor.

The Revolutionary Council appeals to the world to support this freedom movement.

Now is the time for countries who have pledged themselves to help all freedom movements against imperialism to come to our assistance.

We have nothing against the people of India but their Governments have established a record of treachery and dishonesty in the world. We expect all same and freedom – loving elements in India and particularly the brave Sikhs, the South Indians and the Rajputs who have always given us moral support to lend us active assistance.

The people of Pakistan have stood by us in our fight. To our regret they have not done as much as we expected of them. Now is the time for them too to join us in our struggle for life and liberty.

Let the nations of the world remember that if we go down the light of freedom will be extinguished forever.

And above all, you the people of Kashmir, you are the ones who are on trial. You are the ones who must win this war for the sake of coming generations, for the sake of freedom and for the sake of the glory of your motherland.

Arise : now or there will be no tomorrow:

Issued by the Revolutionary Council of Kashmir

Sadi Kashmir Press, Srinagar.

Appendix – C

THE INFILTRATION CAMPAIGN

Training and Organisation

The training of Pak Infiltrators had commenced in May 1965 and was carried out in commando training schools at Shinkiari, Mang Bairi, Dungi and Sakesar under respective Sector Headquarters.

A number of Task Forces were raised, each comprising three to six companies. A company consisted of 35 to 40 Pakistan Occupied Kashmir Soldiers, a group of three to four Other Ranks (OR) from Special Service Group and about 66 Mujahids. The Pakistan Occupied Kashmir soldiers were tapped from various POK battalions in each sector and the Mujahids were forcibly recruited from local areas in Pakistan Occupied Kashmir. The Pakistan Occupied Kashmir soldiers formed the hard-core of the companies and the Special Service Group personnel handled explosive for sabotage activities. The companies comprising the Task Force were commanded by regular Pak or Pakistan Occupied Kashmir Army officers of the rank of Maj, Capt or Lt. Each Task Force was placed under the charge of the 2IC of the Pakistan Occupied Kashmir battalion already located in the vicinity of the projected area of operations.

The infiltration forces were equipped with Pak arms, ammunition, equipment and clothing. Pak markings were however, erased from most of the weapons and equipment before launching the infiltrators across the CFL. In addition, to personal arms, the companies were equipped with light machine guns, 2 inch Mors, 83 mm Blendicide

Rockets, shotguns and Verey Light pistols. Force Commanders were issued with wireless sets 62/19/ANGRC-9 for communication with sector Headquarters and the nearest Pakistan Occupied Kashmir Battalion Headquarters. Company Commanders were to use runners for communication with, their respective force Headquarters. They were however issued with transistor sets to listen in to messages to be broadcast by the Azad Kashmir Radio at a fixed time every day. Each individual carried five to seven days cooked rations in the form of sweet chapathies, gur, shakarparas and three days ration of atta, rice and dal. Company commanders were given Rs 9,000/- each in Indian currency to buy rations locally thereafter. Companies were issued with faked registration cards to facilitate local purchase of rations.

Tasks

The following general tasks were assigned to the infiltrating forces-

(a) Destruction of bridges and disruption of lines of communication.

(b) Raids on ammunition and supply dumps.

(c) Raids on Formation and Unit Headquarters.

(d) Ambushing of convoys and patrols.

(e) Distribution of arms and ammunition to local civilians across the CFL, and enrolling them as Razakars.

(f) Creating situations which would result in paralysing the Jammu and Kashmir administration and encourage an open rebellion in the State.

Operations of the Infiltration Force

The whole force of infiltrators, known as the Gibraltar Force, was launched in the first week of August 1965 and was divided into the following Task Forces.

Tariq Force in Area Kargil.

Qasim Force in Area Gurez.

Khalid Force in Area Tithwal.

'F' Force in Area Uri – Rampur.

Salahuddin Force in Area Gulmarg – Srinagar – Mandi.

Nusrat Force in Area Rajauri – Mendhar.

Ghaznavi Force in Area Darhal – Thanamandi – Budil.

Babar Force in Area Naushera – Chhamb.

Sector Commanders and Force Commanders were assembled in Murree during the second week of July 1965 and addressed by Field Marshal Ayub Khan, Maj Gen Akhtar Hussain Malik who controlled the operations of the force from Murree, addressed the Force Commanders on 1st August 1965 and impressed upon them the importance of the mission, stating that it was their last chance to liberate Kashmir. The operations of each force is described under various divisional and brigade sectors in the succeeding paragraphs.

Tariq Force in 121 Infantry Brigade and 19 Infantry Division Sectors

This force consisted of elements of Karakoram Scouts and Mujahids, and was raised by Headquarters Northern Scouts at Skardu during May-Jun 1965. The force was composed of five to six companies each under a Captain and operated in six different columns.

One Column went along River Suru and set on fire the suspension bridge at Kunore. The second column operated along Wakka Chu and partially damaged the bridge at Paskyun. The third column operated between Kargil and Dras and damaged the bridge at Shamshah NN 9972. The fourth column operating between Dras and Zojila attacked the Base Headquarters of one of our Border Roads camps at Dras. They also attempted to blow up a bridge approximately two miles Northeast of Zojila, but could only damage it slightly. Another column, approximately 300 strong, entered through Gultari NN 5489 and established a hideout in Sirbal Jungle on Road Baltal NN 4739 – Sonamarg. The tasks given to this column were to ambush convoys on Road Sonamarg – Baltal and destroy bridges at Sonamarg. It succeeded in damaging the Hamilton Bridge at GR NM 299435. The sixth column, approximately 300 strong, infiltrated from Minimarg NH 0801 through Karobal Gali NN 2584 and Gujran NN 2672 in Tilel Valley and created a safe area at Gujran. From here the column moved towards Sumbal. Bridge NM 1033 and partially damaged it. A party from this column succeeded in infiltrating upon Gandarbal NM 8131 where it raided the Government Sheep Farm, the Power House and the new Water – Works.

The Force was continuously hounded and harassed by our own forces from the very start and eventually disintegrated into a number of parties to slink away unobtrusively across the CFL into their own territory.

Qasim Force in Area Gurais

19 Infantry Division Sector

Two columns of this force known as "Murtaza Force' and 'Sikandar Force' consisting of Northern Scouts, infiltrated from Gultari – Kel NG 3400 Sector and operated around Kangan NM 9436 and Bandipur NM 6753 through Tilel Valley, and around Kapowar through Lulab Valley. These columns raided our forward posts, gun positions at Ringpain NM 4094 and Ringbala NM 3889, and Headquarters 268 Infantry Brigade at Kapowar. They also raided Shumberail Bridge at Kapowar. On account of the stiff opposition from own troops and lack of cooperation from the local population these columns started retiring to Pakistan Occupied Kashmir by the end of August 1965.

Khalid Force in Area Tithwal

19 Infantry Division Sector

Khalid Force consisted of men from several Pakistan Occupied Kashmir battalions and 300 to 400 Mujahids recruited from Keran – Mirpur Areas. It was grouped into five companies out of which one company was later sent to join Salahuddin Force. They crossed the CFL via Keran and formed firm bases in areas North East of Tithwal and North West of Chokibal. The exploits of these columns included the followings :

a) An attack on a battalion Headquarters at Naugam on 13th August 1965 during which a few casualties were inflicted.

b) Damage to bridges at Karalpur and Chokibal.

c) Raid on Ammunition Dump at Chokibal. In addition, attempts were made to incite the locals against the administration. Due to relentless chase by own troops and lack of food and ammunition, this force soon disintegrated into small parties and dispersed over a vast area. Most of the force returned to Pakistan Occupied Kashmir in the second week of Sep. 1965.

A second wave, consisting of 23 Pakistan Occupied Kashmir Battalion and a few Mujahids, infiltrated into the same area in the middle of August 65 crossing the Kishanganga at Jura. The unit was given the task of covering Tangdhar Area from the rear by establishing road blocks combined with harassing attacks. This could not be achieved since the force had to be used in a defensive role around Puran, Sunjoi (Point 9013) NM 8952 and Mirpur Ridge when our troops attacked Sunjoi.

'F' Force in Area Uri – Rampur

19 Infantry Division Sector

This force, consisting of three companies, was to operate in Area Uri – Bamramula and was given the task of destroying the Mahura Water Channel NM 1514 and raid other opportunity targets. Only one company was active for some time on Road Uri – Baramula, and the remaining two companies were intercepted by our troops at the start, compelling Pak use them for the defence of Bedori Bridge.

This force consisted of men from several Pakistan Occupied

Kashmir battalions and approximately 400 to 500 Mujahids recruited from Rawalkot No 8280 – Chakothi NL 9211 and Bagh No 8295 Areas. The force was organised into five companies. Another company from Khalid Force joined it later. Of all the forces that operated in 19 Infantry Division Sector, Salahuddin Force played the most important part.

The tasks given to this force were as follows :-

(a) Four companies to move towards Srinagar through Chor Panjal Pass and Jamian Wali Gali and establish themselves in Srinagar – Badgam Area. One company was to capture or destroy All India Radio Station Srinagar.

(b) One company to advance on Baramula, attack Divisional Headquarters, cut all telephone wires, destroy all culverts and bridges on Road Uri – Srinagar, and blow up the Mahura Power House.

(c) Force Headquarters and one company to form firm base in Area Bunna Danwas and create disturbances in Tangmarg – Gulmarg Area.

(d) To create a sympathetic section among the local population and enroll and train Mujahids in the Valley.

Elements from this force also trickled into the Mandi Valley.

The Salahuddin Force crossed the Cease File Line at Chor Panjal Pass on 1st August 1965, left two companies in Gulmarg Area and with the remaining companies made for Badgam. They established bases and hideouts, in Bunna Danwas, Chhanz NR 5982, Yusmarg NR 7286 and Sutahran Forests NR 6090. From these hideouts, columns and small groups moved towards Srinagar, Khunamuh, Khundru, Shupiyan, Anantnag and Pahalgam.

A large party of infiltrators clashed with the Punjab Armed Police at Bimna in Badgam Area on 08 August 65 and inflicted some casualties on our post. An attempt was also made to blow up Bimna Bridge. Another party attacked Qasha Beru Police Station and then advanced on Srinagar Airfield. Some of these infiltrators later appeared in Village Tangpur and fired on Srinagar City and the Tatoo ground. Their attempts to get closer to Srinagar Air field and to storm the Radio Station Srinagar were however, foiled. Raids on Ammunition Depot at Khundru on 21st and 22nd August were successfully countered.

When our security force started combing the concentration areas of the raiders, clashes took place around Badgam, Magan NM 6413, Yusmarg and in Sutahran Forests as also in Areas Dor NR 9349, Nagbal NX 2514 and Sanglipur NR 6092. As a result of these operations, the force was completely dispersed and slipped away in driblets across the CFL via Chor Panjal Pass NR 4195, Jamian wali gali NR 4692 and Nurpur Gali NR 5277.

Nusrat, Ghaznavi and Babar Force

25th Infantry Division and 191 Infantry Brigade Sectors

The task forces operating in 25 Infantry Division Sector were the Nusrat – Ghaznavi – Babar Group of columns whose sphere of activities extended from Punch in the North to Chhamb in the South. In addition, a group from the Salahuddin Force known as the Mann Column branched South through the Gali into the Mandi Sector while the main force made its way into the Valley. The enemy's strategic aim in this Sector was to cut off Punch and Rajauri and capture them if possible. The plan envisaged was to take shape as follows :-

(a) A two pronged deep infiltration on a massive scale via the Mandi Valley in the North and through Mendhar Valley in the South, to establish a link-up at Kalai Bridge NR 2668. Simultaneously the envelopment of Rajauri by infiltration through the gallies adjoining Galuthi and lodgement in Area Thanamandi – Darhal NR 5139 – Budil.

(b) The establishment of a series of concentration areas and control points in and around our defences with particular reference to Punch town and Rajauri.

(c) A raid on the administrative installations at Khenetar NR 2267 and Narian for replenishing their supplies and ammunition requirements.

(d) The capture of the vital Kalai Bridge for severing out line of communication to Punch.

(e) Shelling of the Punch Airfield to disrupt air traffic.

(f) Bombardment of Punch town to create confusion and to demoralise the local population.

(g) Depending upon the successful progress of the above missions, to put in a conventional full-fledged attack on Punch town from the West or North West in coordination with an infiltration thrust via Mandi or Pir Mangot Ghazi NR 1865 Areas.

(h) Raids in strength on the line of communication in the Chhamb – Jhangar Sector to disrupt administrative traffic.

The succeeding paragraphs describe in detail the operations of each of these infiltrating columns.

Mann Force in Area Mandi

This column consisting of approximately two companies strength made its presence felt on 07 August 1965 when it concentrated in force against Gali picquet. As this picquet was not tactically sited and was beyond the range of our artillery, we were compelled to abandon it. Simultaneously with this action a large number of infiltrators bypassed this picquet and established a base at Loran. Within a short space of time their activities dominated the Mandi Valley.

To deal with this menace which posed a serious threat to the line of communication to Punch from Rajauri including the vital Kalai Bridge,

52 Mountain Brigade was rushed to Mandi Town on 11th August 1965. This was followed by a slow and slogging match between the grit and determination of our troops and the elusiveness of the infiltrators operating in terrain ideally suited for guerilla action. After a series of tough fights in most of which our troops bested the enemy the Mandi Valley was finally cleared by 27th August 1965.

While the hunt for the infiltrators in the Mandi Valley was on, a number of them concentrated against Khanetar, the administrative base for all troops deployed South of River Punch. The garrison at Khanetar consisted of a small police detachment and for a time it appeared as if the infiltrators would easily overpower it. The artillery however stepped into the breach and through a series of well directed concentrations, disorganised the impending raid.

Nusrat Force in Area Rajauri

Mendhar: 25 Infantry Division Sector

This force consisted of five companies. Three companies operated between Rajauri and Bhimber Gali and along Roads Rajauri – Thana Mandi and Bhimber Gali – Surankot NR 356. Two companies operated between Bhimber Gali – Mendhar and Mendhar – Punch. These infiltrators were first contacted six miles west of Rajauri on 6th August and in Area Bhimber Gali on 7th Aug. They attempted a raid on Headquarters 120 Infantry Brigade at Galuthi. They also succeeded in ambushing several of our convoys, on road Bhimber Gali – Surankot between 13th to 15th August 1965 but in spite of these interruptions the road was kept open by our troops throughout.

The force was reinforced between 17th and 18th August and then started moving to Shupiyan over the Pir Panjal Pass. A small party left behind remained active on Roads Rajauri – Mendhar and Rajauri Thana Mandi and succeeding in damaging a few unimportant bridges. This party also raided our administrative base near Mendhar but without much success.

The raiders made a show of establishing administration in Areas Kot Bhrote NR 2167, Darhal and Thana Mandi. Even at the best of times our civil administration had made little impact on these remote areas, which had remained comparatively isolated from the main centre of government like Jammu and Srinagar. Hence the selection of these areas by the infiltrators to create an administrative set up.

Combing operations against these raiders were launched as soon as the tactical situation was clear. The Mendhar and Mandi Valleys were cleared of the infiltrators by early September. The areas east of Galuthi and Rajauri were searched thoroughly in September and the raiders were driven back across the CFL. During these operations, heavy casualties were inflicted on them and a large quantity of arms, ammunition and explosives recovered. Before pulling out, the raiders burnt the houses of the local population and indulged in indiscriminate killing of civilians.

Ghaznavi Force in Area Darhal – Thanamandi – Dudil

25 Infantry Division Sector

This force consisted of five companies. The tasks assigned to respective companies are given below :-

(a) No 1 and 2 companies – To penetrate to Budil and remain there for further operations.

(b) No 3 company – To proceed to Ramban and destroy the bridge.

(c) No 4 company – To function in conjunction with Nusrat Force.

(d) No 5 company – To raid Headquarters 80 Infantry Brigade and our administrative dump at Narian. They were then to proceed to Budil, merge with the local population there and await further instructions from force Headquarters.

This force established hideouts in Gol Forest, Darhal, Budil and in Gulabgarh NR 92 in Riasi NW 9793. After the leading column had formed a firm base for guerilla operations, it was reinforced by approximately 600 men from 21 Pakistan Occupied Kashmir Battalion. The force tried to enroll the local population in the interior of Rajauri for guerilla operations but met with limited success only. It suffered heavy casualties at the hands of our security force. The commanding officer of this force retreated with his men towards Pir Kalewa NR 3939 and then withdrew into Pakistan Occupied Kashmir after the Cease Fire. Own administration was established in all areas by early Oct 1965.

Babar Force in Area Naushera – Chhamb

25 Infantry Division and 191 Infantry Brigade Sectors

Down in the south, the Babar Force, 400 strong, entered Jammu and Kashmir through the Bhimber NW 2075 and Sadabad NW 2887 gaps. Groups of this force mainly operated in the Kalidhar – Chhamb area. On 8th August 1965 approximately 30 to 40 Pak infiltrators raided our camp at Jaurian NW 7261. We suffered some casualties. Apart from a few desultory raids on our forward posts the only other activity of any significance was the ambushing of our maintenance column in area nine and a half miles north – west of Akhnur on 20th Sep. A few infiltrators penetrated as far as Riasi and Udhampur but achieved nothing of any consequence. The force infiltrated back in small batches through the Pir Badeshar Area just prior to the Cease Fire.

Appendix – F

Excerpts from the comments of Col. Bhagat Singh Ex-CO, 7 SIKH, on the report of Battle of OP Hill fought on 2/3 Nov 65, submitted during review of the situation on 18 April 1982.

Sit Before The Battle

Pak forces had EST a coy post at NR 1052 and NR 1152 in between 2 DOGRA pqt No. 636 NR 0953 and 11 J&K MILITIA pqt 475 (pt 5136) NR 1151 as early as 05 August, 65. The enemy called it "MALL" denoting free passage of infiltrators without any interruption to and from our territory.

Enemy Defs.

Although the objectives of all the three bns in assault role were sparsely wooded out except for TWIN PIMPLES, the remaining parts of the obj were completely intervened from view by pine forest in the NORTH & EAST. The view from the side of pt 5136 in the South would have been quite clear but the enemy had taken suitable measures to prevent our recce parties from getting closer view of the obj. This made difficult, not only for the attackers, but also the Bde Cdr to delineate the features when allocating tasks to different bns. Despite the help of map, allocation of obj particularly to 7 SIKH, as eventually turned out, was a bit too complex as the pimples now shown on the enlargement att to the report as TWIN TREES formed part of the ridge beginning with WHITE ROCK & it was quite distinct from the JUNGLE/OP HILL. 5 SIKH LI would not have been able to hold for long only on one pimple i.e. WHITE ROCK (as allotted to them as their task in phase I) without pressing their attack into other two adjoining pimples i.e. TWIN TREE which were located within an area of 50 yds. There was nothing at LONE TREE. Phase 3 of the attack was planned out of ignorance about the actual layout of the obj. Similarly, the marking of OP HILL on a pimple in the enlargement att to the bde report is also an after thought. If the loc of OP HILL had been as now shown in the enlargement, no sensible Cdr would have allotted this task to bn other than 5 SIKH LI. Apparently, OP HILL was conceived to be part of the JUNGLE, hence allotted to 7 SIKH as their task in Phase II.

The JUNGLE was the largest amongst the obj of three bns & somewhat rectangular in shape. It had 10-15' high precipice & ledges in the NORTH, SOUTH, & SOUTH WEST. Along the edges of the cliff were series of bunkers flushed to ground & interconnected with a continuous comn trenches all around the obj. The location of Comd Post, & Arty OP being at JUNGLE, and it's commanding posn right in the centre of the OP HILL COMPLEX, clearly showed that the JUNGLE & OP HILL were one & the same obj. Had OP HILL been a separate feature as now shown in the enlargement, it would not have been allotted to 7 SIKH as their task (see Para 11 of Phase 2 in 120 Inf Bde OO). Hence there was no question of any doubt as reflected in part 50 of the bde report as to who reached the OP HILL first. It was indeed 7 SIKH which captured the OP HILL & correctly reported as such.

On the other side, 5 SIKH LI had captured their obj & secured TWIN TREES except that of an LMG posn on the NORTH- EASTERN slope of TWIN TREES which kept on sweeping the front of JUNGLE/OP HILL till it was captured by 7 SIKH after the capture of their own obj.

Appendix – G

TRIBUTE TO A SOLIDER

Lt Col Mohd Akram Raza Officer Commanding 35 FFR who led the counter attack on Indian position of Village JARPAL at 0400 hrs on 17 Dec 71 has died a real solider's death, Our hats off to him.

He was personally leading the attack by being in the front line of assault, when he was hit by an MMG burst from our positions right on the face killing him on the spot.

We had recovered his body on 18 Dec 71 after having been told by one of the prisoners of war captured by us. The prisoner also helped us in identifying the dead body. We found both his arms frozen after death in the position in which he was holding his sten gun which indicates his determination to go ahead.

In this action Lt Col Mohd Akram Raza displayed courage, determination and personal bravery of the highest order in keeping with the traditions of the soldiers.

This heroic deeds of Lt Col Raza, a brave soldier should not go unnoticed.

Praying for the departed soul.

Field

SD/- x x x
(VP Airy)

Note: Citation of Lt Col Mohd Akram Raza written by Lt Col VP Airy commanding officer 3 Grenadiers was handed over with the remains of Lt Col Akram Raza to Brigadier Sher Baaz Khan of Pakistan Army, who had come to collect their dead bodies.

BIBLIOGRAPHY

A Matter of Honour	Philip Mason
Kashmir - Resolving Regional Conflict	RG Wrising
Overcoming Crisis in Leadership	Brig K Kuldip Singh
Top Brass	Brig HS Sodhi
Men Against Fire	SLA Marshall
Conduct of War	Col (Dr) Narender Singh
Missed Opportunities	Maj Gen Lachhman Singh
Indo-Pak Conflict over Kashmir	Lt Col Bhupinder Singh
Friends Not Masters	FM Ayub Khan
Pakistan Meets Indian Challenge	Brig Gulzar Ahmad, Pakistan Army
War Despatches	Lt Gen Harbakhsh Singh
India-Pakistan War Vol 1 & 2	HR Gupta
Slender was the Thread	Brig LP Sen
The Far Flung Frontiers	Maj Gen OS Kalkat
Military Leadership in India	Maj Gen Rajinder Nath
Indo-Pakistan Conflict	Russel Brines
Operation Rescue	Maj Gen SK Sinha
General Trends	Maj Gen Sukhwant Singh
Crush India or Pakistan's Death Wish	GS Bhargava

Kashmir-Pakistan's Proxy War	DP Kumar
The Sikhs Today	Khushwant Singh
The Kashmir Story	BL Sharma
Kashmir in Conflict	Victoria Schofield
The Armies of India	Macmunn
Jammu and Kashmir	DN Panigrahi
Kashmir Panorama	KL Kalla
The Vali of Kashmir	Kaul LN
The Charismatic Leader	Sikander Hayat
In The Line of Duty	Lt Gen Harbakhsh Singh
History of Pakistan Army	Boughley
Military History of British India	HS Bhatia
Military Plight of Pakistan	Col MN Gulati
Pakistan's Downfall in Kashmir	Col MN Gulati
The Killer Instinct	Maj Gen OP Sabharwal
100 Great Lives	HD Sharma
Guide to Places of The World	Reader's Digest
Right of the Line, The Grenadiers	Maj Gen AHE Michigan
The Rajputana Rifles	Maj Gen CN Das
Mountbatten	Richard Hough
Article 370 – A Thorn	Prof Chamanlal Gupta
The Madras Sappers 1947-1980	Lt Gen PM Menon
Sir Chhotu Ram	Dr Balbir Singh
Pakistan Occupied Kashmir: under the Jackboot	Jasjit Singh

Bibliography

Pakistan Occupied Kashmir: The Untold Story	Virender Singh and Alok Bansal
Are We Two Nations	MS Vairanpillai
Demystifying Military Leader	Lt Gen HB Kala
The Pakistan Army	Stephen P Cohen
Low Intensity Conflicts in India	Lt Col Vivek Chadha
Inside the Pakistan Army	Carey Schofield

INDEX

1947-48 War and Afterwards, 70-79
  accession, 73-74
  brig rajinder singh and his state forces, 72-73
  british officers in pakistan army, 75-77
  empathizing britain, 77-78
  invasion by armed looters and marauders, 71-72
  landing of indian troops in kashmir, 74-75
  looters at village peta hir, 77
  nehru and mountbatten 1st governor general of india, 78-79
  partition and jammu and kashmir, 70-71

2 DOGRA, 188, 191, 195, 197, 198, 199, 205, 207, 208, 209, 210, 215, 219, 221, 229, 254, 274, 320

2/Lt SS Ahlawat, 22, 111, 113, 114, 116, 117, 120, 121, 122, 125, 126, 127, 152, 160, 166, 167, 168, 170, 178, 179, 250, 255

5 SIKH LI, 188, 191, 195, 198, 204, 209, 212, 213, 215, 221, 229, 274, 322

7 SIKH, 19, 20, 21, 22, 24, 26, 27, 28, 30, 31, 32, 33, 67, 68, 77, 98, 99, 101, 102, 104, 105, 107, 110, 111, 112, 113, 116, 122, 123, 125, 126, 130, 131, 133, 134, 135, 136, 39, 140, 141, 147, 151, 152, 153, 154, 156, 159, 60, 164, 165, 166, 168, 171, 176, 178, 181, 185, 188, 190, 191, 192, 195, 197, 198, 199, 208, 209, 212, 213, 214, 215, 218, 219, 221, 222, 229, 230, 231, 232, 233, 248, 252, 254, 256, 261, 262, 272, 273, 274, 275, 276, 282, 301, 311, 312, 318, 322, 323

A

Abdali, Ahmad Shah, 226
Abdullah, Sheikh Mohammad, 43, 48, 71, 72, 74
Afganistan, 72
Akbar the Great, 59
Aksai Chin, 56
Amarnath Temple, 152
Ashoka Chakras, 306
Azad Kashmir, 64, 94

B

Babur, 226
Baramula, 72, 73, 74
Battle of Gali, 128-150
  changing scenario, 143-144
  commencement of hostilities, 135-136
  composition of force at gali post, 136-137
  critical appreciation, 147-150
  destruction of post, 145-147
  developing into defended locality, 130-132
  fiercest battle ensued, 144-145

first series of attacks, 137-139
importance of gali post, 133-134
infiltration, 132-133
own intelligence agencies and enemy, 134-135
police check post, 130
post in bowl, 128-129
reinforcing a success or failure, 141-142
second series of attacks, 142-143
views of commander 93 infantry brigade, 140-141

Battle of OP Hill, 186-222

7 sikh in OP hill, 221
aberrations, 222
addressing of troops by lt col bhagat singh, 195-196
attack by 2 garh rif, 193
breaking crust, 203-204
catering for all eventualities, 196-197
ceasefire and after, 188-189
clarification, 211-213
critical appreciation, 215-218
crux of matter, 210-211
elimination of last enemy, 208-209
enemy, dug down, 192-193
enemy dispositions and own plan of attack, 194-195
junior leaders and ground realities, 213-215
launching of attack, 202-203
leading company commander, 199-200
local intelligence, 190
lt gen harbaksh singh and op hill, 191-192
multi-directional attack, 218-219
op hill complex, 187-188
pakistan's intensions and designs, 189
phase I of attack, 197-199
planning for brigade attack, 191
position of commander in battle, 219-220
readjustment of junior leaders, 200-202
reorganisation at op hill top, 209
reorganisation stage and its imperatives, 220-221
role & place of reserves, 206-208
situation, 186
table top/op hill top, 204-205
tactical advantages of op hill complex, 190

Bedori, 76, 112, 152, 182
Belliappa, KG (Maj), 21, 105, 112, 113, 116, 117, 122, 126, 127, 171, 176, 248, 273
Betar Nala, 22, 94, 165, 166, 167, 168, 169, 170, 171, 172, 177, 178, 179, 180, 181, 184, 313, 315, 316, 318
BMGs, 102, 119, 143, 193, 210, 282, 320
Britain, 41, 45, 51, 70, 77, 87, 90, 258, 325
Bhutto, Z A, 80, 81, 87
Buddhism, 236

C

Capture of Mandi, 108-127

arrival of hq 52 mountain brigade and a unit, 115-117
capture of pimple, 117-119
capture of ring contour, 119-121
casualties, 127
conduct of operations, 114-115
deployment of own troops, 110-112
enemy guerrillas and irregulars, 108-109
honours and awards, 126-127
mandi town under enemy, 110
operational analysis, 123-126
restoring of situation in mandi town, 121-123

task force and its composition, 112-114

China, 52, 53, 54, 56, 66, 67, 80, 81, 328, 330

Congress, 41, 55, 59, 60

Cunningham, Sir George, 46, 78

D

Dealing With Pakistan, 325-334
  conclusion, 333-334
  genesis, 325
  measures to deal with pakistan, 328-333
  nehru and army, 326-327
  pakistan and its army, 327-328

Defence At Sauji, 100-107
  7 sikh in mandi valley, 101-102
  administration at sauji, 106-107
  battalion hq at sauji, 107
  beginning of hostilities, 100
  clearing of sauji, mandi area, 105-106
  molsar ridge becomes active, 104-105
  redeployment of own troops, 102-103

Deoxyribo Nucleic Acid (DNA), 333

E

Emperor Ashoka, 236

Engagement At Molsar Ridge, 151-157
  clearing of mandi valley, 156-157
  enemy at molsar top, 152-153
  enemy's pattern of operations, 153-154
  establishing of sher post, 154-156
  importance of molsar ridge, 151-152

England, 45, 53, 57, 85, 258

F

First Things First, 26-37
  causes of delay in documenting battle accounts, 28-30
  certain overlappings, 36-37
  history of unit starts with first commanding officer, 33-34
  old 7 sikh (redesignated as 5 sikh) vis-a-vis new 7 sikh (op hill), 30-31
  old pearls of wisdom, 35-36
  publishing of combat accounts, 34-35
  sanctity of operational accounts, 31-33
  soldiering and combat, 26-28

First World War, 307

France, 93

G

Gandhi, Mahatma, 41, 49, 50, 60

Ghori, Shahabuddin, 226

H

Haji Pir Pass, 22, 52, 68, 152, 156, 159, 164, 180, 324

Haryana, 269, 297

Honours and Awards, 267-280
  7 sikh in battles of mandi and gali, 272-274
  7 sikh in op hill, 274-275
  maintaining merit a must, 269-270
  man and machine, 267-268
  operational analysis and relations among senior officers, 275-276
  out of context, but, 277-279
  rights of leaders and men, 268-269
  some home truths, 279-280
  welfare of troops and our own commanders, 277

Hyderabad, 42, 78

I

India, 39, 40, 41, 43, 44, 45, 46, 47, 48, 49, 50, 51, 52, 53, 54, 55, 56, 57, 58, 59, 60, 61, 62, 64, 65, 66, 67, 68, 69,

70, 71, 72, 74, 75, 76, 78, 79, 80, 81, 82, 83, 84, 85, 86, 87, 88, 89, 90, 91, 92, 93, 108, 109, 169, 190, 197, 209, 223, 224, 225, 226, 227, 234, 235, 237, 251, 252, 258, 59, 269, 275, 277, 323, 324, 325, 326, 327, 328, 329, 330, 331, 332, 333, 334

Indian Military Academy (IMA), 20, 248, 250, 259, 262, 264, 269, 294, 297, 301

Indonesia, 93

Infiltration by Guerrillas, 89-99
causes for venturing against india, 90-91
crisis game, plan, 93
effects of new weaponary for pakistan army, 94-96
guerrillas in pre-selected basis, 98-99
launching of enemy columns, 96-98
obsession – kashmir, 89-90
planning of operation gibraltar by pakistan, 92-93
succourers of pakistan, 91-92

Irony After Irony, 38-51
british and jinnah, 45
employability of jcos and ncos, 42
geo-political, 43
indian political leadership and jinnah, 43-44
insertions on instrument of accession, 48-51
instrument of accession, 47-48
pangs of division of army, 38-39
problems in kashmir, 46
reorganisation of army of independent india, 41-41
shortage of officers, 39-41

ISI, 331

Islam, 49, 81, 223, 225, 237, 325, 331

J

Jamaat-ud-Dawa, 330

Jammu And Kashmir, 24, 26, 27, 28, 30, 32, 42, 46, 47, 48, 52-63, 64, 65, 66, 67, 70, 71, 72, 74, 76, 77, 78, 83, 86, 89, 90, 92, 93, 94, 96, 99, 108, 109, 151, 164, 225, 230, 248, 326, 330

british and pakistan, 52-63
british interests in kashmir, 54
checking of expansion of communism, 54-55
congress and hindus, 59-60
geography of kashmir, 51-54
importance of pakistan, 60, 61
importance to india, 61-62
india for destroying pakistan, 56-57
keeping roots in india, 57-58
middle east defence organisation, 55-56
paying debt, 58-59
valley and convergence of expeditionary routes, 62-63

JCOs, 20, 21, 32, 42, 116, 160, 166, 177, 182, 207, 222, 242, 250, 253, 257, 258, 259, 260, 261, 262, 263, 264, 269, 314, 315, 316, 317, 319, 320, 337

Johnson, Lyndon, 323

Jihad, 46, 93

Jinnah, MA, 43, 44, 45, 46, 49, 50, 52, 71, 76, 325

Junagarh, 42, 78

Jungle Hill, 24, 68, 188, 194, 195, 202, 208, 209, 210, 212, 213, 215, 218, 221, 254, 272, 320

Junior Leadership, 257-266
beating back deadly raid, 264-266
creation of jco rank, 257-258
factors affecting performance of jcos, 259-261
food for thought, 263-264

jcos and mercenary army, 258-259
junior leaders, 257
making best use of jcos, 261-262
ncos and their contribution, 262-263
performing team, 263

K

Kabar-Ki-Dheri, 158-163

Karakoram Pass, 56, 66

Kargil, 85, 88, 95, 226, 324

Kautalaya, 244, 253, 279

Kennedy, J F, 323

Khalsa, 111, 146, 238

Khan, Akbar (Maj Gen), 77, 129, 225

Khan, Ayub (Field Marshal), 61, 80, 81, 83, 86, 87, 88, 96, 323, 330

Khan, Liaquat Ali, 61, 71, 77

Koak, NS (Capt), 21, 174

L

Ladakh, 53, 62, 64, 88, 95

Lahore, 77, 279

Last Few Yards,
  bitter truths, 283-284
  characteristics of junior leaders, 285-286
  layout of the ground, 286-287
  making best use of everyone, 287-288
  moving from start line to enemy and his reaction, 288-290
  personality of company commander, 284-285
  planning as phenomenon, 281-282
  remedy, 290-293
  training schedule at each level of command, 282-283
  what happens at unit level after battle, 293-294
  what should be done in peace time, 294-296

Lessons Learnt, 310-324
  administrative functioning, 321-322
  appreciation and awards, 314
  attending the wounded, 319
  bold, audacious offensives, 312
  commanding officer, best judge, 313
  conduct of withdrawal/fallback, 318-319
  creating of reserves, 311-312
  digging tools, 317
  disposal of dead bodies, 321
  enemy's information, 319-320
  familiarisation and knowledge of area, 311
  general, 310
  jawan, 317
  jcos, 315-316
  lt col bhagat singh and recording of historical facts, 323
  move of reserves, 320
  offensive defence, 313-314
  organisation of enemy, 318
  physical courage & fitness, 317
  position of commander, 322-323
  provision of supporting fire, 312-313
  ruthlessness, 314-315
  signal operators and others, 320-321
  taskent declaration, bargaining table, 323-324
  time, 316
  training of troops, 316
  young officers, 315

LMGs, 96, 104, 120, 133, 137, 138, 144, 145, 161, 162, 193, 203, 204, 205, 208, 210, 212, 214, 215, 282

Lockhart, Sir Robert (Gen), 326

M

Mahavir Chakra, 274

Malaysia, 93

Malta, 92, 223, 224, 225, 226, 227

Mandi, 21, 22, 23, 24, 29, 65, 67, 68, 95, 97, 99, 100, 101, 102, 104, 105, 106, 107, 109, 110, 111, 111, 112, 113, 114, 115, 116, 117, 118, 119, 120, 121, 122, 123, 125, 126, 127, 129, 130, 132, 133, 134, 139, 151, 152, 153, 154, 155, 156, 157, 158, 159, 164, 166, 169, 187, 189, 196, 201, 228, 229, 230, 232, 233, 234, 250, 254, 255, 262, 272, 273, 274, 276, 282, 287, 310, 311, 312, 313, 314, 315, 319, 320

Capture of, 108-127

Manekshaw, Lt Col Sam (later Field Marshal), 47

Maurya, Chandra Gupta, 279

Mediterranean Sea, 224, 225

Meerut, 19, 20, 31, 248, 249

Mahmood of Ghazni, 226

Menon, VP Krishna, 47

MMGs, 113, 116, 117, 121, 124, 127, 141, 144, 145, 162, 168, 202, 250, 254, 276

Mountbetten, Lord, 41, 46, 47, 48, 74, 76, 78, 79

Mushrraf, Parvez, 76

Muslim League, 44, 46, 50, 52, 55, 72

Muzzafrabad, 69, 71, 73, 95, 251

N

NCOs, 20, 42, 120, 182, 257, 262, 315

Nehru, Jawaharlal, 41, 46, 47, 48, 55, 56, 60, 70, 78, 81, 326, 330

North Africa, 93, 224

O

OP Hill, 24, 25, 28, 30, 31, 32, 33, 67, 68, 123, 127, 174, 176, 186-222, 228, 229, 253, 254, 255, 262, 274, 275, 276, 282, 314, 315, 319, 320, 321, 322, 323

battle of, 186-222

Operation Gibraltar, 92, 93, 94, 158, 233, 265

Operation-Phanne-Shah, 164-185
changed scenario, 164-165
crossing site, 171
crowding of ring contour, 171-173
earmarking for offensive action, 165-166
enemy dispositions and plan for attack, 169-171
enemy's reaction, 168
hard times, 178-179
home truths, 185
lack of arty support, 175
launching of fighting patrol, 166-168
non-occupation of knoll and pt 6061, 173-175
occupation of own langur, 178
only choice, 176-177
operational analysis, 179-185
planning and conduct of battalion attack, 168-169
plastering of area by pak arty, 175-176

P

Pakistan, 26, 30, 39, 40, 41, 42, 45, 46, 47, 48, 50, 52, 53, 55, 56, 57, 58, 59, 60, 61, 62, 63, 64, 65, 66, 67, 68, 69, 70, 71, 72, 75, 76, 77, 78, 80, 81, 82, 83, 84, 85, 86, 87, 88, 89, 90, 91, 92, 93, 94, 95, 96, 98, 108, 121, 129, 133, 147, 158, 165, 167, 168, 169, 171, 174, 182, 189, 190, 204, 208, 214, 215, 223, 225, 226, 227, 228, 251, 255, 256, 258, 265, 272, 277, 278, 279, 307, 310, 312, 318, 319, 320, 323, 324, 325, 326, 327, 328, 329, 330, 331, 332, 333, 334

Pakistan Occupied Kashmir (POK), 64, 65, 69, 94, 95, 96, 102, 109, 128, 156, 159, 228, 229

Param Vir Chakra (PVC), 75, 273, 277

Patel, Sardar, 326

Phenomenon of Gibraltar And It's Crumbling, 223-234
7 sikh, saviour of punch, 231-233
conclusion, 233-234
enlarging hold on punch basin, 228
gibraltar, 224-225
malta, 224
northern pincer, 228-230
obsession kashmir, 226-227
pakistan hatred towards india, 225-226
planning by enemy, 230-231
religion as weapon, 223-224
what is in name, 225

Preamble, 17-24
actions fought, 21-22
case study, 19
general, 17-19
last action, 24
misplaced notions at phanne-shah, 22-24
raising process, 19-20
recording of historical facts, 24-25
team of officers, 20-21

Pritam, 22, 68, 76, 94, 115, 127, 165, 166, 169, 170, 174, 177, 182, 230, 276, 318

Punch, 20, 22, 24, 25, 27, 32, 52, 64-69, 77, 90, 91, 93, 94, 95, 97, 98, 101, 105, 108, 109, 110, 111, 112, 122, 123, 126, 129, 132, 133, 146, 156, 158, 159, 163, 164, 165, 166, 175, 178, 187, 191, 197, 226, 227, 228, 229, 230, 231, 233, 248, 249, 251, 253, 255, 256, 264, 272, 301, 310, 313, 317, 324

and its specific importance, 64-69

capturing and cutting off punch, 66-67
conclusion, 68-69
lone unit on independent axis, 67-68
mangla dam, 65-66
past history of punch, 65
regions of kashmir, 64-65

Punjab, 44, 45, 53, 62, 75, 105, 152, 174, 189, 204, 251, 269

R

Raid At Kabar-Ki-Dheri, 158-163
composition of team, 160-161
conclusion, 163
conduct, 161-162
enemy's modus operandi, 158-59
mission, 159-160
operational analysis, 162-163

Rajasthan, 269

Rann of Kutchh, 80, 81, 82, 83, 84, 85, 86, 87, 93

Red Fort, 30, 74

S

Sauji, 21, 22, 30, 99, 101, 102, 103, 104, 105, 106, 107, 110, 111, 112, 119, 121, 122, 125, 126, 137, 138, 140, 141, 151, 152, 153, 187, 229, 230, 231, 232, 234, 313

Second World War, 18, 38, 39, 41, 57, 58, 59, 65, 74, 167, 264, 274, 307, 315

Sharma, Som Nath (Maj), 75

Shastri, Lal Bahadur, 84, 323, 324

Singh, Bhagat (Lt Col), 19, 28, 33, 99, 101, 110, 111, 127, 130, 137, 140, 141, 143, 155, 166, 171, 195, 200, 204, 214, 219, 222, 231, 233, 248, 252, 265, 274, 275, 313, 323

Singh, Bikkar (Sub), 113, 187, 201, 203, 204, 205, 208, 210, 211, 315, 320

Singh, Darya (Capt), 21, 27, 174

Singh, Guru Gobind, 237, 238

Singh, Harbakhsh (Lt Gen), 30, 31, 76, 151, 191, 230, 263, 274, 275

Singh, Maharaja Hari, 43, 46, 47, 48, 54, 55, 70, 71, 73, 74, 75, 89, 238, 307

Singh, Maharaja Ranjit, 238, 307

Singh, Pritam (Brig), 68, 165

Singh, Ravel (Lt Col), 105, 109, 113, 115, 118, 122, 147, 174, 182, 196, 236, 250, 254, 315

Singh Sansar (Capt), 23, 24, 104, 174, 196, 199, 202, 203, 205, 206, 207, 208, 209, 210, 211, 216, 253, 315

Sikh Regiment, 19, 20, 30, 39, 74, 252, 263, 307

Singh, Bhagat (Lt Col), 19, 28, 99, 101, 110, 111, 127, 130, 137, 140, 141, 143, 155, 166, 171, 195, 200, 219, 222, 231, 233, 248, 252, 265, 274, 275, 313, 323

Singh, Trilochan (Maj), 21, 27, 196, 206, 207, 209, 210, 248, 253

Singh, Zora (Brig), 98, 100, 134, 137, 140, 233

T

Testing of Metal and Might at Rann of Kutchh, 80-88
background, 80
chance in thousand years, 80-81
current of history-theory, 84-85
escalation of activities in kargil sector, 85-86
foreign powers, 81
india and non-alignmen, 82-83
new weaponry for pakistan army, 83-84
operation ablaze, 86-87
operational analysis, 87-88

The Last Word, 335-339
command, 336-337
essential safeguards, 338-339
free exchange of views, 335-336
junior leaders, 337
summing up, 339

Tibet, 52

U

United Kingdom (UK), 56, 82

United Nations (UN), 48, 78, 89, 179, 188, 278

United States (US), 56, 57, 66, 67, 80, 81, 82, 83, 88, 90, 92, 93, 133, 166, 214, 245, 265, 323, 325, 328, 331

USSR, 80, 81

UP, 269

Uri, 22, 68, 69, 73, 77, 105, 152, 156, 158, 159, 163, 164, 165, 166, 324

V

Vietnam, 93

Young Commanders and Leaders, 235-256
ambitious commanders, 241-242
command as an element of power, 238-239
commanding officer and his team, 252-253
conventional training, 248-249
foreign invasions, 237-38
leadership as an obligation, 243-244
leadership of 7 sikh, 248
men joining armed forces, 242-243
military leadership, complex art, 244-46
nature of the man, 235-237

officer's training cadres, 250-251
practical training on posts, 249-250
role of officers, 239-241
sense of commitment, 255
they made things to happen, 256
traits of military leadership, 246-248
young leaders and an active area, 253-254

W

What Makes Man Fight, 297-
age and performance, 306-307
army and its ethos, 298
conclusion, 308-309
general, 297-298
men, 305-306
officers and men, 302
officers, 302-304
on job training, 301-302
soldiering and state, 299-300
special characteristics of sikh soldier, 307-308
system of working in army, 300-301
training of junior officers, 304-305
war and its causes, 299